Winning the Long Game

"Given the disruption in our industry, developing the strategic capability of our leaders is a major focus for us. *Winning the Long Game* offers a clear path to build strategic thinking in a very digestible style."
—ANNE BOWERMAN, vice president,
executive development, Thomson Reuters

"I loved the anecdotes, from so many angles. Finally, a book on strategic leadership that is grounded in real word situations! This is definitely a practical, insightful, easy-to-read guide to becoming a better strategist and more effective leader."
—JEAN-PIERRE GARNIER, former chief executive of
GlaxoSmithKline and current chairman of Actelion Inc.

"In the global wealth management industry, leadership comes from those who have successfully advised clients and then step up to lead others across diverse markets and teams. Our challenge remains to convert star performers into strategic leaders. *Winning the Long Game* provides a clear roadmap to that end."
—NICK GORNALL, managing director, head of learning and
professional development, Coutts /Royal Bank of Scotland

"Success in business requires agile leaders adapting to a changing world, especially in banking. Steven Krupp and Paul Schoemaker offer a comprehensive yet practical approach providing insight and advice on the disciplines leaders must master to thrive today and in the future."
—ALEX HILLER, head of leadership and
organizational development, UBS

"Delivering results in an uncertain world calls for seeing ahead, thinking long term, and navigating sharp, inevitable curves. Strategic leadership is a necessary rather than optional skill to create high sustainable performance. The authors have done a great job of decoding this skill

for everyday use in a compelling and useful manner. This important book, combining strategy and leadership, makes it one of a kind."
—RAGHU KRISHNAMOORTHY, vice president, executive development and chief learning officer, General Electric

"*Winning the Long Game* weaves keen insights about strategic leadership, fun stories, and very practical tips into a power packed narrative sure to raise any leader's game. My COO devoured it and thought we could apply many of the recommended actions immediately. A must read."
—FRED KRUPP, president, Environmental Defense Fund

"One of the dilemmas that chief executives face is finessing the competing challenges of delivering results both in the short term *and* over the long term. *Winning the Long Game* provides invaluable insights as to how to negotiate this trade-off to great effect. Stories based on real events and situations where executives have reconciled these competing priorities illuminate how to navigate the rougher seas of corporate life successfully. This is a compelling and extremely useful book, not only for chief executives but for all leaders who face these decisions."
—QUINTIN PRICE, senior managing director, global head of alpha strategies, and global executive committee, BlackRock

"The authors take a complex concept and neatly unpack what it means to be strategic. The wisdom, insights, and stories jump off the page, showing leaders how to navigate through uncertain terrain. This can be a game changer for those who take the advice to heart and distinguish themselves as strategic leaders."
—JUAN CARLOS RIVERO, chief talent officer, Marsh & McLennan Companies

"As the business landscape has been changing dramatically in our industry, truly strategic thinking has become more critical than ever for continued growth. *Winning the Long Game* provides a practical playbook for senior and high potential leaders to increase their strategic aptitude and business impact."
—WILLIAM STRAHAN, executive vice president, human resources, Comcast Cable

"Krupp and Schoemaker have produced a practical, readable guide for developing the mental habits and reflexes that undergird visionary leadership. Leaders with strength in all six of the skills they identify are needed at all levels of the organization to create competitive advantage in today's ever-shifting global economy. They are the central nervous system of the dynamic capabilities of the firm and will be of great interest to scholars and practitioners alike."
—David J. Teece, professor, Haas School of Business,
University of California at Berkeley; chairman and
principal executive officer, Berkeley Research Group, LLC

"Thinking in time sounds easy but is really hard. In this masterful synthesis, we learn why—and learn how to cope more effectively with a Black-Swan/Gray-Swan world."
—Philip E. Tetlock, Annenberg University professor,
department of psychology and Wharton School,
University of Pennsylvania

"Steven Krupp and Paul Schoemaker make a captivating case for strategic leadership, thinking broadly and acting decisively. Through extended accounts of strategic actions by leaders ranging from Tesla's Elon Musk to Lego's CEO and even Pope Francis, *Winning the Long Game* offers a tangible and comprehensive playbook for becoming a strategic leader when it really matters."
—Michael Useem, professor of management and
director of the Center for Leadership and Change
at the Wharton School, University of Pennsylvania

"This important strategic leadership book captures exactly what we are doing at Cancer Treatment Centers of America, from the ability to think strategically long term to enacting game changing new practices in cancer care that place the patient truly at the center of all our activities. We are re-imagining cancer care and our leaders need to master the six strategic disciplines laid out so clearly and practically in this highly engaging book—a must read for any strategic leader and those aspiring to be one."
—Gerard van Grinsven,
CEO of Cancer Treatment Centers of America

"*Winning the Long Game* hits the mark. It's a compelling read with engaging stories and practical tips. The integrated view of the six disciplines in the context of ambiguous and uncertain times differentiates *Winning the Long Game* from other work in the leadership development arena. Leaders who want to be more strategic will eat this up and organizations will surely benefit from the impact it will inspire. We have tracked success cases from the work we've done with Decision Strategies International to develop 'outside in' and 'future back' perspectives to improve decision-making in critical commercial roles. This book brings new lessons and fresh ideas about how to build strategic leadership capability in any organization."

—THERESA ZELLER, executive director, learning
and development, Merck Manufacturing

"*Winning the Long Game* helps us move from execution to strategy, and back. The down-to-earth stories and 'how to' tips about what strategic leaders do, and the traps to avoid, offer practical advice to our leaders. he stories make the reading fun and the ideas pop."

—LESLIE TEICHGRAEBER, vice president of PepsiCo University

WINNING
THE LONG GAME

How Strategic Leaders
Shape the Future

STEVEN KRUPP &
PAUL J. H. SCHOEMAKER

PublicAffairs
New York

*To our many clients, colleagues, and partners
from whom we learned so much about leadership
in the real world. We hope this book will help them
become even more strategic in how they lead
and serve their teams or organizations.*

Copyright © 2014 by Steven Krupp and Paul J. H. Schoemaker.

Published in the United States by PublicAffairs™, a Member of the
Perseus Books Group

All rights reserved.
Printed in the United States of America.

No part of this book may be reproduced in any manner whatsoever
without written permission except in the case of brief quotations embod-
ied in critical articles and reviews. For information, address PublicAffairs,
250 West 57th Street, 15th Floor, New York, NY 10107.

PublicAffairs books are available at special discounts for bulk purchases
in the US by corporations, institutions, and other organizations. For more
information, please contact the Special Markets Department at the Perseus
Books Group, 2300 Chestnut Street, Suite 200, Philadelphia, PA 19103;
call (800) 810-4145, ext. 5000; or e-mail special.markets@perseusbooks.com.

Book Design by Linda Mark

A catalog record for this book is available from the Library of Congress.
Library of Congress Catalog Control Number: 201495317
ISBN 978-1-61039-447-5 (HC)
ISBN 978-1-61039-448-2 (EB)

First Edition

10 9 8 7 6 5 4 3 2 1

CONTENTS

FOREWORD

THIS BOOK OFFERS A WELCOME EXAMINATION OF HOW strategy and leadership are highly intertwined even though most writings treat them separately. The authors' focus on the long game—with the attendant needs to make frequent adjustments—underscores the role of leadership in the dynamic capabilities framework that I and others co-developed. The framework is a multidisciplinary approach to understanding the long-term performance of enterprises. The best firms are able to rapidly leverage opportunities and constantly renew their structure and resources. The competences that enable firms to do this are known as dynamic capabilities. A firm's dynamic capabilities rest on two pillars: (1) the vision and leadership skills of managers, and (2) the cohesion and flexibility of the organization as a whole. Leaders must fashion sound strategies for the enterprise, and the organization itself must be agile enough to adapt as required. An organization's culture and values are much slower and more difficult to change than its structure or processes, and can hamstring even an excellent strategy if its leaders cannot show the way forward.

One way to think about dynamic capabilities is to divide them into three groups of activities at which successful firms must excel:

+ *sensing* needs, threats, and opportunities in a timely fashion
+ *seizing* attractive possibilities by mobilizing resources, and
+ *transforming* the organization to maintain its effectiveness.

This approach connects closely with *Winning the Long Game*, since adaptive leadership is crucial in all of these activities. For example, anticipating changes (Chapter 1), challenging assumptions (Chapter 2), and interpreting data (Chapter 3) are all deeply tied to *sensing*. This requires not only leadership but also an organizational structure and culture that encourages the free flow of information.

There are other key connections as well. For example, the ability of leaders to decide what to do and when (Chapter 4) is a crucial element of *seizing*, whereas aligning teams and incentives (Chapter 5) is a critical aspect of *transforming* the organization. Learning (Chapter 6) and Vision (Chapter 7) are important cross-cutting aspects of dynamic capabilities that apply to all three challenges (sensing, seizing, and transforming).

Winning the Long Game is replete with well-chosen examples that illustrate how leaders can enhance as well as destroy the dynamic capabilities that firms need for long-term sustainable advantage. Krupp and Schoemaker provide deep as well practical insights, for both scholars and practitioners, about how to integrate strategy and leadership for the long run. Leaders who apply these ideas, and the many tips throughout the book, will have a distinct advantage in navigating today's complex environment.

DAVID J. TEECE
Thomas W. Tusher Professor in Global Business
Director, Center for Global Strategy and Governance
Haas School of Business
University of California at Berkeley

INTRODUCTION:
THRIVING IN A WORLD OF VUCA

Why Strategic Leadership Is So Crucial Now

I T WAS *THAT* TIME OF THE YEAR AGAIN, TIME FOR THE annual performance review that leadership experts say is so important and participants find so stressful. Nonetheless, Jing "Jane" Wang felt confident and upbeat going into her meeting with Lee Azner, vice president and director of Asia Pacific operations for "Brazelton Global".* Her division met budget, no easy accomplishment given the economic downturn. She got along well with Lee, and they had talked regularly throughout the year about the performance of her division. Her only problem with Lee was that he could be, well, somewhat vague and rely too much on American sports metaphors to make his point. All things considered, though, Jane believed she'd had a pretty good year.

Lee agreed. For the first hour of the session, he was full of praise, telling Jane, "You're one of our top up-and-coming managers" and "a very promising candidate for our high-potential program." He

*This is a disguised name; other fictitious company or person names (to protect confidentiality) will likewise be in quotations marks when first used.

1

commended her division's financial discipline and cost-cutting initiatives. She was feeling good, starting to relax and thinking about promotion opportunities. Jane was ambitious and had anticipated making a move up within the next year. She was getting the feeling that Lee was delighted with her work.

But then the performance review took an unexpected turn. Lee shifted uneasily in his chair and said, "Jane, you're a great operational leader but you need to be more strategic. We can't just keep reacting to what our competitors are doing in Asia, or how our customers are changing. You need to work on being more strategic. We are beginning to lose market share."

Be more strategic, Jane wrote on her note pad, underlining the phrase. Moments earlier Lee had been so positive. Now he made it clear that her next promotion hinged on being more strategic—whatever that meant. "Okay," Jane said, "can we get a bit more specific? What do you suggest I do?" Lee's face went blank. After a few seconds of silence, he said, "Well, do what Wayne Gretzky did; you know, learn to skate to where the puck is going. I'm sure you've heard of 'The Great One,' four-time Stanley Cup winner, hockey hall-of-famer." With that, the session came to an end. Walking back to her office, Jane muttered, "Oh those sports metaphors." She shut her door and googled "Wayne Gretski." Up popped "Wayne Gretzky" on Wikipedia. Ah, she misspelled his name. More importantly, she learned that "despite his unimpressive stature, strength and speed, Gretzky's intelligence and reading of the game were unrivaled. He was adept at dodging checks from opposing players, and he could consistently anticipate where the puck was going to be and execute the right move at the right time."[1]

We've experienced countless situations like Jane's: leaders get the message during their performance reviews or in high-potential programs that they need to be "more strategic," and they intuitively understand why. In a changing environment, old ways of seeing the world become obsolete. And those who fall victim are often among the last to notice or respond. The need to become strategic is widely recognized. As Robert Kabacoff notes, "When asked to select the leadership behaviors most critical to their organizations' future success, executives chose strategic thinking 97% of the time."[2] What is sorely lacking, however, is clear, specific advice about how to develop strategic acumen.

The term *VUCA*, which appears in the title of this Introduction, gained currency in the military during the late 1990s to describe an environment of volatility, uncertainty, complexity, and ambiguity. It reflects a shift from traditional Cold War military conflicts to asymmetric warfare with agile, dispersed opponents fighting under different rules for causes we don't fully understand (e.g., terrorists). Businesses are increasingly encountering VUCA conditions as well, and this poses deep new challenges. Operational whizzes who rise to positions of leadership during relatively stable times often struggle when markets become turbulent and unpredictable. They are more comfortable with certainty and want clarity of direction so they can build a plan and direct a team. Yet, in this more uncertain world, successful leadership is less about a detailed plan than about a long-term approach built around capabilities that can be constantly adapted and reapplied to changing circumstances.

Peter Drucker was one of the first to emphasize that management is doing things right and that leadership is about doing the right things.[3] *Operational excellence*, for example, is about determining where to source and how to optimize supply chains to meet near-term objectives as efficiently and reliably as possible. *Strategic excellence* is about seeing the bigger picture, being aware of pitfalls that might blindside you, spotting undercurrents in or outside the organization, seeing connections to other decisions, and winning the engagement of key players, or at least noticing how well they are aligned. It also entails setting direction, knowing how to get there, and making vital adjustments along the way. Adjusting strategy requires the ability to anticipate shifts in the environment, challenge long-standing assumptions, interpret disparate or complex information, and make strategic choices under ambiguous conditions.

Leadership is by definition about getting people on board to achieve a shared goal. It often involves developing an organizational culture and creating strong collective commitment to the cause. Leading requires the abilities to get buy-in for tough decisions, inspire people to follow you in the desired direction, and create a climate for continuous learning so that the team is prepared for the challenges ahead. But sometimes mainstream leadership is not enough. In times of crisis and change, when people are confused about what to do, ordinary leadership must rise to the level of *strategic* leadership. This means navigating the unknown, recalibrating the strategy, pointing out where to go, and getting the team back on track to prevent paralysis.

✦ ✦ ✦

"Unusual uncertainty" is how Ben Bernanke, former chairman of the US Federal Reserve Bank, characterized the business environment at the start of the financial crisis in 2008.[4] Earlier he had written: "Uncertainty is seen to retard investment independently of considerations of risk or expected return."[5] Today's business environment is still full of uncertainty, from economic and political to social and technological. The present level of uncertainty is such that many leaders consider it an impediment to spending and investment.[6] In such times it is tempting to scale back and play it safe, but strategic leaders stay focused on the future, wary of curtailing investments and plans needed to win the long game.

Elon Musk, an entrepreneur par excellence, realized full well that his electric-car company Tesla could easily fail. At one early point, he was out of money but still highly committed to continue even when many others thought he had lost his mind. When asked about Tesla in a *60 Minutes* interview, Musk replied, "If something's important enough you should try, even if . . . the probable outcome is failure. . . . With Musk's personal fortune dry and cars stockpiled in California warehouses, Tesla had to turn to outside investment to keep afloat."[7] George Buckley, as Chairman and CEO of 3M, put it succinctly: "If you don't invest in the future and don't plan for the future, there won't be one."[8] Although uncertainty need not impede investment, and entrepreneurs routinely exploit uncertainty, it still tends to paralyze many leaders and companies. There is an abundance of excellent operations managers in companies around the world, but there is an acute shortage of leaders who can think and act strategically when confronted with volatility, uncertainty, complexity, and ambiguity—that is, the world of VUCA.

Why is there such a shortage of strategic leaders, the special kind who can handle VUCA well? One reason, illustrated through Jane and her vice president Lee, is that few managers get or give concrete advice on how to become more strategic. The problem is not just a general lack of feedback but a poor understanding about what it really means to be strategic. To most leaders, the notion of "being strategic" is fuzzy, poorly defined, hard to grasp, and shrouded in mystery. As a consequence, organizations often exhibit a lack of urgency or effectiveness in developing strategic leadership ability at multiple levels of management.

Our book seeks to bridge the gap between what most people superficially see as two separate domains—strategy and leadership. In practical terms, we want to empower managers to develop leadership plans for themselves and their teams. Companies need more people who are equipped to lead in an increasingly uncertain and complex world. Once you master the disciplines of strategic leadership, as Jane plans to do, the path to bigger roles and more influence to shape the future will be within your reach. The good news, as we have seen with many successful leaders, is that *you can learn how to be more strategic*.

WHAT IS STRATEGIC LEADERSHIP?

When times are stable, meaning that economic, political, social, and technological forces are reasonably predictable, leaders can formulate a straightforward plan to help execute a strategy. Their challenge in such cases is twofold: setting the right strategy and then delivering the desired results efficiently. Of these, execution will receive the most attention since the strategy is clear and stable—akin to the way a conductor executes a score in orchestral music. In a stable environment, the ability to execute consistently on a quarterly or annual basis can make a good leader great and widely admired. In times of volatility, however, the right strategy can quickly become the wrong strategy, and even flawless execution will not help. The game will have shifted from classical music to jazz, since improvisation around broadly agreed themes is now called for. Strategic improv is hard for just a single player, let alone a whole team. For example, Kodak was for many decades the leader in producing film for making photos. It fully mastered the process of chemical emulsion technology that went into making the photon-sensitive paper widely used in pre-digital cameras. Yet this operational excellence meant little as the world shifted toward digital imaging.

What Kodak lacked was sufficient *strategic leadership* to guide the organization's ongoing exploration, discovery, investment, and implementation of a new strategy that embraced the digital revolution. Although Kodak had the digital technology and capacity to invest, it was not able to turn the organization around quickly enough to keep pace with the disruption of its industry.[9] Strategic leaders constantly test and revise their strategy while managing and adjusting execution. They seek to deliver results in the short term while securing long-term viability. This balance is tough to get right. Since the stakes and challenges are higher in uncertain times, companies must tilt more toward strategic leadership than toward operational excellence. Importantly, strategic leaders not only respond well to uncertainty when it hits; they can actually create it by pursuing strategies that disrupt or destroy well-established business models. In the last few decades, we have seen great business success emerge from such creative destruction by agile entrepreneurs and companies that exploit new technologies, emerging markets, and sociopolitical trends.

A strategic leader must look at strategic decisions from two perspectives: "outside in" and "future back." By "outside in," we mean that a strategic leader starts with the external marketplace when addressing problems, without getting wrapped up by internal organizational issues. For Kodak, this meant downplaying the chemical-emulsion business model and asking what the future of digital imaging might be five to ten years hence. Deep down, Kodak needed to see and act sooner since digital cameras were displacing the company's film. Ultimately, years later, smart phones would become smart cameras and kill Kodak's traditional business. By "future back," we mean that strategic leaders play the long game. Their long-term vision guides short-term decision-making in a flexible way. Strategic leaders plan backward from their idealized future images to what they must do now to be ready in five years or more. Being *more strategic* means reimagining your future and adapting your strategy or business model appropriately to changing times, to give your business the best chance of staying vital and sustainable. Kodak took too long to mobilize its middle management layer, even though its leaders recognized the tsunami of digital imaging ahead.[10]

In a rapidly changing world, strategic leaders engage not only with the competition but, more broadly, with an ecosystem of diverse and potentially disruptive forces such as customers, suppliers, partners, organizational cultures, capital markets, and technological innovations. The continual threat of disruption requires the capacity to envision the future and catalyze change. Strategic leaders can spot, avoid, or neutralize threats to the business, much as soldiers can neutralize improvised explosive devices if they get to the IEDs before anyone is harmed by them. This is the point Lee was trying to make when he asked Jane to do what Wayne Gretzky did—namely, skate to where the puck would be.

You can do this, too. Every leader can become more strategic. Having surveyed more than twenty thousand global leaders, and examined the actions of strategic leaders for more than two decades in industries and countries around the globe, we were able to identify what makes some of these leaders highly successful in shaping their future. Specifically, we found that relying on what worked in the past was often not an asset but a liability in times of uncertainty and change. At Kodak, for example, experienced managers stuck with technologies familiar to them and, deep down, resisted developing new competencies needed for future success. When regime change occurs, when the success formula or rules of the game in your industry are shifting, your instincts and past recipes may no longer work. That was exactly Jane's experience at the time of her review.

In this book we focus on cases entailing serious stakes and high uncertainty, conditions common to many markets, industries, and countries today. Our research has identified six disciplines—meaning habits, attitudes, and capabilities—that are essential for leaders to thrive in VUCA environments. We devote a chapter to each discipline, illustrate success factors, and describe how strategic leaders can develop the ability to:

1. *Anticipate* changes in the market environment by staying closely connected with customers, partners, and competitors, rather than becoming disconnected and reactive.

2. *Challenge* assumptions and the status quo by surrounding themselves with people who think outside the box and are open to new ideas.

3. *Interpret* a wide array of data and viewpoints rather than looking only for evidence that confirms their prior beliefs.

4. *Decide* what to do after examining their options and then exercise courage to get it done rather than waffling or belaboring the decision-making process.

5. *Align* the interests and incentives of stakeholders, based on understanding different views, rather than relying on their power or position.

6. *Learn* from success and failure by experimenting, making small bets, and mining the lessons from both the good and the bad outcomes to create quick learning cycles.

These six disciplines are multiplicative in nature: when exercised together, they mutually enrich a leader's situational awareness and strategic aptitude. Mastering only a few may not cut it for you or your team. Like the playmakers in a live-action competition, strategic leaders hone these six disciplines so that they can make the right

The Six Disciplines

moves at the right times to produce the desired results. Sometimes, leaders apply the disciplines to advance their vision. Other times, they use these disciplines to reimagine and envision their future. At all times, the most strategic leaders apply these skills with purpose and rigor. Let's examine two examples.

Adapting to Changing Circumstances Can Win Many Followers

Oprah Winfrey had the strategic vision and discipline to redefine the talk show genre at a time when social values and mores were changing profoundly. Through an innovative blend of charisma, intellect, and emotion, she strategically shifted the paradigm of daytime talk shows in line with social trends.[11] In the late 1980s and early '90s, the world was increasingly complex, diverse, and unpredictable. The Cold War was coming to an end, social experimentation was increasing, more women and minorities were achieving success, and massive globalization was under way. Anxiety was high and norms were changing. Oprah's emphasis on spiritual values, healthy living, and self-help spoke to the anxieties her viewers felt. Rather than ignoring these concerns, she embraced them and achieved new levels of viewer intimacy.[12]

Because Oprah didn't fit the image of the traditional talk show host, who was typically white, male, and more conservative, she worked diligently to perfect a new style of audience engagement. Instead of using comedy for laughs or shock effect, she asked her viewers to think and feel. Compared to Phil Donahue, whom Oprah was originally slotted against, she was better able—through her dramatic stories and painful self-revelations—to connect with viewers.[13] Donahue's persona was familiar and appealing, yet he did not relate emotionally as Oprah did. Donahue touched on controversial topics without revealing his vulnerability. Oprah had an autobiographical and confessional component that blurred public and private personas. Her authenticity fostered empathy. In a refreshing and strategic breakthrough, she positioned herself essentially as one of her own guests. Even as she became famous and wealthy, she kept that personal bond.

At its peak in the early 1990s, *The Oprah Winfrey Show* drew an average of 12–13 million viewers each weekday. (The figure was about 6 million when the show ended in 2011.) Hers was by far the most popular show of its kind. As a result Oprah became one of the most influential and successful businesswomen on the planet.[14] After twenty-five years, she left the show to launch her own TV network—twenty-four hours of programming seven days a week, all inspired by Oprah. The Oprah Winfrey Network (OWN) had a rocky start but turned a profit in the second quarter of 2013, six months ahead of schedule, and has grown in both ratings and revenue since then.[15]

Oprah's strategic leadership discipline enabled her to realize a strong personal vision, anticipate audience interests, challenge TV conventions, make controversial decisions, and rally talented people to her cause.[16] She built a trusted brand and maintained its integrity while diversifying across multiple channels, including production companies, acting roles, magazine publishing, book clubs, diverse charities, and Oprah's Angel Network. She even launched a school focused on leadership for girls in South Africa. Oprah dreamed big to achieve her strategic intent and, in the process, reinvented herself. She took risks, learned from mistakes, and embraced new media opportunities. Her innovations built unmatched audience rapport and brand loyalty needed to win the long game.[17]

Embracing Uncertainty Can Pay Off Big

Whereas Oprah adapted her brand to changing times and fashioned a winning strategy in the media industry, Nathan Mayer Rothschild confronted uncertainty head-on in finance. Rothschild, the legendary financier whose eponymous bank became a global powerhouse, realized that uncertainty was a vastly underrated source of wealth creation. He summed up his investing philosophy with the aphorism "Great fortunes are made when cannon-balls fall in the harbour, not when violins play in the ball-room." Nathan, the third of five brothers—all German Jewish bankers in the late eighteenth and early nineteenth centuries—understood that the more unpredictable the environment, the greater the opportunity, provided that you have the right combination of strategic thinking and leadership skills to capitalize on the moment.

The Rothschilds had just such a combination and, indeed, capitalized on the unpredictability of their time. Each brother set up banking operations in a different city of Europe. During the Napoleonic era, the British government struggled to dispatch money to its generals in battle on the Continent. "N. M.," as Nathan was called, pioneered a payment system whereby he could move British coin from London to his brother James in Paris. James transferred it through Paris bankers to Spain, where the Duke of Wellington was fighting Bonaparte. The system enabled Wellington to replenish supplies, pay his troops, and rally his allies. According to Fritz Redlich, "Napoleon, who was almost completely ignorant of financial matters, was pleased by the imports of coin into France, and did not suspect at all that these funds merely passed through France and served to finance the war against himself."[18]

The Rothschild brothers leveraged their network from the Jewish Diaspora to inform and implement their flexible financing strategies across Europe. They struck financial agreements with the English government that appreciated in value as the war dragged on and, over time, accrued vast amounts of British bullion. During the Battle of Waterloo in June 1815, N. M. took his usual trading position near a pillar on the London Exchange. He began to sell British consols, the primary trading debt instrument at the time. Other traders saw him and assumed that, with his superior information network, N. M.

was receiving news about Wellington's military conflict with Napoleon at Waterloo, Belgium. So, like N. M, they began dumping their consols on the market, driving the prices down sharply.

"Buy when there's blood in the streets," N. M. reportedly said, *"even if the blood is your own."*[19] Buy he did, knowing that his fortune derived from superior information flow and willingness to bet when others were afraid. N. M. actually had advanced knowledge of Napoleon's defeat at Waterloo, thanks to fast couriers and carrier pigeons. But he did not want to tip his hand, and so he implied, through his trades, that Napoleon was winning the battle. In the meantime, he privately bought British consols at rock-bottom prices. By the time the truth reached London, prices had skyrocketed—and N. M. made millions of pounds in these trades.[20]

Strategic leaders like N. M. are prepared to adapt and flex their strategies and can do so more nimbly than those who are entrenched. When times are uncertain, the best move is often not the one you planned. Strategic leaders recognize this reality and the potential trap within it: they size up the situation and create new options as N. M. Rothschild did when risking his fortune on a war's outcome. Importantly, however, N. M. had an edge with superior information, insight, and guts. He played his hand to the fullest and helped create a banking empire in the process.

THE ROADMAP TO STRATEGIC LEADERSHIP

Strategic leaders enable their Wellingtons to win at Waterloo with timely information, excellent situational awareness, and smart tactics. Whether you're an executive, the head of a business unit, an entrepreneur, or an aspiring leader, the six disciplines of strategic leadership provide immediate benefit in your current job, prepare you for promotion, and equip you to shape the future. We guide you through these six disciplines to enhance your own strategic leadership for the long run and to provide assessment tools to measure your progress. The focus of our book is on you, the reader, in your role as an individual leader en route to becoming more strategic. Organizations can also use our framework to build strategic leadership training into development programs so that leading strategically becomes an organizational core competence.

Chapter 1: Elephants and Black Swans examines the discipline of anticipation. How far can you see into the future? How quickly do you spot ambiguous threats and opportunities on the periphery of your business? These are important skills that require time and perseverance to master. Elon Musk, co-founder of PayPal, Tesla, and SpaceX, has shown that he can see pathways for technology innovation sooner than others. Contrarian Wall Street investor Steve Eisman is another rare exception who saw the impending demise of the subprime bubble early on. By contrast, leaders at the Lego Group all but missed the digital revolution in toys and gaming. Digital entertainment was outside their comfort zone and beyond their planning horizon. Strategic leaders see sooner and scan wider to outpace disruption. Accordingly, this first chapter demonstrates how customer intimacy, peripheral scanning, scenario thinking, and war-gaming can help you to scan wider and see sooner.

Chapter 2: What Are You Afraid Of? explores the discipline of challenge. Are you comfortable with conflicting views and differences in opinion? How often do you question your own and other people's assumptions? Do you challenge the underlying assumptions of your industry or team to redefine the customer's experience, as Sir Richard Branson did at Virgin Atlantic? Branson works hard to solicit candid feedback from his staff and customers. Strategic leaders rarely isolate themselves. We discuss how Pope Francis, soon after his election, traveled to Brazil where he walked and talked with the crowd. He continually connects with regular people to stay close to the true mission of the Church and get input from diverse members of his flock. Sheryl Sandberg, of Google, Facebook, and *Lean In* fame, promotes equal risk-taking by women and men with messages such as "Fortune favors the bold" and "What would you do if you were not afraid?"

Chapter 3: The Dog That Did Not Bark covers the discipline of interpretation. Can you pick up on signals to distinguish anomalies from leading indicators of change? Finland's former president J. K. Paasikivi, who served from 1946 to 1956 and whose nation had long been under threat from the Soviet Union, was fond of saying that wisdom begins by recognizing the facts. Paasikivi usually asked a lot of questions and invariably elicited complex and conflicting answers. We recount how Charles O. Holliday Jr., former CEO of DuPont, picked up several weak signals in the fall of 2008 that prepared DuPont for the deep recession that followed. We show you how strategic leaders see the future in the data at hand and provide tips for amplifying signals, connecting dots, spotting patterns, and testing hypotheses in clever ways.

Chapter 4: Sailing into the Storm breaks down the discipline of decision-making. How often and how quickly must you make tough calls with incomplete information? Maybe 10 percent of the time? That's Bill Clinton's estimate: "You really hire the President for the 10 percent of the decisions that advisors cannot agree on. The most difficult decisions were the ones where nobody could know the answer."[21] We look at such prominent decision-makers as Chancellor Angela Merkel in Germany and Laurence Golborne, the Minister of Mining in Chile. Golborne, new to his job, faced a collapsed mine that had trapped many poor workers. These decision-makers did not go maverick; they followed a disciplined process that balances rigor with speed, considers the trade-offs involved, and accounts for both short- and long-term goals. We also examine the unconventional decisions made by Zappos's leaders, who broke the rules, saved the start-up from going under, and transformed it into one of the hottest online retailers.

Chapter 5: This Matrix Is Killing Me addresses the discipline of alignment. Do you regularly engage your managers' direct reports in decisions that affect their work? According to one study, 47 percent of managers said that their leaders did not appropriately involve them.[22] That's why the leaders of Whole Foods, for example, have formed autonomous, self-managing work teams who manage their own business, run their own profit-and-loss statements (P&Ls), and make merchandising decisions. We also examine how fabled soccer coach Alex Ferguson managed to get brash young soccer stars at Manchester United to win again and again. Managing big egos is one major challenge; getting alignment across diverse cultures is yet another. This chapter looks at different approaches to rallying key players, building bridges, and achieving buy-in among stakeholders who may have competing agendas.

Chapter 6: My Gift Was Not Knowing focuses on the discipline of learning. When was the last time you admitted you were wrong—in public? We describe what CEO Reed Hastings did after one of his decisions riled the Netflix customer base enough to drive hundreds of thousands to drop their subscriptions.[23] We examine why Sara Blakely, the youngest self-made female billionaire in America, attributes her startling success at Spanx to learning from failure.[24] Strategic leaders study setbacks and defeats openly and constructively. The US Army routinely conducts immediate after-action reviews. Google has created a community of learning modeled after Stanford University, where the company's founders studied. Samsung sends high-potential leaders overseas to immerse them in different cultures. In examining this sixth discipline of the strategic leadership framework, we discuss how to experiment widely and probe deeply so as to learn from your experiences, flops, and surprises.

Chapter 7: Two Visionary Leaders provides an integrated view of all six disciplines. We profile Nelson Mandela to illustrate how these disciplines were instrumental, each on its own and especially in combination, in his remarkable journey. The key to Mandela's success was a strong vision of social justice and the ability to deploy the six leadership capabilities as he confronted challenges and opportunities. His transformational leadership to help with the long game evolved over decades, whereas for Albert C. Barnes, another strategic leader profiled in this chapter, harmonizing multiple skills was problematic. The very gifted Dr. Barnes rose from humble beginnings to assemble a world-class collection of paintings and had a vision to achieve social democracy through art education. His great business success early in life afforded him time and money to pursue his passion for art. He collected paintings from artists such as Cezanne, Matisse, Soutine, and Modigliani before they were well known. Nevertheless, Barnes's story illustrates how an enormously gifted leader with a transformative vision can fall short of a far-reaching goal.

Epilogue: Be More Strategic guides you in developing your own strategic leadership plan. It introduces a strategic leadership survey to diagnose patterns and gaps in your capabilities, establish your personal skills–building agenda, and measure your progress. We look at Jane Wang's approach to becoming more strategic. We discuss how you can set priorities according to your career plan and organizational setting. And, finally, we show how to select the right tools for bridging major gaps as well as how to leverage resources such as training, coaches, and mentors.

The aim is to tailor a strategic leader plan just for you. We illustrate how to structure your plan around the six disciplines by revisiting Jane's case in each chapter.

✦ ✦ ✦

The problem is the world changes out from under you if you're not constantly adding to your skill set.

—JEFF BEZOS

1 ELEPHANTS AND BLACK SWANS

The Discipline to Anticipate:
See Sooner and Scan Wider

Tesla, the brainchild of Elon Musk, has shaken up the automotive industry. In February 2014, the Model S was rated greatest car in all the land when it received the number-one ranking by *Consumer Reports*, becoming the first US car ever to receive a "best overall" pick. The reviewers singled out the Model S for its "blistering acceleration, razor-sharp handling, compliant ride, and versatile cabin." "We don't get all excited about many vehicles, and with this car we really did," said Jake Fisher, head of auto testing for *Consumer Reports*.[1] "You get into it, and it really stands out. It's the very best car I've ever driven."[2]

Just a year earlier, in 2013, the Model S was named Automobile of the Year by *Automobile* magazine[3] and Car of the Year by *Motor Trend*. The breakthrough of the Model S and, indeed, these unparalleled accolades speak to Musk's prowess in spotting new market opportunities and then seeing them through.[4] Not only is the car admired by critics and envied by environmentally oriented car enthusiasts, but many financially oriented doubters jumped on board when Tesla announced a profit in the first quarter of 2013 and surpassed established rivals like Mercedes, Audi, and BMW in sales growth.[5] Tesla stock has been a Wall Street darling, with meteoric growth during 2013 and early 2014 despite the fact that various hedge fund investors bet against it.

How did this happen? Students of the automotive industry and clean energy are aware of the long-term quest to build and commercialize an environmentally friendly car that would be independent of oil and gas and usher in a new age of transportation. The powerful forces and barriers arrayed against this future vision were dramatized in the movie *Who Killed the Electric Car?*[6]

Entrepreneurs like Elon Musk, Apple's Steve Jobs, and Amazon's Jeff Bezos excel in spotting unmet market needs and figuring out how to serve them profitably. They have an eye for change that they leverage through innovative business models. In short, they excel at *anticipation*. This skill is innate to some degree, but we've found that leaders can enhance it through deep curiosity, superior information, smarter analysis, and broad touch points with those in the know.

Elon Musk is an anticipator in chief with game-changing ambitions, and we can learn from his successes and struggles. Born in South Africa, Musk started his studies in physics and completed his university education in North America where he studied economics, engineering, and high-energy physics. His innovative eye and entrepreneurial drive made him a multi-millionaire in his late twenties. Before the dotcom bubble burst in 2000, Musk sold his digital publishing business to Compaq for more than $300 million. He then co-founded the ecommerce payments system PayPal, with its innovative software and business model, bought by eBay for $1.5 billion in 2002.[7] Next he turned to clean transportation with his Tesla car and his SpaceX private rocket ventures.

Tesla's Fortune on the Rise

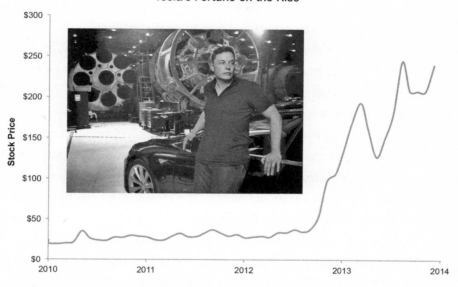

Ever since his college days at the University of Pennsylvania, Musk had a vision of commercializing electric vehicles for the mass market.[8] He recognized full well that getting into the electric-car business could be "one of the stupidest things you could do." Mitt Romney proclaimed the Tesla a "loser" during his 2012 presidential election campaign.[9] Ron Adner, professor of strategy at Dartmouth, concurred: "The current approach to the electric car is doomed to fail in the mass market."[10] Even Takeshi Uchiyamada, known as the "father of the Prius," expressed reservations: "Because of its shortcomings—driving range, cost and recharging time—the electric vehicle is not a viable replacement for most conventional cars."[11]

Musk played the long game and recognized "a need for acceleration of electric vehicles. It became clear to me that, if it was simply left to the big car companies, we wouldn't see compelling electric cars, not for a long time. It would be some time before we would see sustainable transport."[12] Musk believed that "the industry was operating under two false premises: One, that you could not create a compelling electric car. And two, that no one would buy it."[13] In his view, "the current challenge is not to prove that an electric car will work, can be mass-produced, that people will buy it, or that a profit can be made but to convince people that electric cars (Model S) can be a mainstream product and to reassure consumers that infrastructure (chargers) can be developed to give them the freedom and reliability of a regular car."[14]

Musk founded Tesla Motors in 2003 because he saw these opportunities in automotive technology and distribution well before others saw the possibilities. He wanted to make affordable all-electric roadsters that, unlike hybrids such as the Prius, consumed no fossil fuel. Musk saw that an electric-powered car could maneuver just as well as a sports car powered by an internal combustion engine. It could also be stylish, dynamic, and a statement car for at least one segment of the well-to-do population. According to Musk, "with the Model S, you have a compelling car that's too expensive for most people. . . . And you have the Leaf [a 100 percent electric car made by Nissan], which is cheap, but it's not great. What the world really needs is a great, affordable electric car. I'm not going to let anything go, no matter what people offer, until I complete that mission."[15] During a 60 Minutes program aired on March 31, 2013, Musk discussed how he had dealt with great adversity, including financial ruin after having been worth hundreds of millions.[16] Through it all, he remained true to his vision and said he fully expects more big challenges ahead.

Despite Tesla's engineering, technical, consumer, and stock market success to date, Musk's effort to secure its long-term commercial viability is still a question mark. In the commercial arena, Musk is challenging conventional practice. Tesla set up a distribution network so that consumers could buy cars directly from the factory rather than using the traditional franchised dealership model that prevents Detroit's automakers from selling directly to consumers.

Tesla insists on selling its cars directly to consumers: "You walk into a Tesla store—much like you would an Apple Store—to sample the products and order a custom version of their car."[17] And if you wanted to take it for a ride, you can make an appointment to be picked up at your home or office. Not surprisingly, litigation quickly followed. Dealers are suing Tesla in New York State for violating state franchise laws. Similar suits by dealers are pending in other states, and there have been legal setbacks for Tesla in New Jersey, Texas, and elsewhere.[18]

Musk remains undeterred, convinced that he is right about the urgent need for an affordable clean car. Tesla is pursuing what the top three US automakers have failed to do—namely, to overhaul their outdated fossil-fuel business models to support a low-carbon economy. In a radical move in June 2014, Musk went a step further by opening over five hundred of Tesla's patents to the world. In two highly competitive industries where patents are considered sacred (technology and automotive), Musk defied convention by allowing his competitors use of these patents without fear of intellectual property litigation. This gutsy gambit challenges the industry's traditional mindset as well as misguided perceptions about Musk himself. On Tesla's blog, Musk reflects, "We felt compelled to create patents out of concern that the big car companies would copy our technology and then use their massive manufacturing, sales and marketing power to overwhelm Tesla. We couldn't have been more wrong. The unfortunate reality is the opposite: electric-car programs (or programs for any vehicle that doesn't burn hydrocarbons) at the major manufacturers are small to non-existent, constituting an average of far less than 1% of their total vehicle sales."[19]

Looking to win the long game, Musk realizes that Tesla's true competitors are traditional gas-powered cars. Electric cars comprise less than 1 percent of the entire automobile population worldwide. In order for electric cars to compete against gasoline-powered automobiles, Musk believes the electric-car industry needs to catch up quickly. Industry-wide collaboration, instead of competition, is necessary to move the auto industry toward cleaner electric cars, especially if the ultimate goal is to curb the carbon crisis. By embracing an open-source philosophy, Musk hopes to promote Tesla's leading-edge technology as a starting point from which the electric-car industry can grow. This is a rare but powerful example of a strategic leader who adopts an industry rather than just a firm perspective, to the benefit of many.[20] As he puts it, "We believe that Tesla, other companies making electric cars, and the world would all benefit from a common, rapidly-evolving technology platform." The world is responding in kind. Soon after the announcement, several automakers, such as Nissan and BMW, embraced the opportunity to work with Tesla. Through such partnerships, Musk hopes to see growth in the charging station network, a shared infrastructure, improving economies of scale, and reducing battery costs.

Near term, Musk marches on, convinced that he is right about the urgent need for an affordable clean car. Tesla is pursuing what the top three US automakers have failed to do—namely, to overhaul their outdated fossil-fuel business models to support a low-carbon economy. Given continued pushback by traditional industry players in the United States, and the greater openness to green-energy solutions in other countries, Tesla expects the combined sales in Europe and Asia to be almost twice those in North America in 2014. The company said it will introduce right-hand-drive versions of its Model S sedan in the United Kingdom and offer leasing and financing programs in Europe. The electric-car maker has forecast a more than 55 percent jump in global sales in 2014.[21] Tesla sold 22,477 cars in 2013, including a record 6,892 vehicles in the fourth quarter.[22] BMW is paying close attention to Musk's effort to create a mass market for electric cars and is launching its own versions as a fast follower.

To produce its own batteries, Tesla plans to spend as much as $5 billion to build a so-called giga-factory employing some 6,500 US workers. The facility will allow Tesla to manufacture its own batteries, thereby creating cheaper versions of its cars, potentially doubling its worldwide market share to about 1 percent.[23] The giga plant is key to Tesla's goal of producing 500,000 or more electric vehicles a year. The cheapest model, the Model S, starts at $71,000, still too expensive for mass appeal. The planned expansion would be large enough to drive down lithium-ion battery costs by at least 30 percent and lower the price of the car as well. It would also make Tesla a power storage company, benefiting Musk's other enterprise, SolarCity. A rendering of the facility on Tesla's website shows it in the desert with adjacent solar and wind farms to supply electricity.[24]

We may not know for years, perhaps decades, whether Musk will achieve his ultimate goal of transforming transportation as we know it. But we do know that Musk has an eye for the long game and a stomach for risk and resistance. He makes big bets on what he sees down the road. Consider his ambitious venture, SpaceX. After several failed rocket launches, Musk reached that defining moment familiar to many strategic leaders, where his next effort had to succeed or he would go out of business. Since Musk's team had learned from each launch attempt, we weren't surprised by SpaceX's triumph over gravity in what could have been its final launch.

The Musk story illustrates that strategic leaders who take the long view are highly observant and discerning in their judgments. They can separate signal from noise. The antennae of contrarians work overtime to tune in weak signals that others miss, such as a growing US market for eco-friendly, upscale cars or battery technology. Moreover, to leverage their superior insight, such leaders spring into action when they spot opportunities, whereas lesser souls are too timid—or unable—to see the future through the smog.

Contrarians delight in exploring ideas outside the mainstream, especially when traditional arguments fall apart or collide with a transformative vision. They are wary of status quo views and prefer honest, transparent assessments that reflect how much, or how little, is really known about the issue at hand. This openness allows them to be creative and to *see sooner* what lurks around the corner. In the face of uncertainty, their skepticism frees them to catch the meaningful anomalies that their overly confident colleagues will likely miss or simply dismiss.

Strategic leaders are stubbornly certain only in their belief that the world is far more complex than the overconfident prognostications of experts imply. And that brings us to an intriguing paradox: to *see sooner and scan wider* you must proceed with equal parts passion and humility. Start by assessing how well you anticipate the future and play the long game. Answer the questions below, and ask your colleagues to score you as well with brutal honesty.

See Sooner

1. *How well do you track industry trends that pose threats or opportunities for your business? What did you see sooner than others? What did you miss?* Musk looks at trends and spots breakthrough technologies that prompt him to look more deeply into new opportunities. He is not just lucky; his career provides ample evidence of a commitment to disciplined independent thinking.

2. *Closer to home, how well do you foresee the changing needs of your customers or end-users? Do you see their evolving needs sooner than they will themselves?* Again, Musk and his collaborators have been able to see sooner that investors who bet narrowly against battery-powered vehicles are in for a rude awaking. Musk is reinventing the entire value chain end to end. By watching how Apple engaged and inspired consumers in its new-age stores, he is fashioning a direct-to-consumer model.

3. How well do you anticipate the moves of your competitors and their likely reactions to new initiatives, products, or services? Musk realizes that most traditional competitors are blinded by their short-term focus and incremental strategies. Tesla is prepared for the attacks on its direct-to-consumer sales strategy. Whether the various state courts side with Tesla or not, it is ready to battle, has more wins than losses so far, and is pursuing a market strategy that transcends the provincial barriers of the United States.

Scan Wider

4. Do you see market uncertainty as a source of potential advantage because you are better informed, scout more broadly, and look under many rocks? Rather than gloss over the issues, Musk looks broadly as well as deeply until he better understands complex market dynamics and possible future scenarios. This aptitude ultimately led Musk to start making his own batteries since they are so central to Tesla's cost structure and push to make cars cheaper.

5. Do you gather information from a wide network of experts and other sources both inside and outside your function or industry? Musk is a sponge, talking to people from all sides of the transportation community and well beyond it. By collecting many different opinions, he is able to see new patterns and anticipate options.

6. Do you think in terms of multiple futures and new business models, different from today, by studying innovators inside and outside your industry? Musk learned from Apple about designing a special customer experience and generating demand by engineering a "must-have" car for a niche market of early adopters. Musk understood the dynamics of technological disruption and positioned himself for a future where driving without gasoline would become the norm and not the exception.

Now that you have done a quick self-assessment, let's probe deeper into the skills of seeing sooner and scanning wider.

SEEING SOONER

Seeing Threats and Opportunities: Lessons from Microsoft

In a volatile, uncertain world, your leadership effectiveness and sustainability will in large measure depend on your ability to anticipate well. Many companies that grew fast, such as Microsoft, Virgin, or Google, recognized an emerging need in the marketplace and moved quickly to fill it. But even the entrepreneurial geniuses behind these companies often get tripped up later. For example, in the early 1990s, Bill Gates, co-founder and former CEO of Microsoft, was slow to see how Netscape, a new start-up, would gain traction and change how people consume information on computers. Before Netscape, people "surfing the web" had to wait for browsers to download every single byte before displaying any information on the screen. Netscape changed all that with its browser Navigator. By allowing content to load when any piece of data was ready, the Netscape Navigator displayed content faster and allowed for more media diversity.

Thanks to this and other breakthroughs, Netscape conquered nearly 80 percent of the Internet browser market by 1995. This paradigm shift caught even Gates by surprise. On December 7 of that year, a date coinciding with the Japanese attack on Pearl Harbor in 1941, Gates wrote one of his big priority-setting all-hands-on-deck memoranda. It became known as the Pearl Harbor memo; and, in it, Gates quoted Japanese Admiral Isoroku Yamamoto to suggest that Netscape, like Japan, had awakened "a sleeping giant." Rick Sherlund, an analyst with Goldman Sachs at the time, advised Netscape investors to "hold onto your seat," since Microsoft would surely initiate a strong counterattack.

Microsoft acquired a small browser company and swiftly launched its own offense. By 2000, Netscape's share of the browser market had dwindled to 20 percent, while Microsoft's had gained steadily.

Microsoft finally won, only to be sued by the US Department of Justice for anticompetitive behavior. The subsequent settlement required computer manufacturers to install Netscape's Navigator on all machines that licensed Microsoft's operating system.[25]

Though Microsoft eventually defeated Netscape, its leaders were slow in spotting the threat and overcompensated by trying to stifle competition. The software business is fast moving, with surprising twists and turns. Gates was always scanning the horizon for new clues about future change. For example, while surfing Google's help-wanted section, he noticed that the search giant was seeking software engineers with profiles similar to those hired by Microsoft. Gates dashed off another big memo to his management team: What does this mean? What is Google up to? The management team apparently missed the prescience of Gate's memo.[26] Google outflanked Microsoft in the all-important search algorithm market and associated advertising segments.

Each of these blind spots cost Microsoft in terms of growth, prestige, and market capitalization. Once a company becomes the master of its own universe, as Microsoft was with respect to operating-system software, seeing new developments in adjacent markets becomes harder. Consider Steve Ballmer's statement in April 2007: "There's no chance that the iPhone is going to get any significant market share."[27] Ballmer, who by then had become CEO at Microsoft, was wrong not only about Apple's iPhone but also about Google's Android. Microsoft was one of the early innovators in smartphones but failed to see their growth potential and, more importantly, the disruptive entries of its competitors. Failure to anticipate threats and opportunities tied to key market developments can be costly to a company and to your career as a leader. Amid investor clamor, Ballmer announced his retirement in 2013.[28] After a year-long search, Microsoft promoted another insider, Satya Nadella, to lead the firm. But can and will this inside CEO offer the company sufficient outside perspectives? Some of his early moves and observations suggest he intends to shake up Microsoft. Nadella himself noted that "Microsoft is no longer the dominant force and . . . needs to act like a hungry startup."[29] Still, investors wonder whether an insider can fully reimagine Microsoft amid massive industry transformation.[30]

Leaders can run red lights only so often before the sirens go off and the powers-that-be pull them over and slap them with a fine in the form of demotion or termination. For the CEOs of Eastman Kodak, Blockbuster video, Borders Bookstores, Nokia, and, more recently, BlackBerry and HMV, the ability to anticipate was so important—and so lacking—that they barely saw their own pink slips coming. Up until 2013, the British music chain HMV (His Masters' Voice) was still selling music CDs and DVDs through its two hundred stores in Britain, Ireland, Singapore, and Hong Kong. The company employed more than four thousand people at the time, reflecting its long-standing role in Britain's music distribution business. But its risk averse management missed the signs and failed to invest sufficiently in its Internet presence, and eventually online ventures such as Spotify completely disrupted HMV's retail business model. Spotify lets its customers listen to an unlimited number of songs for less than $16 a month. In January 2013, HMV entered into administration, a form of bankruptcy protection in the United Kingdom.[31] In a relatively short time, it went from the top of the charts to off the track.

Missing a Tectonic Shift at Lego

At the time of this writing, Lego is on top of the movie charts. *The Lego Movie* fully capitalizes on the brand and uses creative animation to connect more widely with audiences. Only a decade ago, the company was on the ropes, posting massive losses and laying off thousands of workers.[32] It had failed to see that the toy manufacturing and entertainment industries were at a creative cross-roads. Let's review the turnaround.

Ole Kirk Christiansen, a master carpenter who crafted wooden toys, founded Lego during the Great Depression. At its peak in 1994, the company employed one in four residents of Billund, a small hamlet in the farmlands on the Jutland Peninsula of Denmark, "three hours from anything," as its citizens like to say.[33] The pioneer of those neat plastic bricks had a truly remarkable run of double-digit growth for fifteen years starting in 1980. But then profits plunged from 752 million Danish kronen (about US$186 million at the time) to losses of 194 million kronen (US$48 million) in 1998. It was the first down year ever in Lego's sixty-six-year history.

The tiny community of Billund was shocked. How could this happen? In early 1997, Peter Eio, then US chief of operations for Lego, proposed that the company sign a partnership with Lucasfilm Ltd. to bring out a licensed line of Star War toys. George Lucas was preparing for the 1999 launch of *The Phantom Menace*, the first of three prequels to the original Star Wars franchise. After a fifteen-year hiatus, the Jedi would be returning to the big screen! Star Wars science fiction fanatics—and there are many—were ecstatic. Parents now, many fans couldn't wait to introduce their children to the wonders of The Force.

What's more, Star Wars fans love merchandise almost as much as they love trivia. There would be new action figures, dynamic video-games, cool costumes, and toys. The deal had the potential to generate revenue from three movie tie-ins and could catapult Lego into the sci-fi fan collectible market, not to mention popular culture, for the next eight years.[34] But the senior vice president who had to approve the deal did not concur. His curt response was "Over my dead body."[35] It was a strong visceral reaction born of suspicions about Hollywood (a world he did not know) and his deep pride that Lego's innovations had always come from inside the company. Why would Lego need outsiders, he wondered? It seemed insulting.

In the end, wiser heads prevailed and Kjeld Kirk Kristiansen, a grandson of Lego's founder, signed a deal with Lucasfilm.[36] When the new Star Wars films became a global smash, Lego profited greatly. Like Kjeld, the best strategic leaders anticipate where their business is headed and see change before others do. It's not a Jedi mind trick. Instead, these leaders excel at the "outside-in" thinking that hones their ability to anticipate well. They know customers intimately, foresee competitors' moves, and understand changing market dynamics. We examine these key domains further below.

Changing Needs of Customers: How to See Sooner

The leaders of Lego missed important social and psychographic changes in the lives of its customers. Children raised in an environment of instant gratification often lacked the patience or vision to build complex Lego configurations from scratch. Their lives were more highly scheduled than ever, with the parents filling extra hours of the day with planned activities. There was little time left for hours of imaginative self-directed play.[37]

Getting close to ever more demanding and overbooked customers requires "getting inside their heads," whereas Lego's innovations had primarily come from inside the company. Open innovation was not yet common practice and would not have fit the Lego culture. The effort to anticipate what consumers want, perhaps even before they know it themselves, was lacking at Lego.

Like most companies, Lego paid the price by not seeing these changes soon enough. Strategic leaders such as Kevin Tsujihara, CEO of Warner Brothers (Time Warner Inc.'s movie studio), are vigilant about looking ahead in their environment for signals of change. "Consumers' expectations don't allow us to wait for the silver bullet that doesn't exist," says Tsujihara. "We need to anticipate where the market is going."[38] Many were surprised at the success of the film. But Tsujihara, who engineered *The Lego Movie* deal

for Warner Brothers, had clearly seen the potential from a consumer point of view. One reason he became CEO was his experience with disruptive technologies such as digital that are upending
industry business models and customer strategies.[39] Although staying ahead of or even shaping customer expectations is difficult,
especially in manufacturing companies such as Lego, CEOs like
Steve Jobs of Apple showed how to do it. Success requires a total
market-driven orientation, as opposed to a production or efficiency
mindset.[40] The key is to open your eyes to where your customers are
heading, ideally before they fully realize it themselves. As Henry
Ford said, "If I had asked people what they wanted, they would
have said faster horses."[41]

Perhaps the single most important challenge for strategic leaders
is to develop and maintain an external mindset. There's a great
temptation to lock in on internal organizational issues where you
can immediately add value. But getting sucked into doing so means
losing sight of the forest for the trees. Because being customer-
centric is so fundamental to anticipation, we highlight how to tune
in to customer signals.

1. *Stand in your customer's shoes.* Look beyond your core business to understand a customer's full range of choices as well
   as the ecosystem of suppliers, partners, and end users. One
   leader we know emphasizes the importance of knowing
   your "customer's customer." Lego sold to retailers and distributors but needed to experience the hectic schedules of
   the kids and parents who were their target audience. They
   needed to ask why parents chose one activity over another
   and to understand where and how children were exercising
   their creativity. Akin to drivers of Coke trucks who go in
   and out of restaurants and bars all day making Coca-Cola
   deliveries, they may not stop to notice what people are

drinking or see that water bottles have become the norm in some markets. And if they do notice, no one asks for their observations.

2. *Staple yourself to a customer's order.* Track the key experiences of your customers as they traverse your company's pathways and note where the experience breaks down. For example, some hospitals ask interns to experience the check-in process as fake patients or ask outsiders to role-play and understand the patient experience.[42]

3. *Learn together with customers,* as General Electric does by inviting some of its top customers in growth markets like China, along with local executives and account managers, to seminars on leadership and innovation. Customers value such face-to-face exchanges with high-ranking GE executives. These meetings also help GE executives to better understand the world of their customers and to better explain GE's innovations and business approach. Such interactions promote trust, co-creation of mutually beneficial solutions, and opportunities to understand and anticipate customer needs.[43]

In short, you need to get out of your own way to understand how your customers are changing and then foresee what they will need before they do. One cartoon captures this challenge nicely. It shows a couple discussing whether to eat at home or to go out. They decide to stay home and order a pizza. While they're still narrowing down the toppings they want to order, the doorbell rings. There stands a delivery person from *Psychic Pizza* with exactly the toppings they desire. The subtext of this cartoon reflects the growing emphasis on *life-cycle modeling,* which, enabled by in-depth customer information and smart data mining, lets sophisticated companies anticipate your needs better than you might. Of course, such an analysis can be annoying if they call you during dinner or target you on the Internet.

But it can also be helpful, as when your accountant reminds you to file an obscure tax form within two weeks or your bank asks whether you need a loan for your eighteen-year-old's college tuition. When you listen only for problems that concern your own company's offerings, you may be blind to customer cues signaling new business opportunities. Try to listen with a third ear, analogous to what Taoists call a "third eye" that gets activated during states of deep contemplation, when your ability to perceive without prejudice is heightened. Anthropologists use this approach when conducting ethnographic research. Their challenge is to leave their own values and mental filters at home so they can study a particular tribe entirely on its own terms, without prejudgment.

Seeing Competitive Moves and Reactions Sooner: War-Gaming

Copyrights and patents have predictable expiration dates. For example, Pfizer, Novartis, and Merck are acutely aware of the dates when their best-selling drugs go off patent. That's the day when generic drug manufacturers start cranking out competitive capsules and tablets for private labels and store brands around the world at a fraction of the price. To offset the dramatic loss of sales, these pharmaceutical giants are continually exploring partnerships, acquisitions, adjacencies, product extensions, co-branded generic medicines, and other novel solutions.

So, it's a bit of a head scratcher that, when Lego's patents expired, its leaders were surprised that Chinese and other manufacturers deluged the market with cheap imitations. More disquieting to Lego, these knock-offs snapped right onto Lego sets. As companies often do when they fail to anticipate, Lego sued. But its patent and trademark infringement lawsuits couldn't curb such low-cost rivals as Mega Blocks from Canada, Cobi SA from Poland, and Oxford

Bricks from China.[44] Well in advance of patent expiration, Lego could have applied several techniques to see sooner, by anticipating the likely moves of these aggressive competitors.

One such technique is *war-gaming*. Before the US Navy SEALs conducted their 2011 raid on Osama bin Laden's hideout in Pakistan, they spent months crafting their strategy. They studied satellite pictures of his compound, constructed a detailed model of the buildings, and rehearsed how the mission might unfold. In these rehearsals, some participants played the role of the enemy—bin Laden and his security team as well as Pakistani police—to simulate how various players would react. They not only practiced the raid on a life-sized replica but did so using different game plans. The SEALs ran many scenarios to prepare them for the unexpected. When one of their modified Blackhawk helicopters crashed, no one panicked; they had actually rehearsed this possibility. The overall aim in SEAL training is to remain one step ahead, by always anticipating the possible actions of others.

War-gaming in the business world serves exactly the same purpose. It helps organizations to spot the moves of rivals sooner, especially if combined with good competitive intelligence. War-games are as much about the preparation as the results. For the game to surface new strategic insights, every player must be willing and able to adopt the mindset of a particular competitor and plunge deeply into its business realities.[45]

For example, one Midwestern pediatric hospital was grappling with rapid consolidation in its metro area, where larger hospitals with primarily adult patients were actively looking to merge or to form strategic alliances. To prepare for any eventuality, the pediatric hospital's CEO engaged his board in a simulation in which five teams played the roles of the five major competitors. They were asked to explore possible alliances that might occur in the next twenty-four months.

The teams documented each competitor's behavior, decisions, and tendencies. During the game, the CEO introduced a hypothetical scenario: "a merger between two particular adult-patient hospitals." He asked the members of each team to evaluate their hospital's attractiveness given the shift in marketplace dynamics, to identify potential alliances, to decide on a strategic action relative to competitors, and to assess their hospital's preparedness to execute such actions.

Once the board examined the merger scenario, the CEO introduced a second strategic surprise, a disruptive technology coupled with overly demanding legislation. The teams repeated the process and recorded all plays. The games produced a tactical playbook that outlined optimal responses to various situations that helped the CEO crystallize a plan. He initiated informal conversations with a wide cross-section of his rivals. He learned, for example, that a billionaire benefactor and board member of another adult-patient hospital was itching to shake up the market and that this visionary benefactor had the clout, smarts, and means to do so through a strategic acquisition. The CEO also learned that, if certain adult hospitals merged, their most direct pediatric competitor would likely want to merge as well. Within months of the simulation, two adult hospitals announced a major consolidation. The CEO and his board were ready to act. They approached the other pediatric hospital about partnering on an opportunity they might otherwise have missed.

Old ways of thinking in today's "new normal" can be dangerous. The same worn scripts, with the same cast of players, may not suffice. War-gaming brings to the surface unexpected events, black swans, and unfamiliar choices so that you can be prepared. In this way, it can help you anticipate major market shifts early and prevent a lot of unproductive drama later, such as crisis management, finger pointing, and rushed decisions that are poorly thought out.

Seeing Shifts Sooner to Capitalize on New Market Dynamics

What really stopped Lego in its tracks was the shift "from bricks to clicks." Toymakers began embedding digital technology into their products, moving the toy market away from mechanical, engineering, and architectural models to audio, video, and online entertainment. By the turn of the millennium, interactive games such as SimCity were delivering amazing building experiences online that connected with changing consumer preferences. The digital special effects of Game Boy, Xbox, and Nintendo left that old bucket of bricks in the dust. Once reality fully set in, Lego embarked on an undisciplined innovation binge. This time the company went overboard in a misguided attempt to compensate for its earlier blind spots. A few of its efforts took off, such as the Star Wars line that hit record sales by 2001. But many of the other innovative attempts lacked focus and did not get traction.[46] When you are gripped by today's business challenges, grasping changing market dynamics is difficult. That's why strategic leaders discipline themselves to step outside the immediacy of the battle periodically and take the long view.

In the marketplace for clean and accessible energy sources, Brent Alderfer had the focus and readiness to take advantage of rapidly evolving market forces, regulation, and consumer preferences. Alderfer and his partners launched Community Energy when they (1) saw viable wind energy technologies in use in Europe and soon to be viable for the United States and (2) believed that some US consumers, if given the choice, would choose clean energy over conventional energy, even at a higher cost.

"I went to some solar and wind conferences," said Alderfer, who is a lawyer, "and what struck me was—wow, this industry needs some marketing, some outreach, and some political savvy. Not that I brought all those, but I wanted to be part of the group that was moving it forward, moving it from alternative technologies, basically unaccepted politically and economically, to something that could make a difference."[47] Alderfer believed the time had arrived and it was important for wind to become a meaningful energy source in the eastern United States.

Community Energy was a pioneer in the marketing of wind energy because it saw an untapped space. It understood that many energy consumers would pay a bit more to support renewable energy. Just as Musk battled fundamental beliefs about electric vehicles, Alderfer battled "the conventional wisdom that there's not enough wind on the US East Coast." Like Musk, Alderfer understood how "technology was converging—the blade length was getting longer, the towers were getting higher, and the generators were getting larger—becoming better-suited to more moderate winds." Community Energy's business plan was basically to get regulators' permission to tap the market: "That's one of the premises of our business: we can lead and innovate more quickly by tapping the market rather than simply tapping the regulators." It wasn't easy. "We made a bold proposal to PECO [Philadelphia Electric Company]: allow their customers to choose to pay more, voluntarily, on their bill, for wind energy in Pennsylvania." PECO ultimately agreed, but Community Energy was challenged from start to finish by other providers who didn't want PECO to offer the wind option. Community Energy went to the Supreme Court of Pennsylvania, a process that took about three years for approval. Then they had to negotiate with environmental groups—the Clean Air Council—to get this program approved; but they knew this was essential to their mission of having a meaningful impact, so they stayed the course.

Since penetrating the residential market would be the greatest challenge, the Community Energy team focused first on institutional accounts. They started with major universities, which would create the foundation to approach residential customers. Eventually they signed up forty thousand residential customers in the Philadelphia area. The bet paid off big, as they went on to implement similar programs with some twenty utilities across the United States and to develop a pipeline of 700 megawatts of wind projects. It paid off handsomely for investors as well: Community Energy was eventually sold to Spain's Iberdrola, one of the world's largest renewable-energy companies.

After achieving success with wind energy, Alderfer's team decided to explore other scenarios for clean energy and concluded that solar was next. "We started investing in the development—land, regulatory, and team—to build out solar in preparation for the markets to be ready." The goal is to reach 1,000 megawatts of solar by 2016, which would be enough energy to make a real impact in the supply to households. "One thousand megawatts requires big capital," Alderfer explains. "We're convinced in this industry that there are huge amounts of capital—you've got to attract capital. . . . Elon Musk and Solar City had a lot to do with turning around Wall Street."

"We just hit a big project in Colorado, which is with 120 megawatts," said Alderfer. "This project is big—not only because of its size, but also because we want to make a difference." That project beat out natural gas and showed that solar at scale has a place in our national energy portfolio. Still looking ahead, Alderfer's team identified a point on the energy price curve where natural gas prices lose their current competitive edge in the United States. At that price point for natural gas, more of Community Energy's larger projects will become economically viable. Ahead of the crossover point, Community Energy laid the foundation by pursuing medium-sized solar projects (2–10 megawatts) in targeted states that have the most favorable conditions. Back in the eastern United States, the management team was asked to triangulate: "If we want to get to the target, we need multiple paths in order to get there. So, that means developing medium and large projects, and it means going to New

Jersey, North Carolina, and Massachusetts and other states, to get enough solar developed."

Community Energy and Tesla both demonstrate how leaders can see sooner to anticipate changing market dynamics driven by technology and social needs. Strategic leaders keep moving and adjusting to stay in front because the marketplace, regulators, competition, and customers are all shifting too. In addition to their external focus, strategic leaders also anticipate better internally, as illustrated below.

Internal Anticipation

Mostly we think of anticipation as looking outside, left and right, to see what might be around the corner. But internal anticipation, within your own organization, matters as well. Executives at Shell in London had formed an internal committee to evaluate three promising employees—Adam, Abhishek, and Clive—for promotion to a senior position. Internal promotion was the norm in this large multinational and the straightest path to the top. The committee laid out the main criteria for evaluation, such as job fit, analytic rigor, internal reputation, strategic acumen, and leadership ability. Using this scoring frame, they interviewed each candidate to understand motivations, interests, talents, and limitations. Since all three had worked at Shell for years, the committee already had good data on their track records.

After careful reviews, the committee recommended Abhishek for promotion, since he scored especially well on job fit as well as on analytic ability and was broadly liked in the organization. The senior Shell executive to whom the committee reported agreed that Abhishek scored best against the criteria laid out. Then, to the committee's great surprise, he announced that he would give the senior position to Clive because Clive would be better suited for the promotion *after* this one. The committee had ranked the candidates in light of the current promotion and failed to anticipate the long-term consequences of its decision. They failed to consider how well each candidate would fare beyond five years, a common blind spot in succession and career planning.

Action Plan to See Sooner

Below is a checklist of activities to integrate into your operational rhythm or to schedule on a daily, weekly, or monthly basis to see sooner. Not all may work for you—but at least try to experiment, shake up your routine, and win the long game. Socialize these ideas within your organization and start incorporating several of them into your strategic leadership toolkit.

1. *List important threats and opportunities that you recently missed.* Be honest with yourself. Why did you miss them? Also study cases where you spotted threats and opportunities ahead of rivals. What did you or others do differently in those instances? Remember the lessons from Elon Musk, who spotted the opportunities in technology innovation that others missed or underestimated, and the Lego executive who dismissed a big move because he was too insular.

2. *Talk to your customers, suppliers, and other partners regularly to understand their challenges.* Block out at least an hour each week and make an initial list of people or organizations to contact. List and discuss the key uncertainties in their industry. Consider creating a program like GE's to learn together with customers or immerse yourself with clients to get inside your customers' experience, as with the hospital interns we described earlier.

3. *Conduct a war-game to understand the perspectives of competitors, legislators, and other key stakeholders.* Gauge their likely reactions to new initiatives, changes in regulation, or

disruptive offerings. This worked for the CEO of the pediatric hospital we discussed, so why not for your team?

4. *Analyze fast-growing rivals, especially nontraditional ones, and examine which of their moves puzzle you and why.* This type of analysis would have helped Microsoft understand and prepare for the game-changing nature of Netscape and the iPhone.

5. *Envision future technologies that will redefine the market dynamics in your industry.* Make some bets to position your organization for those possibilities. Remember how Brent Alderfer at Community Energy envisioned the market potential of wind and, later, solar power and built a plan to capitalize on them.

SCANNING WIDER

Looking Beyond Conventional Domains: Failure to Appreciate Risk at Fukushima

"This was a disaster 'Made in Japan,'" wrote Kiyoshi Kurokawa, chairman of the Fukushima Nuclear Accident Independent Investigation Commission.[48] In its official report on what happened at the Fukushima Daiichi nuclear power plant, his commission addressed the question "How could such an accident occur in Japan, a nation that takes such great pride in its global reputation for excellence in engineering and technology?" The answer has little to do with Japan's technical prowess. Kurokawa pointed instead to Japanese culture—"our reflexive obedience; our reluctance to question authority; our devotion to 'sticking with the program;' our groupism; and our insularity"—as more fundamental causes of the accident.

The report elaborates: "At a time when Japan's self-confidence was soaring, a tightly knit elite with enormous financial resources had diminishing regard for anything 'not invented here,'" including lessons learned from Three Mile Island in the United States and Chernobyl in the former Soviet Union. Worse was "the collective mindset of Japanese bureaucracy" whereby "the first duty of any individual bureaucrat is to defend the interests of his organization" at the expense of public safety. Resisting regulatory pressure and covering up small-scale accidents had become a widely acceptable practice.

How can leaders anticipate the systemic failures that precipitate financial collapse, political upheaval, shortages in mission-critical resources, and great loss to human life, property, and the environment? Failure to anticipate these dynamics, either at the level of the firm or the industry as a whole, can deeply harm customers, partners, and societal trust. Just consider the damages caused by the collapse of Arthur Andersen for those in the accounting field, the class-action lawsuits over drugs like Vioxx or Avandia for pharmaceutical players, the Gulf of Mexico oil spill for offshore drillers, or the subprime mess for bankers. Such systemic mishaps often reflect flawed perspectives, thinking traps, and emotional barriers that prevent leaders from seeing what they *need* to see on the periphery—as opposed to what these leaders *want* to see. The above problems also call for new approaches for dealing with systemic risks that can damage entire industries and even societies.[49] Avoiding systemic risk starts with leaders of individual companies improving their scanning and anticipation abilities.

The mindset of Lego's leaders, for example, tainted their initial view of a partnership with Lucasfilm Ltd. First, since they had launched every new product on their own with spectacular success, the Lego leaders believed that they could launch new toys better than Lucasfilm or anyone else. Second, a military tradition has never been deep-rooted in Denmark, which was neutral during World War I. Also, the company's founder never wanted to associate child play with war and violence. So, Lego never developed soldiers, guns, tanks, and other military accessories for its games.

Third, deep down, Lego executives were apprehensive about Hollywood and didn't fully understand the excitement of videogames, movies, and interactive play.

There are three techniques for overcoming such deep and often subtle mental prejudices and emotional barriers: scanning systematically for weak signals, leveraging your social networks, and using scenario thinking to make sense of future developments.

Spotting Weak Signals at the Periphery: Finding Treasure Under the Surface

When Deven Sharma, as president of Standard & Poor's, testified before Congress in the fall of 2008 about the financial crash, he said: "Virtually no one—be they homeowners, financial institutions, rating agencies, regulators, or investors—anticipated what is occurring."[50] Virtually no one, that is, if you ignore prominent economists such as Paul Krugman, Dean Baker, and Robert Shiller and don't count savvy investors like Steve Eisman, Michael Burry, and John Paulson. To paraphrase Nobel Laureate Krugman: he and his fellow "nobodies" didn't view the financial crisis as a black swan; they saw it as the big elephant in the room. And, elephants don't tip toe and sneak up on you.[51]

While much of the global economy was reeling from the dramatic collapse of esoteric financial instruments like collateralized debt obligations (CDOs), Eisman and a few other investors—similar to N. M. Rothschild two centuries earlier—had carefully studied the situation. They scanned widely to see more clearly than others what was about to happen. Rothschild foresaw the outcome of the Battle of Waterloo, and Eisman foresaw the collapse of the subprime mortgage market. To us the interesting question is not "Why can't the presidents of large rating agencies see an elephant coming?" but "How do some investors spot the elephant far sooner among the many specks on the horizon?"

Even though annual housing prices had not declined in nominal terms in modern memory, the forecasts of continued market growth with containable downside risks made no sense to hedge fund analyst Eisman. Mortgages had become too easy to obtain. He and a few colleagues dove into the data, collected input from multiple sources, and spotted inconsistencies in the performance of the housing market. They worked through the longer-term consequences and realized that none of the possible outcomes justified the market's increasing exuberance. They saw the disaster coming and designed financial instruments to clean up big when the housing market would crash.[52]

Eisman's ability to spot ambiguous threats and opportunities at the periphery of his business is rare among leaders, and it served him well when his peers were swept up in Wall Street euphoria. For several years, Eisman resisted the temptation to do what everybody else was doing, going for the quick buck. Instead, he shorted the subprime mortgage market. His fortitude paid off. Eisman's wider scanning and earlier detection yielded around $1.5 billion for his hedge fund, FrontPoint Partners, a subsidiary of Morgan Stanley. Eisman's actions also exemplify what Nate Silver in *The Signal and the Noise* calls the "prediction paradox."[53] The paradox is that the more humility we have about our ability to make predictions, the more successful we can be in winning the long game. Why? Open-mindedness encourages inquiry, debate, and doubt, all of which help overcome our deep-seated human bias toward overconfidence and myopia. Scanning the horizons with an open mind requires a willingness to be surprised, confused, and thrown off your planned course but, in turn, allows you to see that important something that you would otherwise have missed.

Johnson & Johnson operates in a complex and fast-changing sector of diversified healthcare products ranging from Band-Aids, Tylenol, and disposable contact lenses to medical devices and pharmaceuticals. Its decentralized structure, with more than two hundred relatively autonomous operating companies around the world, ensures that each business stays close to its customers.[54] In addition to tracking competitors, managers must pay attention not only to markets and technology but also to healthcare regulations, insurance coverage, and formularies. To scan the volatile periphery of healthcare, J&J created a strategy process called FrameworkS, through which the executive committee poses key questions such as

+ What will the demographic picture look like five years from now?
+ What might our customer profiles look like in twenty years?
+ How will a typical doctor's office or hospital operate? (You can substitute your own point of delivery or customer environment here.)
+ What role will government play?
+ What might technology look like in ten years?
+ What will be the role and power of payers in the industry?

These questions encourage a deep curiosity about the future. They also prime managers to explore different scenarios about what is next. Had Lego managers posed similar questions together with customers and suppliers, they would have been more open to going digital and teaming up with Hollywood sooner.

Picking up weak signals really comes down to three key elements: good information flow, an inquisitive orientation, and open-minded interpretation. Architect Buckminster Fuller, inventor of the geodesic dome, never wanted to miss important trends or developments. So, whenever he traveled, he picked a magazine at random from a kiosk—say, on fly-fishing, basket weaving, golf, or car repairs—and read the entire publication during his trip. This simple habit kept him in touch with parts of the world he otherwise knew nothing about or might never see. It enhanced his information flow, much as satellite television or the Internet can do now. Nonetheless, randomness is often missing today. With access to thousands of channels, people typically set their digital video recorders for only those programs they like. The current digital generation, overwhelmed by an avalanche of data from diverse media, filters out what it deems unimportant or uninteresting. Both the old and the young often miss important signals outside their areas of focus and may have to reintroduce vicarious learning into their routines.

Leveraging Social Networks for a Wide-Angle View

To overcome blind spots and transcend narrow information channels, leaders should tap their organizational networks more fully. We saw how Brent Alderfer got flashes of insight at the wind and solar conferences he attended. Many companies belong to industry trade associations ranging from narrow industry verticals to wide agglomerations such as the Business Round Table, the Conference Board, and the Association of National Advertisers. Members of these networks exchange information, collect different perceptions of shared interests, and develop beneficial business relationships. However, since these associations function as affinity groups, they tend to reinforce existing mental models. In some cases, they become echo chambers where like-minded managers confirm their own biases and convictions.

To combat this tendency toward conformity, strategic leaders plug into important spheres that expose them to people with different worldviews, knowledge, and experience. They look to join small groups of noncompeting companies such as those inspired by former Medtronic CEO Bill George, called True North Groups.[55] By sharing failures and misses, executives turn their blind spots into building blocks for sharper and more authentic leadership. Similarly, the peer-learning network Collaborative Gain organizes peer councils where ten to fifteen digital executives from non-competing companies can candidly discuss strategic problems and receive feedback from peers, all under strict confidence.[56] Over time, these networks start to function like personal strategic antennae. Leaders can then combine such networks into an *organizational* strategic radar, as the Defensive Logistics Agency (DLA) did. This large organization handles all supplies (except weapon systems) for the US Armed Forces and is a world leader in distribution and logistics. In the mid-2000s, thanks to their strategic radar, DLA's leaders were quick to spot the shift from radio frequency identification technology to mobile phones for tracking shipments—a capability critical to military operations in remote locations.[57]

Reflect about how well you create and mine your networks. What purpose does each one serve for you? Do they corroborate or confront your beliefs? How can you push yourself further out on the periphery?

To scan wider: track cutting-edge blogs, tap into the "wisdom of the crowd," join LinkedIn interest groups outside your field, and glean deeper insights from data collected in your business or social networks.

Using Scenarios to Widen Your Aperture

Scenario planning, as it traditionally has been used, provides a useful stress test for your current strategy. By developing different views of how the external environment of your business may change, you can better determine whether your organization has sufficient strategic flexibility to succeed in each of these possible futures. You can also use such scenarios to scan wider and detect signals that foreshadow change or disruption. Scenario planning is like previewing a movie: you can better spot what you should be looking for, when the actual show starts. Scenarios can pick up early indicators about how emerging technologies or social trends might disrupt your current business model, how customers' preferences might change, or why new regulations may alter your industry.[58]

A key challenge in scenario planning is to understand not just the deeper trends at work but, especially, the key uncertainties whose outcomes can materially affect your industry in the years ahead.[59] For Lego, uncertainties included the diffusion rate of online media and videogaming, the number and speed to market of manufacturers that would jump on Lego's patent expirations, and the sustainability of Wall Street's enthusiasm for new dotcoms. For you, on the other hand, the key uncertainties may be quite different, resulting in other kinds of scenarios; the key is to reflect a wide range of future possibilities in your scenarios. Make sure that you especially develop a scenario where it is not business as *usual*. Lego might have run a scenario where all those low-cost manufacturers jump on the digital bandwagon and provide much cheaper options with more sizzle.

While such scenario-based analysis does not eliminate uncertainty about changing industry or consumer dynamics, it can help strategic leaders make sense of new information more quickly. For example, what if Lego had developed multiple scenarios about the consequences of Lucasfilm's decision to sell some of its intellectual property to competitors such as Mattel or The Walt Disney Company? As Louis Pasteur noted, "Chance favors the prepared mind." Think of scenario planning as a tool to prepare the organizational mind for better anticipation.

Action Plan to Scan Wider

Here is a checklist of action items for scanning wider. Incorporate some of these into your routines for better anticipation and strategic leadership to help you win the long game.

1. *Identify the weak signals at the boundaries of your current business model.* Like Steve Eisman and the leaders of J&J,

ask questions that are more far-reaching and ask team members to scout on the periphery for emerging trends that may impact your business in the future.

2. *Practice scenario thinking with your team to envision futures quite different from today.* Inherent in playing the long game is that surprise and change will be your constant companions. Use scenarios to stress-test your strategy, prepare for the unexpected, and watch for black swans or elephants in the room. If Lego had applied this technique, it would have been ready for the digital wave that swept its industry.

3. *Look at and learn from start-ups within or outside your industry.* What are they doing and why? What do they see that you don't? Force yourself and your team to take some of their moves seriously, even a few outlandish ones. Watching start-ups or venture capital trends is a means of seeing emerging market shifts and nonconventional rivals.

4. *Choose conferences, workshops, and even training courses outside your comfort zone, your function, or your industry, where potentially no one knows you or your business.* As part of its "connect and develop" strategy for innovation, Procter & Gamble reaches out to companies outside its own industry to share lessons and explore joint challenges. Follow happenings in other countries and sectors, even if they are seemingly far removed from your business. There will be more connections and opportunities than may be apparent at first.

5. *Leverage your current networks and find new ones to join.* How might you engage your existing networks more systematically to keep on top of developments? Join interest groups outside your conventional areas of focus or in adjacent businesses to expand your worldview. Remember how Brent Alderfer started attending sessions on future energy technologies to surface opportunities on the periphery.

6. *Expose yourself to topics different from what you typically consume.* Read, watch, or attend something aimed at a very different demographic. Consider how you, like Buckminster Fuller, might benefit from serendipity in your week.

THE DISCIPLINE TO ANTICIPATE: PULLING IT TOGETHER

When we left Jane Wang, her head was still spinning from her performance review at Brazelton Global. She quickly regrouped and realized that her manager was right: she'd have to get better at *seeing* what was coming *sooner,* or she'd fall short of her professional goals. She had worked too hard thus far to falter in the long game. But how to change?

Though she had no time for fools, Jane did not see herself as an Elon Musk or a Steve Eisman type with a grand vision and a risk appetite to *shape the future.* She worked hard, had some visionary goals, and focused her team on achieving them. Her manager's tough appraisal of her response to the business slowdown and loss of market share was a wake-up call. She was clearly not looking ahead enough, scanning sideways, or taking sufficient risks. She understood now that she had to take very concrete actions to start improving her ability to anticipate.

She made a commitment to work hard on developing these skills. Jane's parents had set high standards for her in their tight-knit family. She'd excelled at school, achieved at work, and made a mark in all her roles thus far. Her parents were very proud: she had surpassed their professional expectations for their daughter. Her determination was her greatest strength—until now. In roles with a diversity of responsibilities and a faster-moving competitive environment, she had to adjust her mind- and skill sets. The drive to climb the next hill had caused her to miss the shifting weather conditions. She had to change her habits.

To *see sooner*, she started by listing threats and opportunities she had missed, the most important of which was a nontraditional competitor who had entered her market. Jane started to block out time to talk with customers about their concerns. She scheduled several dates with field representatives and actually looked forward to shadowing these reps on customer visits in the future. Beyond customers, she scanned more widely by gathering information from stakeholders inside and outside her industry. In particular, she registered for an event about new technologies adjacent to hers, where both suppliers and customers would attend. Also, as part of Brazelton's high-potential program, Jane was invited to attend a session on scenario planning. None of these activities were easy time-wise, and changing her focus would take practice. But she knew that this commitment to change was essential in restoring her confidence and becoming more strategic. She was glad to put a practical plan in place.

2 WHAT ARE YOU AFRAID OF?

The Discipline to Challenge:
Open the Window and Look in the Mirror

THREE MILLION DEVOTEES, MOSTLY YOUNG, SWARMED TO Copacabana Beach to hear the newly elected leader of the Roman Catholic Church on his first official tour. Brazil has the largest number of Catholics in the world. But the church's share slipped from three-fourths of Brazil's population in 2000 to about two-thirds in 2010.[1] Pope Francis, a native of Buenos Aries, knew the challenges facing his organization, not only in Argentina or Brazil but throughout the world.[2] He criticized the church's expenditures on luxuries while children are still starving in many parts of the world. Equally off-putting were the cover-ups of scandals and the corruption in Rome. "Sometimes, we can be like [Pontius] Pilate, who did not have the courage to go against the tide," he said.[3] The pope faced a turnaround situation that called for a deep change of hearts and minds in a two-millennia-old institution steeped in tradition, dogma, and hierarchy.

From day one, Pope Francis eschewed the elaborate costumes, palaces, and pageantry of his predecessors. On this trip to Brazil, he carried his own bag and traveled in a modest compact van. During a traffic jam at rush hour, he climbed out to walk among the poor shanty dwellers of Rio de Janeiro.[4] During the flight back to Rome, he called a surprise press conference. For more than eighty minutes, he answered journalists' unvarnished questions, no topic off-limits. Of the leaking of internal correspondence, including that of the former head of the Vatican office and the pope's personal assistant, he said "It's a big problem" and he committed to looking into how his office handles information.[5] Those who elected him want his office to "be more efficient and more clearly at the service" of the global organization.[6] To that end, he appointed an outside advisory council to reform operations, starting with the Institute for the Works of Religion (IOR).[7]

The IOR, commonly referred to as the Vatican Bank, is a privately held financial institution inside Vatican City. According to former US Treasury official Avi Jorisch, it is "the most secret bank in the world."[8] It accepts deposits only from top church officials, little is known about the bank's daily operations, and its dealings are veiled in mystery. In recent years, the Vatican Bank has been embroiled by scandal and investigation for illicit activities. Pope Francis challenged the current practices of this less than holy institution. "Whatever it ends up being—whether a bank or a charitable fund—transparency and honesty are essential," he said.[9]

In his writings and messages to both the clergy and the more than 1 billion faithful, Pope Francis has chided his Catholic brethren for focusing on contentious issues—such as abortion, homosexuality, the role of women—that he deems less fundamental to the church's mission than embracing all human beings. He calls for a "return to the true basis of brotherhood," the earliest mission of his organization, to care for the ill and the indigent, whereby "every man and woman represents a blessing."[10] To Vatican officials and members of the laity, the meaning is clear: be of service, have the courage to go against the tide, and act with humility, compassion, and transparency. The only mystery in our mind should be how God works, *not* how the Vatican works.

This pope was walking the talk. Within five months of assuming office, Pope Francis surpassed President Barack Obama as the most followed world leader on Twitter. As of Christmas 2013, his approval ratings were sky-rocketing. More importantly, he has prompted a conversation about what really matters in religion and faith. This dialogue has captured the imagination of a broad swath of the global community, from talk show hosts and bartenders to teachers and clergy. The pope's actions allow us all to witness, live, on the big screen and on handheld devices, the power of a leader who challenges beliefs that have outlived their usefulness and undermine the credibility of the institution he leads. His actions refocus the priorities of the Vatican's powerful Curia that governs the church.

The first Papal selfie

As we observe this new pope, named "Person of the Year" in 2013 by *Time* magazine and *Fortune's* 2014 top world leader, we see not just a towering spiritual guide and man of deep faith returning the church to its roots; we see a strategic leader. In taking on the basic assumptions of his organization and the values of society, Pope Francis exemplifies two core practices of leaders who challenge well. First, he is metaphorically *opening up a window* to let in fresh air. In particular, he is bringing in outside advisers and reaching out himself to touch ordinary people, especially those who are hurting or abandoned. Second, he is enlisting Catholics and non-Catholics alike to *look in the mirror*, so to speak, when he reminds us that big battles over marginal issues distract us from the crucial humanitarian mandate to care for those in need. We shall use these two metaphors to explain how leaders like the new pope can effectively challenge the dominant mindset of their organization. *Opening the window* is the practice of promulgating outside perspectives to see complex issues in context. *Looking in the mirror* is the practice of deep self-reflection, whereby leaders confront outmoded beliefs, faulty assumptions, and stubbornness in themselves and others.

Take a moment to consider how you as a leader are challenging yourself and others.

Opening the Window

1. *Do you regularly seek out diverse views to see multiple sides of an important or complex issue?* Can you keep an open mind and open heart so that you can open doors to what you might not understand, as Pope Francis did when he opened himself to the technological zeal of young Italian pilgrims, resulting in the first papal selfie ever snapped?[11]

2. *What practices have you put in place to offset complacency?* Pope Francis has taken risks that his predecessors found unacceptable,

such as stepping away from his bullet-proof motorcade to walk among ordinary people every day.

3. *How deeply do you challenge long-standing assumptions, tradition, and conventional wisdom?* Pope Francis is questioning basic customs that the majority of church leadership has taken for granted, from the gaudy vestments to the veils of secrecy. He is listening to new voices and deliberately bypassing old channels of communication.

Looking in the Mirror

4. *Do you encourage both constructive criticism and creative thinking to surface new perspectives and better options?* Pope Francis certainly fosters healthy debate on taboo topics: "If someone is gay and is searching for the Lord and has good will," he said, "then who am I to judge him?"[12] He wants to embrace the person, not the behavior that violates church doctrine. The pope fearlessly ventured into sensitive political terrain when he challenged world leaders to reflect on the dysfunctions of unfettered capitalism, such as poverty, dehumanization, growing inequality, indifference to human suffering, and environmental degradation.[13]

5. *Do you purposely reframe important problems from several angles to understand their root causes?* At the advice of eight cardinals, Pope Francis has appointed a new council to deal with pedophile priests under secular law and show more compassion to their victims.[14] This council will include outside experts to guide the church in protecting the well-being of its followers, especially the innocent and vulnerable, and not just its own reputation.

6. *Are you able to confront your own biases as well as those of your team?* The pope must have engaged in some deep soul-searching—as Jesuits are known to do—before signing on to his transformational agenda. Now he is ready to reorient the thinking of the entire church leadership back to its basic mission.

OPENING WINDOWS

To open windows is to look outside for fresh perspectives, to understand what outsiders see when they look in. That's why we call these "outside-in" views. The selection of Jorge Mario Bergoglio as pope reflects the foresight of the College of Cardinals, who realized that a nonconventional leader outside Europe might be better positioned to rejuvenate the Roman Catholic Church. By electing Bergoglio, a lifelong ascetic whose evident humility differs from the majority of his colleagues, the College chose a transformational maverick. Pope Francis looks at the church from a fresh vantage point, much as an outside CEO would.[15] Consider what Lou Gerstner did at IBM two decades ago, or what Alan Mulally did at Ford during the current decade. Both CEOs were recruited from outside the computer and auto industries, not just outside IBM and Ford. To revive these two limping global giants, Gerstner and Mulally brought fresh thinking and strategic leadership.

However, you don't need to come in from outside the company to provide that all-important outside-in perspective. Brian Roberts is CEO of Comcast, the largest cable company in the United States and the son of its founder. He continues to open new windows and lead profound change in the company and industry. "It's an exciting time. Technology is changing everything really fast," says Roberts, acknowledging Comcast's many service iterations. "By probably next year, we will have more broadband connections to people's homes than cable connections and we started as a cable company."[16] Comcast acquired NBC and continues to reinvent its various businesses.

Another example of window-opening by a long-term insider is Larry Fink, CEO of BlackRock, which he founded in 1988 with a number of partners. Fink stresses the need to continuously adapt and challenge your business model. "If you don't evolve and change, you go backwards. It's pure physics. There have been times we fell backwards because we didn't adapt fast enough."[17] But overall, Fink and his partners have pushed boundaries and continuously challenged themselves to keep their edge. BlackRock has grown from a niche investment firm focused primarily on fixed income and vigilant risk management into the largest asset management firm in the world with over $4 trillion under management. This enormous growth has involved game-changing moves; innovative technology platforms; major acquisitions to diversify the company's funds, geography, and customer base; reinventing its architecture; and challenging the status quo to drive transformation. A recent growth initiative is BlackRock's leading role in marketing iShares directly to main-street investors and consumers—an approach quite different from its original focus on institutional investors.

In Booz & Company's recent study of CEO succession, the type of outside-in thinking we've described surfaced as an important capability for future leaders.[18] "Rather than breadth of experience, boards and recruiters should look for a proven track record of challenging conventional wisdom and experimenting with unconventional ideas—especially those that pay off," say the study's authors. This quest for alternative views demands two qualities: humility in accepting that no leader can see all angles and courage in flinging wide the window to whoever might look in or whatever might fly in. Leaders at all levels, not just CEOs, need these two qualities if they want to win the long game.

It's no easy task to pry open a window that has long been shut, coated with layers of paint and corroded by rust. Old patterns die hard. In South Africa, Nelson Mandela's attempts to unbolt the system of apartheid cost him twenty-seven years in prison. Pope Francis is drawing criticism from those who'd like to shutter his comments about capitalism and social injustice or to shuffle the pedophiles back behind the tapestries. There are those who've done much the same on Wall Street. Few banks or investors could break ranks with the herd during the subprime crisis.[19] Chuck Prince, the former CEO of Citigroup, summed up the market mentality nicely: "You have to dance when the music plays." If Prince didn't want to dance, Citigroup's board would quickly find a CEO who would be more eager to do so.[20]

The Benefit of a Diverse View:
Challenging Assumptions at BlackRock

While there was no shortage of happy feet in banking, a few financial services firms had the benefit of diverse views and leaders who were independent thinkers. Ben Golub and his team at BlackRock opened the window and challenged the conventional wisdom that had led so many other investment firms right over the cliff. Golub, the chief risk officer (CRO) and one of the founders of BlackRock, is uniquely positioned to challenge faulty assumptions.

During a personal interview, Golub made it clear to us that you need to trust your intuition about what can go right and wrong. If your antennae go up, you have to act and possibly take controversial actions despite the push-back: "It isn't a popularity contest. If you have a concern about risk, you have to push and advocate for it even if they don't like it. Sometimes you even have to jam your position down peoples' throats and be an enforcer."[21] In the months leading up to the subprime crisis, Golub had exactly this intuition and took a forceful position. Collateralized debt obligations (CDOs) were the hot ticket. Everyone—both inside and outside Black-Rock—was investing in them, but he had concerns.

"It struck me," said Golub, "that all this activity and investment was based on some fairly flimsy analysis. It felt like everyone was rushing into it like lemmings. I insisted that we do a research and development project to study the data from the bottom, understand the underlying assumptions, and refine our models as needed. It was expensive and, at the time, unpopular. But I pushed hard because we had considerable exposure and we didn't know enough about it."[22] This push led to pulling back some of the investments, refining the strategies, and enabling BlackRock to navigate the storms better than just about anyone else during the ensuing financial crisis. Subsequently, the firm expanded its reach, strengthened its brand, and ended up playing a pivotal post-crisis role in managing distressed assets for the Federal Reserve. As a reporter for *The Economist* pointed out, "In the chaos that followed the collapse of Lehman, [BlackRock] also advised the American government and others on how to keep the financial system ticking in the darkest days of 2008, and picked up profitable money-management units from struggling financial institutions in the aftermath of the crisis."[23]

More recently, Golub introduced concepts from behavioral economics and decision science to shine a light on bias in the investment

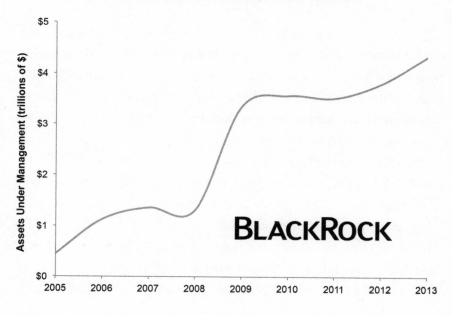

How BlackRock Grew to Over $4 Trillion in Assets

process. His intent was to raise awareness of the economically irrational side of investment decisions and to challenge assumptions about the effectiveness of team dynamics. The outcome was a set of practical tools for investment and risk managers to identify early warning signals of bias and to have a practical guide handy to support better decision-making.

Golub noted that as disruptive companies like BlackRock grow, their leaders can easily become complacent and stray from their entrepreneurial roots as disrupters: "There is a danger that you get entrenched in the status quo. People's jobs and careers are devoted to doing things a certain way. When you challenge that—it can be disruptive. They don't like you."[24]

Despite the challenge and tensions involved, BlackRock founders, employees, and shareholders are delighted that such leaders as Golub keep them honest and protect their flank. Taking a contrarian position may not win you friends, but it could save your company and your career.

The Steep Risks of Complacency

The failure to challenge the status quo can be fatal for leaders—and even more so for their followers. Consider what the Japanese people learned about their nation's energy regulators after the Great Tōhoku Earthquake of 2011. "The TEPCO [Tokyo Electric Power Company] Kagoshima Nuclear Power Plant accident was the result of collusion between the government, the regulators and TEPCO, and the lack of governance by said parties," said members of the Nuclear Accident Independent Investigation Commission. "The root causes were the organizational and regulatory systems that supported faulty rationales for decisions and actions."[25]

The investigation revealed that, as far back as 2006, "regulators and TEPCO were aware of the risk that a total outage of electricity at the Fukushima Daiichi plant might occur if a tsunami were to reach the level of the site."[26] Despite this awareness, they kept the window closed to outside expertise. The prevailing assumption was that Japan had the best technology. No one challenged the "negative attitude toward the importation of new advances in knowledge and technology from overseas," specifically US security measures ordered after the 9/11 terrorist attack in 2001.[27] Even though it had many opportunities to implement the required structural reinforcements prior to the earthquake, "TEPCO did not take these measures, and [the Nuclear and Industrial Safety Agency] and the Nuclear Safety Commission went along."[28]

The system was rigged to favor business over the greater good. That was the status quo. For starters, the commission determined that lax regulations were "biased toward the promotion of a nuclear energy policy, and not to public safety, health and welfare."[29] The commission also identified "the arbitrary interpretation and selection of a probability theory," whereby TEPCO calculated "a low probability of tsunami, and used the results of a biased calculation process as grounds to ignore the need for countermeasures."[30] According to Lake Barrett, a retired nuclear engineer who led the Three Mile Island cleanup, "The Japanese decision-making process, of group decision-making and not individual decision-making, might have been a hindrance to dealing with a situation like this."[31] Culture can constrain individuals from attempting to open a window or two and considering the possible risks and countermeasures.

The key question—which Kiyoshi Kurokawa, chairman of the Fukushima Nuclear Accident Independent Investigation Commission, put to the Japanese people—is how to create conditions that promote and reinforce this fundamental capability to challenge, especially when doing so is culturally taboo, goes against an entire industry, or may cost you your job. As one CEO from India said, when interviewed about the changing leadership context, "The biggest thing in the way of change or transition is the very strong mental models that people have and their inability to shed those mental models."[32]

Challenge Long-Standing Assumptions in Your Industry: Screw Business as Usual

"A bank manager [was] sitting on our doorstep saying on Friday that he would foreclose the Virgin Group on the Monday," said Richard Branson in an interview. "We had to scramble over the weekend to get our overdraft facility down."[33] It was 1984 and, much to the horror of Virgin's board, Branson had just launched a high-quality, high-value airline. What could this record-label executive possibly know that the heads of other airlines didn't? Their companies were already offering first-class cabins, special meals, and preferential treatment. But Branson believed that the major transatlantic carriers, including British Airways, were not providing great service. He challenged core industry assumptions about what customers, especially high-end travelers, really valued and saw room for a radically different airline.

Virgin Atlantic Airways was the first to offer private booths, in-flight massages, pajamas, and a comforter and a nice pillow on a completely flat bed, plus haute cuisine with top-drawer wines. Only now, decades later amid intense industry consolidation, are the remaining giant carriers in the West providing such luxuries in business or first class. "We're a company that likes to take on the giants. In too many businesses these giants have had things their own way," said Sir Richard. "We're going to have a lot of fun competing with them."[34]

Not to be outdone, some Virgin upper lounges now include a health spa, shoeshine service, a personal attendant, a private security passage, sparkling clean showers, clothes pressed, and a chauffeur for its luxury package. Virgin also pioneered the commercial use of bio-fuel on a flight between London and Amsterdam.[35] The airline now flies Virgin America in the United States, runs short flights within the United Kingdom, and has formed an alliance with Delta. These moves, unthinkable in the airline's early days, reflect Virgin's ability to challenge its founding assumptions and keep the window open to new ideas.

In his experiment with Virgin Cola, Branson demonstrated his willingness to challenge incumbency, endure a public stumble, and learn from his failure.[36] "I don't go into ventures to make a fortune. I do it because I'm not satisfied with the way others are doing business."[37] Said Sir Richard, "[The cola] business taught me not to un-derestimate the power of the world's leading soft drink makers. I'll never again make the mistake of thinking that all large, dominant companies are sleepy!"[38]

Those who challenge others need to challenge themselves with equal frequency. One technique inspired by British Field Marshal William Slim is *red teaming*. You designate certain staff members to the red team, which plays the role of both surrogate enemy and friendly opposition. Everyone else plays on the blue team, charged with implementing the current strategy. The red team's assign-ment is to challenge the blue team whenever the strategy gets off course. Slim used red teaming to challenge both strategic and op-erational decisions during World War II.[39] His red team served as a semi-independent unit fully integrated into the commander's planning staffs, but with its own resources. The red team con-ducted its own analysis, problem framing, and strategy develop-ment, often from an adversary's perspective, at every stage of planning and implementation. This method has since gained ac-ceptance in business as a disciplined form of devil's advocacy, open-minded inquiry, and contrarian thinking.[40]

Action Plan to Open the Window

A personal commitment to change and the courage to have an outside-in perspective will contribute to your ability to *open the window*. Make time for personal reflection about the mindsets and behaviors prevalent in your organization and industry, and ask your team to do the same. How do current mental models—including cultural, political, or educational mindsets—affect your business? Are you locked into a pattern that gets in your way?

1. *Surface long-standing assumptions.* Ask a diverse group to come up with the implicit assumptions of your team, organization, or industry. Draw inspiration from Pope Francis, Ben Golub, and Richard Branson, all three of whom showed the vision and courage to put a spotlight on suboptimal practices in their worlds.

2. *Challenge dubious assumptions and outdated mental models from the outside in.* Form counter-teams (i.e., "red teams") to collect data and argue why you should adjust the current strategy. Have the team ask "Which of these assumptions are potentially vulnerable and need to be tested?" and "How are these driving the wrong behavior?" The leaders of Fukushima would have benefited from such questioning.

3. *Explore outside your organization.* Take a fresh look at innovators, other companies, other industries, and other business models. Bring in consultants, academics, and peer reviewers. Ask them to raise tough questions and provoke debate, just as Pope Francis has done regarding the Vatican Bank.

4. *Engage mavericks and respect contrarians.* Listen for those lonely voices that many dismiss. Seek those who truly see the world differently from you and try hard to understand

why they do so. Branson was a maverick himself, and this persona attracted other creative people. He developed a culture that promotes divergent thinking.

5. *Form diverse teams for major initiatives*—not just diversity in the human resources sense but in the cognitive science sense, whereby team members process and interpret information differently. Tap into diverse backgrounds, lifestyles, and points of view.

6. *Break from the pack.* Buck conventional wisdom when facing new challenges or slowly deteriorating situations. Don't settle for incremental thinking or business as usual. Think like Sir Richard, who entitled one of his books *Screw Business as Usual.*

LOOKING IN MIRRORS

Pope Francis deliberately challenged conventional wisdom by introducing a new frame, a "relational way of viewing the world." It calls for inclusion without judgment and insists on greater transparency in operations. That's what strategic leaders do: they reframe the situation. In cognitive psychology, the term *frame* refers to the mental structures that people use to make sense of the world around them.[41] Businesspeople often allude to these in metaphorical terms such as "thinking outside the box," "being on the same page," or "doing it the IBM way." Some joke that "there is the right way, the wrong way, and our way." Disasters, lesser errors, and missed opportunities occur when leaders are unaware of—or in denial about—the limits of the cognitive frames that underlie their own perspectives or those of others. The reasons can be multiple, ranging from complacency to fear, but often people lack the skill of *systematically* reframing how their organization should view the world. Cognitive science clearly shows that most of us too readily accept what we see and what we think. We usually fail to open the window wide enough or stare through the window hard enough to answer two critical questions advocated by Nobel Prize winner Daniel Kahneman:[42]

1. *What narratives besides the one on the table could explain the facts we have before us?* Resist the temptation to latch onto one initial view, especially since the mind locks in nearly automatically. Put that initial view on the table, set it aside, and seek several other views. Suppose that your company launches a new advertising campaign and sales increase the following month. The vice president of marketing might then proudly share the good news and offer praise for the new advertising agency he recently hired. A strategic leader would not instantly accept this analysis but, rather, would search for alternative explanations and consult other experts if needed. The statistician would want to know whether the sales increase is random or statistically significant. The strategist would wonder whether competitive actions, such as a rival's raising prices, played a role. The economist would look for seasonal effects or overall market improvements. The human resources managers would ask whether a recent training program for sales managers had an influence.

2. *What other information—that we presently don't have or cannot see yet—could deeply challenge our current interpretations?* A classic example is NASA's tragic decision in January 1986 to proceed with the launch of the *Challenger* shuttle. Morton Thiokol, Inc., maker of the solid rocket booster, had warned that at lower temperatures the rubber O-rings on the rocket's joints might seal too slowly, thereby allowing gases to leak and further erode the O-rings, opening a path for a flame or explosion. When Thiokol raised this concern the night before the launch, NASA managers plotted the joint temperatures of past flights—seven in total—in which O-ring erosion occurred.

They concluded that there was no correlation between temperature and O-ring erosion and, therefore, no significant flight risk. Thiokol, under great pressure from NASA, relented and withdrew its objection to the launch. If only someone had challenged the assembled team to analyze all twenty-six past flights, including those in which zero O-ring damaged occurred; had they done so, they'd have clearly seen the risk posed by low temperatures. All of these incident-free flights occurred at ambient temperatures above 65° Fahrenheit. The temperature at launch that January morning was 52°. The shuttle exploded shortly after takeoff, killing all seven astronauts.[43]

Encourage Constructive Criticism and Creative Thinking

You probably know people like Bob, a division president in a midsize energy company, set in his ways. His solutions to business problems were thorough, predictable, and rather unimaginative. He preferred incremental moves over bold measures. Bob's colleagues made fun of him behind his back, joking that he'd rather do nothing than try something new. Bob didn't mind; his conservative approach had served him well over the years. Not like that big risk he took once by backing a new venture that went bust. Poof, the money was gone. Ever since, Bob has stuck to the tried and true, which to him meant traditional energy sources. The sexy financial projections of new technologies and new energy markets neither enamored him nor seduced him away from his laser-like focus on core businesses.

Then the energy market shifted and revenues dropped. Bob didn't mind; he had been through many an up-and-down cycle and believed that the core businesses would come back as they had previously, when the market turned around and the next up-cycle took hold. But Bob's CEO, Warren, disagreed. This downturn was different, he felt. Competitors had moved into new technologies and fast-developing markets while Bob's division had done the "same old, same old." The cost structure of Bob's business was too high, and Bob's division was losing market share. Warren confronted Bob: "I need you to cut costs and get into new markets—and fast." These were two big and urgent challenges.

As he always did when faced with complex decisions, Bob gathered all available information and retreated to his office. He thought he did his best thinking alone. The last time he listened to colleagues—colleagues, mind you, who were overly enthusiastic and not objective enough—he made a bad call. In a more recent instance, when Bob needed to streamline the costs of an underperforming business, he decided to consolidate the two offices that were in close geographic proximity—not because this consolidation would cut the most cost, but because it would cause the least disruption. Had he consolidated offices that were further apart, he would have realized even greater savings from much larger operational synergies. The most transformative move would have been to streamline activities across the entire division. That would have yielded the highest strategic impact and largest cost reductions, but Bob ruled it out: "Too much conflict," thought Bob, "and too disruptive."

Warren, his CEO, stepped in when he realized that Bob needed to change *himself*—and time was running out. Warren urged Bob to work with a coach who could help him expand his frame of reference. Bob now had nothing to lose but his job, which had become a big part of his identity, and so he agreed. In itself, working with a coach was disruptive; Bob could no longer hole up in his office. He had to work at willingness to engage, if only to avoid interpersonal conflict and negative reports back to Warren. Together, they explored other industries and business models for reorganization. What an eye-opener! With practice—and that meant going against his initial impulse to isolate himself—Bob learned to invite different views to improve his decision-making and risk tolerance.

After a while, Bob moved beyond the coach and convened his team to probe underlying weaknesses in the business. He even assigned a colleague to serve as a devil's advocate on the streamlining issue, which, to his surprise, yielded an interesting hybrid solution. They restructured one organizational unit to focus more on emerging markets, which allowed local managers to get closer to customers. At the same, they retained this unit's ability to deploy shared services from the corporate center. It was a win-win. Bob's real breakthrough was not just a matter of getting a better solution to the cost and growth challenges. It was his willingness to challenge himself and engage his team in constructive criticism. Bob's boss Warren viewed that as the more remarkable outcome since it would yield benefits many times over.

Engage Your Team in Reframing: Getting at Root Causes

Challenges of Bob's kind are especially critical when the current frame or business model is broken or customer expectations have shifted. Until Warren pushed him to face reality, Bob believed that growth would come back with the next up-cycle. Similarly, Blockbuster's leaders were late in realizing that distributing videotapes and DVDs via stores had become obsolete in the "I-want-it-here-and-now" era of YouTube and streaming video. Leaders like Pope Francis and Richard Branson start with the premise that the game has changed and will continue to change in the future. This mindset is crucial to playing the long game well.

As a leader in an uncertain world, you must force yourself and your team to question the current business model, including deeply held assumptions that may no longer be true, and then explore your alternatives with an eye to the future. Then you must reinforce the point and dramatize the issue through ongoing communication and new incentives because people naturally fall back into old mental and behavioral habits.

Novelist Upton Sinclair put it in simple terms: "It is difficult to get a man to understand something (or see it), when his salary depends upon his not understanding it!"[44] New incentives proved instrumental when a large medical-devices company attempted to implement a new strategy to focus on global accounts. The head of global sales was committed to reframing the company's approach to account management for its top customers. This change was a division priority. Account teams were losing focus on the most critical accounts and missing opportunities to collaborate across regions. Their share of wallet was declining. The sales leader wanted account teams to collaborate on building these key relationships. He engaged in a structured process. Together, they identified the top customers, formed global account teams, redefined team roles, provided new training, and created account management tools. Although they made incremental progress in reframing the strategic sales approach, it wasn't until they introduced account-based, shared incentives that real change happened.

Use the Mirror to Overcome Groupthink

"Conflict is the gadfly of thought," wrote philosopher John Dewey. "It stirs us to observation and memory. It instigates invention."[45] The opposite is "sheep-like passivity," better known as *groupthink*. As we saw in the case of Japan's nuclear governance, groupthink pervades many organizations and systems, tragically so with the Tokyo Electric Power Company. Teams are most vulnerable to groupthink when their leaders are highly directive, there is little time, and decisions are complex. Groupthink also occurs when people seek to avoid conflict and court consensus. During the run-up to the 2008 financial crisis, risk managers often had a different view of the market from the traders on their floor but failed to effectively challenge or hold up the mirror to the traders. They preferred acquiescence over strong debate.

We recently observed the function heads of an IT leadership team in the life insurance industry who described their decision process as "consensus building." They claimed it was important to get all views and the full team on board before finalizing a course of action, given the cost involved in so many of their technology initiatives. But we actually saw a very different process at play: during meetings, team members waited for the strong and successful Marshall, who was the head of IT, to express his opinion before they chimed in, usually in concurrence.

There was no true debate among these team members. And, worse, there was a mild pretense of debate and then a false sense of agreement referred to as "the illusion of unanimity" in the groupthink literature. Afterward, in the hall or in the restroom, people said what they really thought. We discovered that people even held back critical input that might have influenced a different conclusion. But since they did not engage fully in the meeting when it mattered, their silence was viewed as consent—to the detriment of both the team and the decision.

Leaders have a special responsibility to counter herd behavior in any process requiring creativity, which is nearly any problem that involves complexity or uncertainty. The most successful leaders, such as Alfred P. Sloan Jr., are acutely aware of this need. While chairman of General Motor's board of directors, Sloan said to his all-male directors: "Gentlemen, I take it we are all in complete agreement on the decision here. . . . Then I propose we postpone further discussion of this matter until our next meeting to give ourselves time to develop disagreement and perhaps gain some understanding of what the decision is all about."[46] The key in fostering healthy debate is to center the conflict on ideas, not people. Leaders such as John Lasseter, the creative force behind Pixar, is a good example of someone who learned how to disagree without becoming too disagreeable.

Lasseter practiced a powerful, highly effective, and respectful form of team challenge. Each morning, the members of Pixar's creative team picked apart the film output of the previous day and discussed how they could improve it. Usually dissatisfied with prior work and worried about resting on laurels, everyone was expected to give and get candid criticism. Together they put alternatives on the table and cut through the complacency in the room. The goal was to push each other for breakthroughs in bringing stories to life on screen. Lasseter believed this approach was highly effective: indeed, people learned from each other's mistakes, the team shared responsibility for success, and the pursuit of excellence became a group norm. Lasseter's team developed some of Pixar's biggest hits, including the *Toy Story* series, during this time. They worked hard to combat groupthink and pushed everyone to the edge of their creative capabilities.

Research shows that this kind of *creative friction* elicits the best ideas from a group. Psychology professor Charlan Nemeth and her colleagues found that debate and supportive criticism stimulate optimal group problem solving. Specifically, constructive dissent causes members to reexamine their starting assumptions and break free of their comfort zones. The lead animator for *Toy Story 3*, Bobby Podesta, felt strongly that, to pursue excellence and build a winning team, you have to deal with criticism—though your feelings might get hurt in the process. But the hurt is worth it if it leads to the success you envision.[47] The purpose of this type of team dialogue and debate, as with the Pixar morning session, is not congeniality or feeling good but improving the group's IQ. The result can be a group IQ higher than the average of the individual IQs of the people in the group. The converse can also happen: a lower collective IQ as a result of the failure to challenge and debate.

The Pixar team applied another technique called *plussing*: when someone challenges an idea, the other team members add to the idea rather than detracting from it.[48] The aim was to support new ideas without using judgmental language such as "yes but" or outright criticism of the idea. Instead of "yes but," say "yes and." Don't focus on why the idea is wrong but on the parts of it that hold promise. Even if only 20 percent of an idea is sound, it may still merit consideration and improvement. Such positive reinforcement not only encourages people to put ideas forward and build off each other but also creates a safe place for dissent.

How conflict is handled differs strongly by culture. Saving face is especially important in Asian cultures. In traditional or formal cultures such as these, participants need to respect status differences. A group may frown upon a younger person who challenges an older one too quickly or too vigorously or upon junior people who speak before senior ones. This is why in Japan, some wise leaders ask younger associates what they think first, thereby giving them public permission to speak frankly, without risk of contradicting the leader. If opinions vary widely, the senior leaders may not reveal their views at all.

In *Start-Up Nation,* Dan Senor and Saul Singer describe an opposite business culture prevalent in Israeli start-up companies, where teams usually thrive in a high-challenge environment much like the Pixar morning meeting. In contrast to businesspeople in Japan, Israelis value heated debate to generate breakthrough solutions. "If you get past the initial bruise to the ego," an American investor told Senor and Singer, "it's immensely liberating." This approach allows people to truly say what they think. Importantly, participants address key issues in the meeting itself, instead of afterward in the hallways. This means less organizational politics and no pretense of consensus. The authors quote Mooly Eden, an Israeli trainer in cross-cultural communication, who explained: "We are educated to challenge the obvious, ask questions, debate everything, and innovate."[49] Senor and Singer view this willingness to challenge and avoid groupthink as a key success factor in Israel's entrepreneurial and start-up culture. More Israeli firms are listed on the NASDAQ system than those of any other country besides the United States and China.[50] Finding the right balance between openly sharing diverse views and not offending others requires cultural sensitivity, especially in multinational settings. The benefit of frank debate is quickly lost if it causes resentment or backstabbing in teams.

Digging Deep Personally to Challenge Bias

Although creative friction may come more naturally to Israeli start-ups and artistic firms like Pixar, the habit of challenging other people's ideas tests the personal mettle of most leaders. Confronting yourself in the mirror and holding the mirror up to societal or group pressure can be a lonely business. But, remember, *you're not actually alone*. You need to cultivate sounding boards, at the board level (if you are CEO) or through your own kitchen cabinet. Many a strategic leader has been here before you. It takes toughness and belief in your cause to hang in there when you're fighting uphill. High-challenge leaders who question conventional wisdom, or put the brakes on popular practices, must overcome internal and external resistance and persevere. At points in time, the organizational struggle merges with the individual one, meaning you have to look in your own mirror to hold one up for your team or firm. Transformative leaders—Branson in business, Pope Francis in religion, and Mandela in politics—must challenge themselves and society.

In organizations around the globe today, greater diversity among employees, consumers, and other stakeholders puts a premium on the ability of leaders to challenge the habits, viewpoints, and attitudes of themselves and others. In her provocative book *Lean In*, Sheryl Sandberg tackles this issue head-on for women. She describes various invisible barriers in the female mind: "Compared to our male colleagues, fewer of us aspire to senior positions."[51] Modern societies, according to Sandberg, continue to instill in young women expectations, values, and ambitions that differ significantly from those of their male peers. Gender socialization is often invisible or so deeply rooted in culture that women limit their own growth, and society loses their talents. Sandberg challenges herself and other women (and men!) to overcome these internal barriers or biases so that they can assert their leadership and strategic capabilities to the fullest. Sandberg is not alone. She quotes Gloria Steinem, an early pioneer of women's liberation, who said, "We have to both fight against the barriers and get them out of our consciousness."[52]

Much of this deep challenge comes down to surfacing, reframing, and confronting bias. For example, Sandberg points out that most men assume they can succeed equally in business and in their personal or family life. However, women usually hear the opposite: achieving both is difficult if not impossible unless you happen to be Superwoman. Women must make what feels to some like a lose-lose choice. Sandberg says, "Framing the issues as 'work-life balance'—as if the two were diametrically opposed—practically ensures work will lose out. Who would ever choose work over life?"[53] Sandberg challenges this false dichotomy and cites research confirming that this situation can be framed differently. But fear of failing to do it all, or of being judged negatively for trying, remains a huge mental barrier that many women must blast through. As Facebook's chief operating officer, Sandberg helps to promote equal risk-taking by women and men with positive, reinforcing messages such as "Fortune favors the bold" and "What would you do if you were not afraid?"

The research and literature on cognitive, social, and personal psychology—not to mention countless self-help books—make it clear that breaking free of self-imposed, cultural, and institutionalized boundaries is a complex and multifaceted pursuit. Many studies in fields such as decision psychology[54] and behavioral economics[55] document that we are often our own worst enemies in that we cling to dysfunctional beliefs or self-limiting assumptions. Fear can paralyze our ability to question false beliefs, assumptions, and boundaries. It takes personal courage, first, to *open the window* and view yourself through fresh eyes from different angles and, second, to *look in the mirror* and change.

Neither is easy and both seem impossible without a big jolt, such as a public failure or personal crisis. Sometimes a mentor or a coach can help you break through your invisible barriers. Sheryl Sandberg's book has inspired the formation of *lean-in circles* online (leanin.org) and across the country. Former Metronic CEO Bill George advocates for what he calls *true north groups* for developing self-awareness in leaders (www.truenorthgroups.com). The late Stephen Covey wrote of the role of family members and spiritual advisers in reinforcing the newly gained habits of highly successful people. Our point: *Strategic leaders do not go it alone*. They seek feedback and they ask for support.

Action Plan to Look in the Mirror

Are you stuck in a dysfunctional system or team that prevents you or others from challenging often enough? Do you confront your own bias or groupthink on your team? It is not easy to surface invisible biases or hidden assumptions. Create a support system or enlist a trusted adviser to help you. Here is a checklist of practices that have worked for others:

1. *Understand the core problem.* Insist on multiple problem definitions before choosing among them. Consider two additional critical questions advocated by Daniel Kahneman: "How else might we define this problem? What's the core issue here?" Do as Toyota does: ask "why" five times iteratively to get underneath the surface rather than addressing just the symptoms.

2. *Break patterns and disrupt complacency.* Provide opportunities for people to engage, doubt, and ultimately own the new

frame that you want them to adopt, as Bob's CEO did. Or reframe the issue as Sheryl Sandberg did at Facebook and in her book *Lean In.*

3. *Foster open debate and conflicts about ideas.* Disagree without being disagreeable. Encourage debate in meetings and cultivate mutual trust and respect. Try the Pixar technique of *plussing.* Or adopt the mindset of Israeli start-ups and military units to ask the tough questions before accepting the givens.

4. *Push back on quick and easy consensus.* Insist on alternatives, as Alfred P. Sloan did with his board as CEO and chairman of GM. Be suspicious if all members of your team quickly concur on a complex issue. Send them off to reflect more deeply and develop some constructive disagreement.

5. *Create a rotating devil's advocate role.* Playing devil's advocate can teach everyone how to question the status quo in a group setting and appreciate the value of such questioning. Include, as Bob finally did, naysayers and outliers in your decision-making process to help foster early debate.

6. *Create safe zones.* Find a time and place where people can express serious doubts, identify elephants in the room, surface biases respectfully, and disagree on problem definitions and solutions.

THE DISCIPLINE TO CHALLENGE: PULLING IT TOGETHER

Pope Francis inspired Jane Wang. A religious person, she had followed the press on the new pope and admired his approach to shaking up an entrenched hierarchy and resetting the agenda. She never connected his efforts with her own, but upon deeper reflection she saw important lessons. Jane felt she was reasonably good at getting to the root of a problem. She structured her analyses and at times reframed core issues with her team before implementation. Yet, she had to admit that she stayed within her comfort zone at the project management level. She liked familiar routines, and knew she had to practice breaking out of these comfortable patterns. This meant pushing back on quick or easy solutions and disrupting complacency in her own team. She was increasingly confident that she could be more provocative and creative. She had to be, if she wanted to advance and win the long game.

Jane steadily *opened the window* wider. She realized that her narrow focus—her sheer determination—blinded her to opportunities at the periphery of her business. She decided to explore outside her usual circle and beyond her organization and industry. In her company's high-potential program, she met someone who was clearly a maverick in his division, and she resolved to connect with him regularly. He relished playing the devil's advocate throughout their sessions on change management. He wondered why the company wasn't using more provocative tools and models in management training to challenge conventional wisdom. He also felt that managers weren't systematically tapping the outside knowledge of new employees before indoctrinating them to corporate-think. He expressed his challenges in such a respectful manner that everyone in the room was nodding.

Jane realized that her division had recently hired two new employees—one right out of business school and another from a competitor. She invited them to lunch to get their initial impressions of her division and to debrief them on their experiences elsewhere. Challenging her long-standing assumptions and old mental models was more palatable over lunch. She realized she might need a mentor, or even a peer coach, and perhaps she would find such a person—a true maverick—through the high-potential program.

3 THE DOG THAT DID NOT BARK

The Discipline to Interpret:
Amplify Signals and Connect Dots

P EOPLE LOVE A GOOD MYSTERY; THAT'S EASY TO SEE GIVEN
the deluge of books, TV shows, and movies in the genre. A
perennial favorite is the procedural crime drama, such as *CSI:
Crime Scene Investigation*, in which investigators collect all sorts of
data, run them through laboratory tests and computer simulations,
form hypotheses about who did what and why, and then cull
through their list of suspects to identify the perpetrator. Many of
you will remember the endearing Peter Falk who played Detective
Colombo and gave a personal touch to the inner workings of interpretation. He presents a stark contrast with the comical French
antihero Inspector Clouseau, who stumbles cluelessly through
crime scenes in the Pink Panther films.

The archetype for heroic detectives is the exquisitely discerning
Sherlock Holmes, created by Sir Arthur Conan Doyle and reimag-
ined by Nicholas Meyer in the film *The Seven Percent Solution*. Told
through the eyes of Dr. John H. Watson, *The Seven Percent Solution*
contrives a meeting between the fictional Holmes and the very real

Dr. Sigmund Freud.[1] The occasion: Holmes's cocaine addiction has rendered him unusually pale and gaunt, his eyes without their customary twinkle. Watson implores his friend to seek treatment. But Holmes refuses; and so Watson concocts an irresistible mystery that lures Holmes to Vienna where he meets with the young Freud, of whom Holmes has never heard.

Holmes enters Freud's study and asks why the trail has led him there. Freud replies, "Who do you think I am?" With thinly disguised arrogance, Holmes answers: You are a brilliant physician of Jewish faith who studied in Paris. You are at odds with your professional colleagues due to some heretical theory you proposed or support. You are married with a child of five; you enjoy Shakespeare and have a sense of honor.[2] Freud is flabbergasted and asks how Holmes could so quickly and accurately deduce his background, having not heard of him before. Holmes replies:

The dust in your room suggests this is your private study where not even a maid is allowed. Your additional private area with a couch is likely for seeing patients. Your books are arranged in an odd way, not by topic or author but by field of inquiry. For example, you combined the King James Bible, the Koran, Talmud and Book of Mormon. The Menorah here suggests you are Jewish and your French medical books reveal you studied in Paris, which is not easy for a German-speaking doctor. The empty, discolored rectangular shapes on your wall suggest that you removed various diplomas or professional honors due to perhaps radical views that have discredited you in the eyes of the establishment. Your honor shows in having removed them since hardly anyone comes into your private study. Your wedding ring indicates that you are married and the toy soldiers on the floor would especially appeal to a child of about five. This well-worn open book here shows that you like Shakespeare, although I must confess that this is hardly my favorite play.[3]

In this scene, Holmes demonstrates two skills that underlie superb interpretation. First, he marshals his keen observational faculties to *amplify signals* in the evidence around him. In particular, Holmes moves fluidly between specific details and the big picture when making sense of the range of data in his visual field. Second, he *connects dots* from multiple sources to form a theory about the scene. Holmes clearly uses both analytic reasoning and seasoned intuition to see patterns within the data that would elude most observers.

Unfortunately, few of us are as gifted as Sherlock Holmes. Most modern detectives depend greatly on lab tests, video recordings, and electronic paper trails to form their theories of a case and may fail to bring human intelligence and nuanced interpretation into their analysis. Similarly, strategic leaders should at times step back from the data at hand, explore multiple interpretations, and, if possible, test them by probing further. Becoming strategic requires that you as a leader be more Holmes-like in how you *amplify signals* and *connect dots* to dramatically improve your ability to make sense of the many signals in your environment.

Amplify Signals

1. *Do you systematically develop deep insights about customer experiences, competitive perspectives, or the changing dynamics of your marketplace and industry?* Holmes's painstaking and unbiased observations of Freud's study led to his insights.

2. *Can you move fluidly between specific details and the big picture when analyzing complex data?* Holmes zoomed in on the individual books on Freud's shelf, and then zoomed out to draw the implications from the unusual way Freud had arranged the titles.

3. *Are you prone to flawed interpretation, or getting the true story wrong, because you see what you expect to see and miss key signals?* The endearing inspector Clouseau in the Pink Panther movies often falls

victim to this trap as he stumbles from a crime scene and misses one big clue after another. His capacity to misinterpret the situation is both comical and instructive.

4. *How well do your data, analysis, intuition, and judgment approach match the complexity of the problem at hand?* Holmes didn't wallow in all the elements of Freud's study; he focused on those few details that best answered Freud's question of "Who am I?" Holmes's deep denial of his declining health blinded him to the truth—that his cocaine addiction had led him to Freud. This fictional twist made Holmes more human.

Connect Dots

5. *Do you leverage both rich data and analytic reasoning to recognize patterns among disparate data points?* Holmes not only applied a systematic method but also drew on his uncanny intuition and trusted it to be right in most cases.

6. *Do you deploy multiple lenses to connect dots, alone or with others, before jumping to conclusions? Do you seek additional data points to round out the picture?* Since Holmes spotted a variety of religious texts, he had to seek more evidence before concluding that Freud was Jewish. Holmes also noted what was missing from Freud's office—the wall hangings.

7. *Do you ask the right questions to demonstrate curiosity and an open mind about ambiguities and what they might connote?* Given the dust, Freud likely didn't remove the wall hangings for a good cleaning or repair, and so Holmes tied them to Freud's professional stature.

Through experience, crime scene investigators discover which data are relevant, how to collect and analyze them without bias, and whether their findings are conclusive. Our goal here is to show how these skills are relevant to your own capacity to render deeper, more insightful interpretations—a capacity that is a core element of strategic leadership.

AMPLIFY SIGNALS

Most of us naturally pay attention to strong or clear signals in our environment. We notice dirty-bottomed clouds suggesting it might rain, and traffic building up ahead alerts us to begin looking for alternative routes. But because the human mind has limited information processing capacity, we screen out most signals to avoid a dizzying bombardment of sensory stimuli. As a survival skill, we tend to focus on what we deem most interesting and readily available—and end up missing a lot of weak signals that could be quite relevant.

A *weak signal* is a seemingly random or disconnected piece of information that at first sounds like background noise but to the trained ear can emerge as part of a significant pattern. Discerning patterns, however, requires that the signal be heard from a different angle or connected with other pieces of information. Both elements—hearing the signal and then analyzing how it fits into a larger context—are the essence of interpretation: sifting through the data, registering them holistically, shifting frames of reference, and decoding their hidden meaning.

A classic illustration of picking up a weak signal, and decoding the hidden meaning, took place when Steve Jobs paid a visit to Xerox in 1979. He saw a prototype mouse that could navigate a screen as part of an office automation system that Xerox was developing. What he noticed, and few else did, was the potential of this device to serve as a natural interface for the innovative user-friendly personal computer that Apple was envisioning.[4]

Noticing weak signals, amplifying them selectively, and seeing connections among them lie at the root of *re-perceiving*. This leadership skill is especially important when we are facing uncertain situations such as the technology disruptions in consumer electronics, retail, media, and healthcare. The philosopher Immanuel Kant emphasized that there can be no *perception* without *preception*, referring to the mental precepts or categories that underlie our sense making. To Kant, perception was a "representation given by experience."[5] On a practical level, Kant meant that no one is objective: all sensory input is filtered and encoded—largely unconsciously—to create meaning out of a bewildering array of stimuli surrounding us. When Steve Jobs saw the power of the mouse, his mental precepts relating to personal computers rather than office machines primed him exquisitely to what eluded nearly everyone else. How Jobs thought about personal computers, and what he emphasized in them, directed his search for meaning amid an ocean of signals.

Developing Deep Insight from Early Warning Signals at DuPont

Interpreting changing circumstances effectively involves not just observing facts carefully but creatively connecting them beyond routine patterns of perception. Consider what Charles O. Holliday Jr. noticed in October 2008. He was traveling in Japan as CEO of the chemical and life sciences behemoth, E. I. DuPont de Nemours and Company. When Holliday met with the CEO of one of DuPont's top Japanese customers, he learned that this CEO was asking his staff to conserve cash, a step usually taken when a company is experiencing or expecting a decline in revenue and profitability. That got Holliday's attention, in terms of both potential deteriorating economic conditions and DuPont's own cash position. When he returned to the States, Holliday mobilized his leadership team to get a fix on DuPont's own financial resilience. Over the next few days, his team reported that Wall Street's financial woes were spilling over into the general economy and were affecting nearly all areas of DuPont's business.

But how big a problem was it really? Holliday soon picked up another signal: reservations at the Hotel DuPont in Wilmington, Delaware, had dropped a startling 30 percent in ten days, a rather unusual decline at that time of year. Holliday probed further and discovered that corporate lawyers were settling disputes rather than going to court in Delaware. That likely meant that their corporate clients wanted to cap legal fees and eliminate the financial uncertainty of a trial. Although the rate of court settlements before a trial doesn't often mean much in terms of the economy, on this occasion Holliday took it as an early indicator of rapid economic decline. Another bit of information came from Detroit. At the time, DuPont supplied paint for nearly 30 percent of the cars produced in America. DuPont operated a just-in-time system, mixing the paint forty-eight hours in advance of a given production run. But several automakers began dragging their heels on production schedules. Holliday wanted to know why. The answer was simple and devastating: new car sales were collapsing as the US middle class faced mortgage foreclosures. The economy was starting to tank.

Once he had connected the various dots, Holliday sprang to action. DuPont already had a companywide crisis-management plan in place, but the executive committee felt that the risks they were facing now were financial, not the typical external catastrophe risks addressed in management of crises such as hurricanes and terrorist attacks. Holliday activated just nine of DuPont's seventeen crisis teams and asked the chief economist as well as the pension fund manager to communicate internally—in layman's terms—the nature of the crisis. Holliday immersed himself in operational details and revisited plans and progress daily, as the volatile financial crisis became a large-scale, deep global recession.

Within ten days, DuPont's senior managers were explaining the situation to their employees and asking them to conserve cash. DuPont immediately curtailed travel, canceled internal meetings, and eliminated some twenty thousand outside contractors. Within six weeks, DuPont's management had sharply revised each business team's operating targets. When the financial markets hit rock bottom, DuPont was ready. Also, Holliday was far along in his

How DuPont's CEO Triangulated Weak Signals

Reservations down 30% in ten days

Japanese CEO warns of cash flow problem

DETROIT
Carmakers can't provide their production plans

thinking about strategies for recovery, while other CEOs were still reeling from the carnage around them.

What distinguished Holliday from his peers was his ability to amplify various weak signals, connect the dots between them in real terms, and interpret these connections clearly enough to take action. Combining seasoned intuition and vigilant observation of changes in the external environment, Holliday correctly inferred that his company and his clients were about to hit an economic wall. To test his strategic insight of impending doom, he discussed his concerns candidly and insisted upon equally candid feedback.[6] Although we can never fully know the complex neural pathways that fire in someone's brain, asking probing questions does stimulate the mind and generate deeper insight. . . . That's what Holliday did exquisitely to spare DuPont from the financial tsunami that drowned many other firms.

Zoom In and Out: Move Fluidly Between Details and Big Picture

Think about how you approach problems compared to Holmes or Holliday. Many of us tend to dive deeply into the details when planning a vacation. A typical pattern is to pick a destination and then move quickly into logistical preparation. We rarely toggle back and forth to revisit our original intent. We get far down a path, solve lots of technical problems, and somewhere along the way lose sight of why we're doing all this busy work in the first place.[7]

Consider the classic story of a family's trip to Abilene, Texas. During a family gathering, someone suggested a day trip by car to Abilene. Everyone went along with the suggestion, even though several had concerns about making this rather long car trip. Momentum for the trip built, and family members started to address the logistics. Amid the planning frenzy, no one stepped back to clarify: "Why Abilene? Why drive? Why at this time? What are our options?" In the end, the family went on a trip that no one wanted to take.[8]

Many operationally oriented leaders fall into the same trap and start marching down a path, looking at data only in the context of existing plans or assumptions. A key skill in interpretation is the capacity not just to shuttle between various details or data points but also to pull back and look at the overall picture. The chief marketing officer of Tastykake, Vince Melchiorre, appreciates the payoffs of stepping back: by doing so, he re-perceived the real growth opportunity for his company.

Founded in 1914, Tasty Baking Company is a long-standing Philadelphia firm specializing in baked sweets of all kinds. Under the brand name Tastykake, its products include pre-packaged sponge cakes, chocolate cakes, cookie bars, cupcakes, pies, and doughnuts.[9] But a powerful low-carb revolution was afoot following the publication of Dr. Robert Atkins's best-selling book *The Atkins Diet*.[10] In response, nearly every food company in the country was developing a low-carb strategy. Tasty Baking was creating its own low-carb line under the code name "Greta," short for "Greta Carbo," a pun on the famous screen actress's name. The company's new CEO, Charles Pizzi, was pushing for its launch to revive the company's sales, which had been declining since its peak of $166 million in 2001. The low-carb product line was a major part of his new strategy.[11]

In a supermarket aisle in early 2004, Vince Melchiorre had an epiphany: *sugar free*. It came to him after a sixty-something woman and her eighty-something mother interrupted his review of the Tastykake shelf displays. "The mother had eaten Tastykake since she was a child. She could still sing the jingle," said Melchiorre. However, she had developed diabetes and could no longer eat any of the 5 million cakes, pies, cookies, doughnuts, and other sweets baked daily under the Tastykake brand. She and her daughter demanded to know why Tasty Baking wasn't doing anything to serve diabetic customers.

"It took me over the top," he said. This data point got Melchiorre's full attention. He stepped back from campaign details to ask: Was low carb just a fad, or did it signal a long-term change in the American diet? Melchiorre had witnessed the rise and fall of sodium-free soups as a marketing executive at Campbell Soup. "People will say they want sodium-free or low-carb foods. Then they'll leave the focus group and go to McDonald's and supersize everything," said Melchiorre. "I've been in the food industry a long time. I've seen things come and go. The only way people get religion about these kinds of trends is when it affects them personally."

Diabetes is definitely personal, and this elderly customer seemed to take it personally that Tasty Baking didn't offer a sugar-free treat. For her, sugar free wasn't a fad—but was this an isolated case or a piece of a larger pattern? And if the latter, did it mean a larger and more permanent shift in consumer eating habits away from Tastykake? Did it factor into the drop in Tastykake's sales over the last three years?

"I listened to people in stores, the workers who stock the shelves and the consumers walking by," Melchiorre added. "People were beating me up all the time because they love Tastykake and couldn't eat them anymore because they are diabetic. I didn't get one person come up to me and say they couldn't eat them because they are on a low-carb diet." Then it dawned on him: "Carbs are important, but sugar is the bigger issue."

As Melchiorre zoomed in and out, between the consumer data and the evolving bigger picture, the signals became stronger and the strategy became clear: sugar free. Easy to say; tough to do. "We were halfway down the road with the low-carb strategy," Melchiorre said. He was convinced that Tasty Baking needed to change, and so he started internal battles to persuade other managers. Eventually, the company did formulate its line of sugar-free products, dubbed Tastykake Sensables, and launched it in August 2004—just when Project Greta had been slated to launch—with zero grams of sugar and only four to eight net grams of carbohydrates per serving. Sales rose to double their quarterly targets, far exceeding Melchiorre's expectations. By the second quarter of 2005, Tasty Baking's net sales were up 8 percent over the previous year, driven largely by the Sensables line of plain and chocolate doughnuts, orange and chocolate-chip finger cakes, and cookie bars. Did Melchiorre spot this mega-market shift simply by walking the aisles of supermarkets twice a week? Not exactly. He read widely and spoke with others in the industry. He bounced ideas off family and neighbors. He occasionally surveyed the company's fifteen hundred employees on the frontline. "We triangulate from a lot of different sources," he said.

Leaders get blindsided not so much because they aren't receiving signals but because they aren't exploring alternative interpretations, or they get locked into one piece of the puzzle. They seek comfort in traditional views, just as their competitors are doing. As George Santayana put it: "The empiricist thinks he only believes what he sees, but he is much better at believing than at seeing."[12] Our own research suggests that fewer than 20 percent of global firms have sufficient peripheral vision. Because of a strong operational focus, they fail to spot weak signals at the edges of their business.

Dan Simons produced a video to demonstrate the impact of intense focus on peripheral vision.[13] Simons asks viewers to count how many times a team of white-shirted players pass a basketball among themselves. To distract the viewers, Simons inserts members of a black-shirted team who are simultaneously passing another basketball. As viewers intently follow the passes among the white-shirted players, a majority of them fail to notice a guy in a gorilla suit walking slowly through the scene.

Highly focused companies often do not have sufficient capacity to spot, interpret, and act on the weak signals underlying threats and opportunities, even when those signals are wearing gorilla suits. Such weak signals are, by definition, muddled and imprecise—and that's why leaders must be curious and keep their minds wide open.

Missed Signals and Flawed Interpretation

Whenever multiple pieces of evidence point in opposite directions, or when crucial information is missing, our minds operate naturally by shaping the facts to fit our preconceptions. That's why people can form radically opposite views about complex issues. You can flip back and forth between Fox News and MSNBC News to find ample evidence of this phenomenon every night in US cable television. These programs foster a specific political worldview that is largely consistent with that of their viewers and highlights those elements of a given story that are consistent with their ideology.

Strategic leaders realize that people's perceptions are often a kind of Rorschach test: what they see may be as much shaped by their background, training, culture, worldviews, and hopes or fears as by the data that objectively lie before them. We must all be aware of these distortions. Melchiorre saw buying behaviors not just through the filters of his firm's low-carb strategy; he had the strategic leadership capacity to step back and re-perceive what consumers were saying with an open mind and close attention to new facts.

Strategic leaders also look for what is missing when assessing a new situation. What are consumers *not* saying in focus groups, or what are job candidates *not* mentioning? Sherlock Holmes shines once again in this department. In a story titled "Silver Blaze," a winning racehorse disappears and its trainer is found dead the night before a race.[14] While investigating the crime, Holmes notices that no one interviewed during his investigation mentioned that they had heard the watchdog barking during the night. Here is how Holmes turned this negative fact into a positive clue:

GREGORY (Scotland Yard detective): "Is there any other point to which you would wish to draw my attention?"
HOLMES: "To the curious incident of the dog in the night-time."
GREGORY: "The dog did nothing in the night-time."
HOLMES: "That was the curious incident."

The fact that the dog did not bark led Homes to the conclusion that the thief and murderer was a not a stranger to the dog. This key insight allowed Holmes to finger the culprit. The lesson here is that negative data can be as powerful as positive data, and that Holmes once again followed his own advice: "Never theorize before you have data. Invariably, you end up twisting facts to suit theories, instead of theories to suit facts." In business meetings, it pays to ask "What am I not seeing or hearing?" Stepping back to see the larger picture is not always easy, since our views are often like a house of cards: take away one or two crucial facts and the whole story may crumble. Strategic leaders cultivate a climate that helps their teams see this bigger picture, knowing that it will remain challenging nonetheless for most team members.

How We Fool Ourselves

What we expect to see usually determines what we pay most attention to. Psychologists call this *selective perception*. If something doesn't fit, then we distort reality to force it into our mental model rather than challenging the model itself. The leaders of Kodak failed to amplify, interpret, and act effectively on the signals that photography would quickly become digital. This misperception reflected middle management's belief that digital technology was inferior to film as well as top executives' belief that the demands of Kodak's shareholders mattered more than those of its consumers and engineers.

Our cognitive and emotional filters may further suppress data. Countless investment managers suffered from *suppression* when they filtered out dissonant data on the subprime mortgage market so that they could continue racking up short-term profits. Likewise, the mortgage brokers distorted, suppressed, or simply ignored the fact that many applicants could not afford their home loans. Then they *rationalized* their behavior by twisting evidence and noting that everyone else was doing the same.

Wishful thinking leads us to see the world pleasantly, denying subtle or not-so-subtle evidence to the contrary. Consider President George Bush's "Mission Accomplished" banner, President Barack Obama's launch of the healthcare website without proper testing, or British Prime Minister Gordon Brown's pronouncement that "[this is] an era that history will record as the beginning of a new golden age for the City of London's financial district," right before the 2008 collapse of the financial markets.

We routinely see these biases when leaders try to paper over, downplay, or euphemize bad news and poor results. In the oil and gas sector, as well as in other commodity businesses, leaders commonly attribute negative results to external factors such as down-cycles. It is true that the marketplace can have a major impact. Regardless, strategic leaders should explore deeper questions: How well did we read the signals, anticipate the downturn, and prepare our plan against it? How well did we do compared to our competition, or relative to previous downturns? One sales executive in a high-tech company inflated his annual revenue projections on a regular basis because he assumed that the business plan would work out as he wished. Also, he wanted to look like a hero in relation to his peers, who were less aggressive. This actually worked well during the dotcom boom years of the late 1990s, when he had the wind at his back. But when the market turned in 2001, he did not adjust. During the first year his employer gave him a pass, and so he continued with overly rosy projections. Unfortunately, the boom market was not there to save him, and he lost his job and his credibility.

In addition to filtering out discordant information, we tend to search for evidence that confirms our prior views. This is known as the *confirmation bias*. "Groups of guitars are on the way out," proclaimed a Decca Recording Company executive too confidently, when explaining why he declined an opportunity to sign up the Beatles exclusively in the early 1960s.[15] *Encyclopedia Britannica* (EB) was for many generations the number-one brand in its industry, with a dominant market share. In 1989, EB sold over a hundred thousand sets of its multivolume encyclopedia and set a sales record of $627 million. But then a youngish guy with longish hair approached Peter Norton, the CEO of EB, with a preposterous proposal: let's put EB's entire reference content on a CD-ROM and sell it for $100 or less. The boy genius explained that consumers could search one disk more quickly and easily than a whole collection of print books. Given its world-class content, EB could be a pioneer in the inevitable trend toward digital media, with video and interactive features to boot. Peter Norton was puzzled: Why would he switch a print product selling for $1,300 or so to a CD-ROM selling for $100 or less? It meant firing most of his large dedicated sales forces, repurposing his extensive text-based library, creating new multimedia content, and selling through new channels, even perhaps supermarkets! Norton also shuddered when he recalled that several companies had already tried this digital encyclopedia idea and died with arrows in their backs. No, he really did not want to join them in the graveyard of failed businesses remembered for bold bad moves. His fellow executives felt likewise.

They dismissed the hippie scoundrel who turned out to be Bill Gates. Rejection never stopped this visionary and persistent entrepreneur, and it did not take Gates long to find another partner. Grolier was one of the largest US publishers of general encyclopedias and had started its own electronic versions as early as 1986. It had also developed various electronic gaming products using Microsoft operating systems.[16] Gates invited this partner company to help create Encarta and launched the CD-ROM in 1993, forever changing the encyclopedia industry. By 1994, sales of the *Encyclopedia Britannica* had plummeted 53 percent and the company filed for bankruptcy a few years later.[17]

How Intuition Can Enhance Judgment

Intuition significantly influences the process of sense making, especially when leaders are dealing with complex data and weak signals. Gary Klein has studied the power of intuition in such fast-moving environments as firefighting, military combat, and critical care medicine.[18] In one study, he found that experienced nurses picked up the onset of septic shock in premature infants at least a day before the textbook symptoms appeared and a blood test confirmed the presence of the deadly bacterium. These nurses had grown sensitive to weak signals even if the cues varied. This remarkable gift intrigued the attending physicians. How could the nurses make such swift and accurate diagnoses? "Something seemed off" in a baby's skin color or in the crying pattern, the nurses would say, but they couldn't really be more specific or explain how they knew. Such knowing, without conscious thought, is the hallmark of true intuition.[19]

Leaders need many years of experience, with frequent and timely feedback, to develop reliable intuition. When we drive a car or enter a room full of people, our brains respond automatically, quickly recognizing patterns and inferring with accuracy. But when encountering new situations, we must think more consciously, since routine pattern recognition may not work well. General Colin Powell, who was chairman of the Joint Chiefs of Staff when General Norman Schwarzkopf pushed Saddam Hussein's Iraqi army out of Kuwait in the 1991 Gulf War, worked especially hard on getting soft information, such as employees' gut feelings about complex issues. In his words: "With great effort, I tried to have a participative style. I invited my young officers to my office, but I never wore my uniform with all the bars and stars. I just wore a plain sweater, so that they felt relaxed and comfortable. There were no square tables so as to avoid a head seat, always a round table because I wanted to get the best information from them."[20]

General Powell's premise was that in an informal, open atmosphere, his soldiers would loosen up and share some of their hunches and observations from the front lines that could prove invaluable. This was his way of amplifying weak signals from the troops so that he could decide whether he needed to challenge his sense making further. Our general advice is simple: if someone's intuition is well honed and unbiased in a particular domain of expertise, then seek it out and give it due consideration. Just *treat it as one more data point*, akin to more objective inputs, and weigh it according to its predictive value and credibility.

Action Plan to Amplify Signals

To increase the likelihood that you'll interpret the data quickly and accurately enough to act, you often need to enlarge small dots and find new ones. Here are a few practices to do that:

1. *Start with the end in mind; then zoom in and out, between the big picture and the details.* Learn from the trip to Abilene, and question whether everyone shares the same destination and intent. Also, like Melchiorre, step back and re-assess whether the current strategy is the right one.

2. *Define how precise your interpretation must be given the strategic importance of the task.* Given the potential risks at stake, Holliday knew he had to go beyond a few observations and hunches. He asked his people to get more data and conduct different, more targeted analyses.

3. *Jot down your assumptions about customer behavior, and then observe customers in the process of transacting with your organization—buying your products, talking with customer service, using the products—to appreciate what actually happens.* Melchiorre walked the aisles of supermarkets twice a week and spoke with consumers as they made their purchase decisions.

4. *Walk in your customer's or supplier's shoes by interfacing with your organization at key points in critical processes.* Jot down your experiences at every stage. Spend time observing customers or participating in workshops with suppliers and partners.

5. *Search for disconfirming evidence or information that might disprove your hypothesis.* Look not just at the data presented but also at what information is missing. Melchiorre did this; Kodak did not.

6. *Read literature on critical thinking to mitigate cognitive biases and improve interpreting skills.* Books such as Dan Ariely's *Predictably Irrational*, Charles Duhigg's *The Power of Habit*, and Daniel Kahneman's *Thinking, Fast and Slow* can help you understand what tricks our minds may play as we're processing data.

CONNECT DOTS

Strategic leaders have a deeply ingrained habit of connecting the dots, no matter what the situation. Some years ago, one of us (Paul) vacationed with Jean-Pierre Garnier (J. P.), CEO of GlaxoSmithKline at the time, and witnessed his interpretative reflexes in action. We were so taken with the beauty of the island we were visiting that we decided, along with our wives, to check out some vacation homes. We asked a real estate agent to show us homes that met our criteria. When we arrived at the third home, J. P. scanned the building and grounds and whispered, "Why are we here? This place doesn't meet our specifications." The agent heard him, turned around, and said, "This may not be quite the home you are looking for, but it has some special features inside that you may like." We went in. It was indeed a gorgeous place with a kitchen to die for. J. P. exclaimed, "What a kitchen!" The agent smiled, "Thank you, I thought you would like it." Then J. P. stopped to examine a small photo hanging on the wall. "Is that you here in this photo?" he asked the agent. She hesitated and then said, "Yes." J. P. asked further, "Is this your home?" Yes again. The agent had added her own home (also for sale) to our tour, and J. P. was the only one of us to connect the three dots.

J. P. Garnier's insight about the realtor highlights the value of connecting three dots in a relatively simple low-stakes setting. Making sense of complex data, overcoming bias, and separating the music from the noise become far more difficult when the data set is huge, data sources are spread out, signals are conflicting, and the stakes are high. In the right hands, however, big data can be a huge asset. Just consider how Amazon, American Express, and Google use data today.

For decades, the Minneapolis-based Target Corporation has gathered information about the people who visit its stores.[21] Whenever possible, Target assigns them a unique Guest ID so that it can begin assembling their individual customer profiles. Target tracks what they buy, how they buy it, and whether they use e-mail, snail mail, website, or telephone. To each profile, Target links key demographics such as age, gender, changes in marital status, household size, home address, estimated salary, and credit card usage. The company will try to buy from secondary sources whatever data it can't collect directly, such as educational background, employment history, online reading habits, and charitable donations.

Use Data and Analytics to See Patterns

Target's Guest Marketing Analytics department tries to find actionable insights by searching for patterns in the aggregate data of consumers' buying habits. One pattern jumped out as statistician Andrew Pole was analyzing several years of data: when women discover they're pregnant, their buying habits change. They don't even have to buy an over-the-counter pregnancy test at Target to flag the possibility. By comparing one woman's purchases over time with those of pregnant women in her demographic segment, Target can determine whether she is pregnant and when her baby is due. Target also knows that if it reaches out to the expectant mother during her second trimester, it has a good shot at winning her business for years. Because Target cleverly leveraged this knowledge, its Mom and Baby sales exploded. Between 2002 and 2010, total revenues grew from $44 billion to $67 billion. In 2005, the company's president, Gregg Steinhafel, emphasized the company's "heightened focus on items and categories that appeal to specific guest segments such as mom and baby."[22] The key takeaway: Target not only knows which data it needs, and goes after it, but also studies the data carefully, identifies patterns and trends, associates these findings with customer characteristics, and draws up practical insights for promotion, marketing, and sales.

A recent large-scale theft of credit card data at Target and other large retailers in the States highlights the downside of maintaining large data sets. Millions of credit cards were hacked by a criminal gang from Eastern Europe and resold. There is no question that big data is alluring in providing powerful customer insights. Yet strategic leaders must emphasize not just the ability to collect and rigorously analyze data but also the responsibility to safeguard sensitive data.

The Renaissance artist and inventor Leonardo da Vinci (1452–1519) observed that to understand a complex issue, you must view it from at least three different perspectives. For example, you might examine a business problem from strategic, social, and technological perspectives.[23] Similarly, if you have complex data available, you can plot them using different types of graphs, and shift your angle of interpretation. The remarkable work by statistician Edward R. Tufte amply demonstrates the power of shifting your visual interpretations.[24] Using data regarding events ranging from the cholera outbreak in London in 1854 to the explosion of the space shuttle *Challenger* in 1986, Tufte shows how visualizing data from different perspectives can reveal new insights. For example, Tufte illustrates how Dr. John Snow plotted the devastating 1854 outbreak of cholera cases by chronology, by location, and by travel routes. These different representations allowed Snow to infer that water drawn from a pump at Broad Street in London was the source of the contamination.[25]

Getting diverse perspectives, visually or otherwise, is a first step toward generating multiple hypotheses and countering groupthink bias and rigid frames. If managed well, groups can make far better judgments than individuals since two or more people know more than one.[26] Many companies have recognized that data analytics are changing their business procedures, and that technology is playing a bigger role in offering advice to customers. Some now deploy cross-functional teams to look at data from various perspectives such as sales, marketing, product development, compliance, underwriting, and risk. Others are reorganizing around their customers to bring data from various teams to generate customer insights.

A pharmaceutical company we know is strengthening its customer focus by moving from regional, sales-based account teams to global cross-functional teams. Executives want these teams to generate new insights about large, global customers where they do business. Until recently, the organization was structured by country, and each silo worked independently with its customers. The divisional president realized that executives were missing a lot of potential insight and efficiency. He wanted to connect these geographic regions. Executives started with three top customers to design a targeted experiment that they could try, analyze, and mine for insights. From there, they plan to create a more full-blown global account strategy. The teams are studying the customer's ecosystem of consumers, competitors, suppliers, joint venture partners, and strategic alliances as well as creating "what if" simulations to project possible moves in the competitive environment. The intent of this exercise is, first, to triangulate the relevant information and, second, to uncover market scenarios that executives and even their customers haven't yet fully considered. To launch the project, they

+ formed diverse customer teams with representatives from different regions, functions, and divisions.
+ added nontraditional data sources—blogs and online chats—to conventional ones such as feedback on annual reports and investor presentations.

‹ mapped key stakeholders and influencers in and outside the organization and engaged as many of them as possible to capture comprehensive data.

Although the new account strategy is in an early stage, the initial reports are very positive. Team members in a given region are, for the first time, viewing their account in its totality and sharing insights with colleagues from other parts of the world. Account plans are now more complete, effective, and based on inputs from multiple vantage points. Account teams can connect dots in real time during regular virtual teleconference meetings.

Deploy Multiple Lenses to Connect Dots

In 1999, years before electronic media became widely available to consumers through personal digital devices, Xerox introduced a service to deliver customized newspapers electronically to hotels and other locations. This new technology allowed users to print out tailor-made content. Travelers to foreign countries, for example, could now get their hometown news locally delivered and could read the leading national newspaper of whatever country they were visiting in their own language.[27] While hardly remarkable now, this was truly a potentially disruptive technology at the time. To the leaders of Knight-Ridder, one of America's top newspaper companies, it appeared to be not simply a nice-to-have service for readers but an early sign of potential changes to the industry itself. They wanted to win the long game by spotting trends early, monitoring uncertainties, and amplifying weak signals.

Knight-Ridder, which published more than thirty local newspapers across the United States, started asking critical questions. How important was this service? Would it mean that hotel guests would never again hear the familiar thump of a newspaper outside their doors? Knight-Ridder wanted to know. So it developed multiple scenarios about the future of the newspaper from very different perspectives. In a "business as usual" future, this new service would represent a niche market (i.e., the traveler's market) and a welcome alternative channel of distribution for the company. It might enhance customer loyalty and enable some of Knight-Ridder's newspapers to move beyond their current geography. In a scenario called "cybermedia," where customers adopt electronic channels rapidly, customized printing in hotels might lead to customized news printing at home. Such a development could displace the company's physical assets, such as expensive printing presses and a fleet of delivery trucks.

By looking at the information through multiple lenses, leaders were better able to weigh their options, neither overreacting nor undervaluing the new technology. Considering the high ambiguity of the situation, the company decided simply to track the development of remote electronic printing of newspapers. While such scenario-based analysis doesn't eliminate uncertainty around technological advances or consumer acceptance, it can help strategic leaders properly digest new information, such as Xerox's announcement about remote printing capabilities. This announcement could just as easily have remained a weak signal somewhere along the fuzzy and broad periphery, blissfully ignored. In the end, Knight-Ridder failed to win the long game. The online tsunami that hit the newspaper industry forced the company to break up and sell its newspapers to different publishing groups.

Ask the Right Questions: Demonstrate Curiosity with an Open Mind

Managers have long challenged the wisdom of planning for the future using data from the past. Pundits liken the exercise to looking in the rearview mirror while driving at breakneck speed in the dark. The problem of interpretation lies in the nature of data. "Data is heavy. It wants to go down, not up, in an organization," says Harvard Business School professor Clayton Christensen. "Information about problems thus sinks to the bottom, out of the eyesight and earshot of the senior managers."[28]

We attribute one challenge of interpretation to business unit leaders: they are still operating in silos despite their intentions to propagate a "one-company" mindset. Furthermore, division leaders tend to focus on their short-term unit goals, not on longer-term threats or opportunities for the company as a whole. This shorter-term and more narrow agenda may stem from the compensation system that rewards near-term results and a strong divisional P&L. Even when senior executives have incentives tied to corporate re-sults and longer-term stock performance, they still commonly de-fault to focusing on what is under their immediate control. Taking an enterprise-wide perspective typically falls to the board, the CEO, or the chief strategy officer. In Christensen's view, senior leaders can compensate for the narrow focus of people and their reluctance to speak truth to power by learning to ask better questions.

Tailor the following questions to your context and ask them during meetings:[29]

+ Why does the pattern of behavior in the data in *this* case appear to differ from that in previous cases? What might we be missing that prevents us from connecting the dots better?
+ Instead of looking only at today's performance, let's focus on tomorrow's or next year's performance. What do we need to change in order to impact our metrics and our customer growth in three to five years?
+ Which competitors are threatening us, and which are we more likely to threaten? How might the long game shift, and where might nontraditional competitors enter our space in the future?
+ What are the cultural sensitivities and possible risks around this innovation or change?

+ How might a change in this market segment affect or benefit other market segments? Is this segment an early adopter
or a laggard?

Strategic leaders ask such questions to engage a wider group of
people in spotting and assessing potential disruptions. The art of
asking deep, penetrating questions is a key skill set that leaders must
hone and master. Asking questions that focus on the overall enterprise, rather than on one of its functions, allows such teams to find
and connect many dots from many sources. It gives them permission
to explore and question widely. It also primes the teams to think
longer term and react less.

In the end, brilliant interpretation comes down to a relentless
curiosity in the pursuit of meaning. Strategic leaders begin by
observing the facts, amplifying weak signals, staying open to competing perspectives or data, and connecting the dots in multiple
ways. Those who probe deeper invariably elicit complex and
conflicting answers. Instead of reflexively accepting what they
see, they synthesize diverse inputs by amplifying the more subtle
cues. They look for unusual patterns and play with data to see
how the puzzle may fit differently than thought, as leaders did at
Target.

Strategic leaders are also aware of common traps and bad habits
of mind, such as jumping to conclusions and engaging in biased information searches. They are comfortable with ambiguity and, like
Holliday of DuPont or Melchiorre of Tasty Baking, they keep digging until they see reality as it is, not as they wish it to be.

Action Plan to Connect Dots

Connecting the dots is no easy task. The dots can seem random and
at first may appear to lack connection. Fortunately, there are practices you can use to develop this capability:

1. *Generate competing explanations or hypotheses for what you or others are observing.* Melchiorre had a knack for observing and talking with customers and employees. Through questioning, he arrived at a different interpretation and a better strategic choice.

2. *If generating competing hypotheses is hard, invite others outside your group or function to give their perspective.* If possible, get customers, strategic partners, or representatives of other divisions in your own business to weigh in. Remember how Pope Francis brought in outsiders to evaluate the Vatican Bank.

3. *When stuck analyzing complex information, or trying to recognize patterns, step away, refresh yourself, then try again.* Sleep on the data, since the mind continues to process at night. Each time Holliday stepped away and then reengaged with different team members, he enlarged his picture.

4. *Identify the main components of a problem for deeper analysis.* For each component, identify the most critical data points or signals. Remember how the fictional Holmes homed in on signs that would provide a remarkably accurate understanding of who Freud was. Holliday did the same to understand the economy.

5. *Use a fishbone diagram or flowchart to connect individual pieces of the puzzle with the larger picture.* Using his experience and intuition, Holliday built a mental flowchart of factors pointing his economic outlook for DuPont in one direction or another. Leaders at all levels can apply this tool, either on the back of an envelope or with a spreadsheet.

6. *When you travel, select and read a book or magazine outside your normal interests to expand your frame and uncover new perspectives.* Pick one at random from a kiosk, as Buckminster Fuller did.

THE DISCIPLINE TO INTERPRET: PULLING IT TOGETHER

Jane Wang never really liked Sherlock Holmes because she craved more obvious clues and straightforward solutions. Plus, she did not care much for Holmes's cocksure style and perpetual patronization of Dr. Watson. But she recognized that she lacked patience as well as the skills to amplify hidden signals. She also realized that she needed to connect the dots better and was inspired by Holmes in that regard. Besides, Holmes was an exceptional *fictional* character.

Her manager Lee said she had tunnel vision when implementing projects. Her single-minded focus made her great at execution but poor at adjustments. She finally started to accept that her focused determination was actually undermining her ability to see the long game clearly. To *amplify more signals*, she instructed herself not to jump to conclusions so quickly but to give each signal its due respect. She forced herself to pay more attention to a wide variety of inputs and see new connections. She also started searching for disconfirming evidence that could disprove her working assumptions, particularly about customers and competitors.

Jane liked to connect with people, and that had served her well. However, she needed to connect many more dots, and so she had to enlarge her field of observation. She asked her team to research and list external stakeholders who might have different insights and agendas. She closely looked at any new data about changing customer needs, developed several different hypotheses about what the data really meant, and then challenged her own assumptions as well as those of others.

4 SAILING INTO THE STORM

The Discipline to Decide:
Explore Options and Show Courage

O<small>N</small> A<small>UGUST</small> 5, 2010, <small>THE SIMULTANEOUS COLLAPSE OF</small> several mine shafts stranded helpless workers 700 meters (2,300 feet) below the ground near the Chilean city of Copiapó, some five hundred miles north of the capital, Santiago. When the disaster occurred, Laurence Golborne, the mining minister, was traveling to Ecuador along with Chilean president Sebastián Piñera. At 11 o'clock that night, Golborne got a heart-stopping message on his smartphone: "Mine cave-in, Copiapó. 33 victims."

There are few scenarios that highlight the white-knuckle challenge of true leadership like rescue missions, conducted under grave time pressure in the glaring public spotlight. While few leaders will ever find themselves in a position where their decisions will save or lose the lives of thirty-three men, many will make decisions that affect the livelihoods of their employees and their communities. The Chilean mining disaster introduces themes that will resonate for anyone wrestling with the high-stake decisions and public exposure that are intrinsic to leadership.

Making tough calls is the most difficult leadership challenge. Over the course of our careers, through our hands-on work and countless interviews with executives, we are still struck by how rare the truly decisive leader is. In uncertain times, too many leaders hesitate to step up and take full accountability for tough decisions. In many cultures, people are more concerned with avoiding mistakes and dodging blame. They instinctively duck under the table or throw colleagues under the bus. Conversely, those braver souls who do rise to the occasion might rush to judgment without exploring their options fully. The purpose of this chapter is to improve your inner decider-in-chief by striking the right balance between boldly moving forward and coolly exploring options.

DECISION-MAKING DEFINES A LEADER

Laurence Golborne faced the leadership challenge of a lifetime. There was no clear, obvious way forward. The complexity of the problem meant that the government would immediately step in, instantly multiplying the number of stakeholders in the solution and the possible outcomes. Daily media scrutiny was inevitable, guaranteeing an additional source of pressure. Information was limited, and lives were at risk. It would be days before Golborne could ascertain how many of the thirty-three missing men were dead or hurt, how much air they had, and how long their food and water would last.

Just four months into his job when this crisis struck, Golborne was new to government and to the mining industry. He'd been appointed because of his experience as CEO of Cencosud, Chile's largest retail chain. He had majored in civil engineering at Pontifical Catholic University of Chile and studied management at Northwestern and Stanford Universities. Although this training had helped him become a successful corporate leader, he now found himself 700 meters deep in a life-threatening mining problem of major technical and strategic complexity well beyond his experience base.

In the initial hours, Golborne informed and engaged critical stakeholders. He immediately sent word of the accident to the president and then boarded a commercial airliner back to Santiago. A Chilean Air Force plane transported him to Copiapó. From there, he traveled some 45 kilometers by car to the mine, arriving at 3:30 a.m. on August 7.[1]

No other minister of mining had ever visited a crisis site before; the conventional approach would have been to ask those lower down in the government's hierarchy to step in and manage the rescue effort. By quickly getting to the site, Golborne demonstrated his intent to serve as more than a figurehead. Within minutes of his arrival, he took charge. As he later recalled, "We were not part of the problem at the start of the rescue,"[2] meaning that the government would normally not step in and become the responsible party. But given the scale of the disaster, Golborne felt that he was better positioned to tackle the problem and navigate through the mess and figure out how to save lives. He wanted to win the long game, both for the miners and for his government.

Golborne did not, however, assume that he could manage the crisis single-handedly. Instead, he immediately assembled an inner circle capable of providing technical expertise, support, and relationship management with the families of the victims, the community, and the media. Key players included trusted colleagues such as his deputy, René Aguilar, and prominent figures from industry and government such as senior engineer André Sougarret of Coldeco, and Christian Barra of President Piñera's cabinet. The members of this inner circle had both prominence and pedigree and put their egos aside. They coalesced into a real working team, assembling each morning between 9:00 and 9:45 a.m. for laser-focused strategy sessions. Golborne urged all members to speak their minds, make requests, and put forward any viable solutions. "Tell us what you need," Golborne said. "Say it in time. . . . We are not going to tolerate stoppages in the processes because a material, a piece of equipment, or a truck that you did not ask for, but needed, was not there."[3]

With his inner circle in place, Golborne focused on fostering dialogue rather than making final decisions: "As a minister, I did what I normally do, let the experts talk," he recalled. "I started asking questions. Why are you putting in this winch? What alternatives are there?" In doing so, he reframed decisions to avoid such common traps as addressing the wrong issue or falling victim to overconfidence and confirmation bias. He promoted democratic decision-making by asking for solutions by consensus. When consensus proved impossible, however, he made the call, acting as final arbitrator. For example, the Coldeco engineer André Sougarret struggled with the task of objectively evaluating each of the rescue drilling proposals. It was Golborne who asked the critical questions and determined that not *one* approach but a *multiplicity* of approaches had the greatest likelihood of saving the men.

A plan began to take shape—rather, a series of options. Plan A, the option conditionally approved by President Piñera, was to drill straight down at an angle of 90 degrees. Plan B, the cheapest option proposed by one of the subcontractors, was to widen the existing boreholes. Most members of the inner circle dismissed Plan B as "crazy," but Golborne insisted that they evaluate and then execute it. Plan C, the most expensive option that would require presidential approval, was to bring in an oil drilling rig from the States. Golborne needed only one tunnel to retrieve the miners, but he insisted on breaking ground for three parallel tunnels, each representing a different strategy for saving the trapped men.

The three-pronged approach was a major shift from past mining rescues, which typically focused on a single option. Given the un-

Multiple Rescue Options Explored in Chile

Ⓐ **Pilot hole**   Ⓑ **Shaft widening**   Ⓒ **Rescue capsule**

33 Miners Trapped

700 Meters

certain circumstances—the gradual depletion of oxygen, food, and water in the mine—Golborne chose redundancy rather than going "all in" on a single plan. He hedged the risk of failure, prioritizing speed over efficiency. If one plan faltered or failed, the others would proceed apace.

On October 13, 2010, all thirty-three miners emerged from the earth, sixty-nine days after the fateful collapse, and thirty-three days after drilling had commenced under Plan B, the "crazy plan" for widening the existing holes that ultimately saved the miners' lives. The rescue team used a slender hole to deliver fresh food, water, and medical supplies to the men. That bought Golborne's team valuable time to widen another hole to the point where rescuers could pull the trapped miners through it, one by one. On the day of the actual rescue, relatives and paramedics were standing by to embrace the men. The whole world rejoiced. Television cameras projected the victory sign—"Misin Cumplida Chile"—to millions around the globe. It was a proud moment in Chile's recent history, thanks to the strategic leadership of Laurence

Golborne, the expertise of his inner circle, the perseverance of the rescue crew, the devotion of the Chilean people, and the fortitude of the miners themselves.

In retrospect, we might be tempted to view the rescue of the Chilean miners as an uncommon disaster that required both heroic leadership *and* extraordinary serendipity. At its core, however, this is a story of strategic decision-making under grave risk and great uncertainty. We can and should broadly transfer and apply what we've learned from Copiapó. Golborne's approach in the days and weeks after the disaster demonstrate two core elements critical to successful leadership decision-making: *exploring options* and *showing courage*.

Exploring options means having the wisdom, cool-headedness, and perspective to consider all of the alternatives available. Golborne envisaged and evaluated *all* alternatives, drawing on the collective insights of an inclusive team with complementary expertise. This strategy proved particularly effective because time was of the essence, uncertainty was high, and failure was not an option.

Showing courage means demonstrating the fortitude to commit to the right solution and, if that solution proves ineffective, critically stepping back to reconsider. Golborne committed himself from the moment he landed at the crisis site. He was willing to assume individual accountability rather than cowering behind bureaucracy or complaining about others not taking the reins. Because of his courage, the issues that needed to be addressed surfaced quickly. We do not exaggerate when we say that the miners owe their lives to Golborne's broad perspective and steady hand.

The rescue in Copiapó was a scene of joy because Golborne was "ambidextrous" enough to both explore options and show courage. How well and how frequently do you take steps such as these?

Explore Options

1. *Do you always generate and evaluate multiple options for realizing your strategic vision, including an analysis of the status quo?* For Golborne, creating new options was mission critical. His decision to drill multiple parallel tunnels defied the status quo and ultimately saved the miners.

2. *Do you carefully balance trade-offs, assess risks, and consider unintended consequences for complex projects?* When the stakes are high, you can't afford to ignore the unintended consequences of your actions. This is why Golborne had to build in redundancy without regard for efficiency and cost.

3. *Do you balance speed and rigor when making complex decisions, especially in fast-moving environments?* In the Chilean mines, time was of the essence, but so was careful, rigorous evaluation, since the mine could collapse further if the structural damage was misestimated.

Show Courage

4. *Do you show courage in setting a distinctive strategic direction and making tough choices in times of uncertainty?* Strategic leaders have the emotional backbone to make tough calls without knowing all the facts, just as Golborne did in the early hours of the mining crisis.

5. *Do you champion innovative solutions and risk-taking to meet changing business conditions, including evolving customer needs?* In the end, the willingness to invest in a more innovative option paid off for Golborne. In uncertain times, leaders must push beyond the easy choices.

6. *Do you balance long-term investment for growth against short-term pressure for results?* Even in Chile's crisis, the long-term

image of the country and the reputations of those involved still mattered, as the world watched government leaders manage the mining disaster. When besieged by quarterly pressures, strategic leaders must still consider the organization's future well-being in order to win the long game.

EXPLORE OPTIONS

On the afternoon of December 26, 1998, over a hundred yachts lined up for the start of the grueling Sydney to Hobart yacht race, an annual Australian tradition dating back to 1945.[4] During the first day of the contest, a cataclysmic storm whipped up and turned the race into the largest rescue mission in sailing history. All across the Bass Strait, a 200-mile-wide stretch of open water between the southeastern coast of Australia and the island of Tasmania, boats struggled to stay afloat. Despite noble efforts, the lives of six sailors were lost.[5] Only 44 of the 115 vessels completed the course: 5 were abandoned, 2 sank, and 64 others declared defeat. In the midst of this chaos, the skipper and crew of one of the smallest boats, the *AFR Midnight Rambler*, made a bold, counterintuitive choice. While all of the larger yachts were trying to outrun the storm or head for shore, the *Midnight Rambler* opted to sail directly into the storm.

Evaluate Multiple Options When Navigating Storms

The storm's onset was sudden and terrifying. Among the individual crews of each boat, tensions ran high. Some crews spent hours bickering, reaching a decision that few believed in. Others were simply paralyzed by fear. Under these conditions, most of the skippers and crews were able to see only two courses of action. The first option, heading back north toward mainland Australia, seemed the most obvious but proved to be the most dangerous. Most of the smaller boats chose it, heading straight into large waves from "astern," compromising their ability to maneuver. These yachts fell to the mercy of the high seas. Many rolled or dismasted; their crews had to be rescued from the turbulent water.

The second option, pursued by larger boats further south when the storm struck, was to sail southeast, away from the storm, in an attempt to outrun it or sail around the worst of it. But this strategy aligned the course of the boats with the path of the storm, prolonging their time in hurricane-like conditions and diverting them from the finish line. While many of these larger boats survived the storm, they all lost so much time and distance that they had no chance of winning the race.

There was, however, a third option: to sail directly into the storm. Only a few boats considered it, and only one—the *AFR Midnight Rambler*—executed it successfully. The ship's captain, Ed Psaltis, was a strong leader who believed in shared decision-making. He started sailing when he was seventeen years old and had represented Australia in multiple races, winning several times. Psaltis was an accountant, married with three children. His sailing experience and personal stability allowed him, like Laurence Golborne in Chile, to face this crisis with calmness and clarity of purpose. Psaltis methodically considered multiple options and made a very counterintuitive decision. His unusual move saved the lives of his crew—and won the race.

When the storm struck, Psaltis and his team debated their options, quickly but thoughtfully. By orienting their course directly into the storm, they would reduce the amount of time during which they were subject to its wrath. They would also be pursuing the most direct path to the finish line. Although they recognized the risks, they agreed it was their best option. The skill and teamwork of the crew gave them confidence. Everyone had a say, and then Psaltis made the call. It was tough going. Thundering noise and wind made open dialogue difficult. But skipper Ed and his crew recognized that communication and sticking together could help a team under these most trying of sailing conditions.

After eighty-eight hours, the *AFR Midnight Rambler* arrived safely in Hobart and was proclaimed the overall winner—the smallest boat in ten years to win this notoriously difficult race. Experts have since determined that sailing into the storm was not only the best strategy but also the safest. The *AFR Midnight* crew members had not just been lucky; they had applied sound reasoning, made a strategic choice, and committed to its execution.

The story of the 1998 Sydney to Hobart yacht race illustrates that *exploring options* is as vital as committing to bold, often counterintuitive choices. Situations of great stress and complexity demand that leaders consider multiple options before arriving at the best solution. However, the very conditions that typically create a sense of urgency often impede this type of "options thinking." Playing the long game is most difficult when in the midst of a crisis.

Decision research has shown that people innately prefer clarity and certainty over ambiguity. No surprise there! But *ambiguity aversion* (which is distinct from *risk aversion*) is often heightened at moments of crisis.[6] Adrenalin catalyzes the primitive "fight or flight" response. For most people, it imposes a myopia that can be disruptive, even deadly. Tragically, many people in burning buildings die while banging on a single locked door, their panicked brains incapable of recognizing other escape routes.

Strategically weathering storms means overcoming ambiguity aversion by taking a wide perspective on the problem and considering options that, at first blush, seem less appealing. Since leaders often operate under conditions of high uncertainty, they must suppress their natural desire for what is known and embrace the unknown. In business, the known arena often becomes a "red ocean," meaning a hyper-competitive environment,[7] in which everyone participates in the same adversarial feeding frenzy with much blood and little gain. Greater rewards, however, often await those brave enough to venture into "blue oceans"—the new markets, emerging technologies, uncharted regions, disruptive business models, and novel partnerships in which opportunities have not yet been fully arbitraged. That's how you can win big.

Unintended Consequences: Backing Off a Bad Choice

We saw in Golborne and Psaltis a willingness to explore options and arrive at a strategy that defied conventional wisdom, ultimately leading to success. Of course, many counterintuitive strategies end up failing. Unintended consequences often befuddle those plowing into new terrain, as Reed Hastings, the CEO of Netflix, learned the hard way.

Hastings co-founded Netflix in 1998 to offer people the option of receiving videos by mail using a fixed monthly fee for unlimited use. Assuming a three-day time window to receive, view, and mail back a single DVD, the cheapest plan—costing about $10 a month—would allow customers to watch up to ten different videos per month. For a higher fee, customers could have two or more videos at home at any one time. The aim was to disrupt the old Blockbuster model, which required that people visit a store, browse, select, and pay a fee for their video. Headquartered in Los Gatos, California, Netflix had amassed a DVD collection of more than 100,000 titles and over 44,000,000 subscribers by 2010.[8] It was a very successful business model, but consumers were increasingly becoming accustomed to Internet video streaming, which was disruptive to the predominantly mail-oriented model of Netflix. So, Hastings made a bold choice.

In July 2011, Hastings decided to drop the price of DVDs sent via mail by about 20 percent but to start charging for Internet downloads. Until then, Netflix offered a single service that permitted free streaming of movies via the Internet. To accelerate the move toward online distribution and encourage web downloading, Hastings decided to unbundle these two offerings. He created a spin-off company, Qwikster, to focus on video streaming. Qwikster offered a subscription price lower than what Netflix had charged for mailing DVDs. Many consumers liked this but not the ones who wanted both streaming and mail options. For them, the combined cost of two subscriptions (Netflix and Qwikster) translated into an overall cost increase of nearly 60 percent. These dual-use consumers took their rage out on the company. Over the course of a single year, Netflix reported the loss of 800,000 customers. Its stock price plummeted—a 65 percent decline, with a drop of 26 percent in a single day.[9]

We wonder how a successful entrepreneur like Hastings, who had led Netflix through twelve years of successful growth, could have failed to foresee the angry reaction of his customers. Clearly, Hastings and his team had not thought through the unintended consequences of this important business-model change. The company's aim was to better execute two distinct delivery models without alienating its most loyal customer base.

Hastings managed to recover from this error and to regain the faith of Netflix's subscribers. In September 2011, just two months after his ill-fated decision, Hastings sent an apology to all of Netflix's customers via e-mail.[10] In this e-mail, Hastings didn't just ask customers to come back; he asked their forgiveness and took public responsibility for his decision and for his flawed assumptions about what customers valued.[11] This mea culpa was a rare, vital, and career-saving move—for Hastings, as well as for Netflix. It exemplifies what it means to play the long game. Three weeks later, Netflix reversed its decision and pulled back from the spin-off. Richard Greenfield, a media analyst for BTIG Capital, said in an e-mail that the Netflix announcement was a "necessary reversal of a bad decision."[12] By 2013, Netflix had regained most of its customer base and resumed its position among the top-stock performers, increasing its share price by 300 percent in 2013.

Hastings admitted to a lack of rigor in considering the consequences for all key stakeholders, especially valued customers. Moreover, his team did not properly evaluate alternatives before acting. Hastings wrote in a blog post: "Companies rarely die from moving too fast, and they frequently die from moving too slowly." However, as the Greek philosopher Sophocles stated, "Quick decisions are unsafe decisions." While you may need to drive faster decisions in a fast-changing technology arena, the Netflix case highlights the subtle balance between a sense of urgency and a rush to action. Make sure you weigh your options carefully against the right criteria, not least of which should be your customers' reactions. Strategic leaders need to iterate their decisions as they adapt to real-time market feedback.[13] By thinking through a variety of options for any key decision, you can uncover flaws in underlying assumptions or unintended consequences. Ask yourself: How will my decision look if everything remains stable and rational? Conversely: How will my decision hold up when all hell breaks loose and unintended consequences start to shape the outcomes?

Balancing Speed and Rigor

Marisol Hernandes, a division president in a fast-moving computer-parts technology business based in South America, liked to make decisions quickly and keep the process simple. Because it was a rapidly changing industry, she felt the advantage went to first or at least fast movers. This worked well when the competitive landscape was familiar: the competition remained the same from one year to the next and the choices were straightforward. Her industry, however, was shifting rapidly as new competitors from Korea and other emerging Asian markets began seizing market share with lower-priced products. Hernandes's instinct was to make a strategic acquisition of a supplier in a country with lower costs—a clear go/no-go decision. Her team had identified an attractive target through networking. After analyzing the deal, she pushed for a rapid green light. But the CEO and CFO resisted, asking for a stronger case. Capital was short, and playing the long game meant they should take a more cautious investment strategy. Hernandes's first reaction was to become annoyed and frustrated. She started venting to colleagues about the top executives: "They just don't get it, you can't win if you don't move fast. The Koreans are eating our lunch. We should be ready to go."[14] After calming down and getting some sage advice, she backed off from storming into the office of the CEO.

Hernandes gathered the principals involved in the decision and challenged them to come up with other options that could move them beyond a simple yes/no on this specific acquisition. With external facilitation, they were able to achieve more objective outside-in thinking. The team reviewed a broader range of possible acquisition choices, including a joint venture or strategic alliance option. They weighed each alternative in terms of revenue growth, feasibility, impact on customer relationships, and returns on investment. After this more thorough analysis, her team still preferred an acquisition—but of a different company in a more strategic market. Ultimately, she convinced the CEO and CFO by presenting this deeper analysis and pointing to the strategic advantages of the proposed alternative acquisition.

A common problem when making strategic decisions is failing to see all the options and, as a result, becoming myopic. Fortunately for their business, Hernandes's CEO compelled her to explore more alternatives and examine each option more critically. The key is to expand your thinking and balance speed with rigor, since you must also avoid the other extreme: analysis-paralysis.

Chan Medical Center: Exploring Options at an Inflection Point

Outside-in thinking, a tool for exploring options, was as valuable for Hernandes as it was for Dr. Zara Zephari. Dr. Z—as she was called—is the founder, chief scientist, and architect of the "Chan Center," the first to specialize in research and clinical treatment of pediatric and adolescent multiple sclerosis (MS). The center's mission is highly valued by the university, the community, and the research world. It is also a favorite of a large donor who helped the medical system to acquire cutting-edge technology.

After ten years of innovation in research, patient care, and fund raising, the urgent question was whether and how to expand. From Dr. Z's perspective, the university's administrative bureaucracy made it hard to add talent, pursue innovative research, expand facilities, and get internal funding. The center had to fight for resources from a position of relative weakness in the rankings of strategic programs at the hospital. Further, competition for patients from newer centers had increased. As Dr. Z contemplated the long game, she realized that her decisions would affect the center well beyond her tenure.

The first decision was personal: stay with the center or move to another hospital system. After receiving counsel from a trusted board member, Dr. Z began to contemplate multiple growth possibilities relative to the following decision criteria: (1) increasing revenue, (2) improving patient care, (3) increasing patient numbers, and (4) enhancing research quality and output. Considering these four criteria, Dr. Z and her advisers evaluated the following choices.

Don't Rock the Boat: Dr. Z could comfortably stay where she was and pursue incremental change within the institution. This strategy worked in the past but would not be a good recipe for continued growth. Modest expansion might be possible, but strong growth would be unlikely. She was concerned that the market was becoming saturated.

Fight the Good Fight: Dr. Z could push harder for internal resources, using current levers such as big donors and positive public relations. For example, she could fight for expanding her center with a satellite office in a major city nearby. As she considered this approach, several questions arose: Which moves would grow the center most in the current institution? How many new patients would come to the city? Would aggressive marketing, within the university context, get sufficient traction?

Look for a Friend: Dr. Z could relocate to another institution where the center would have greater resources. For example, she could join with an adult MS program or an independent pediatric center. She had explored this option before and it had considerable promise. Other hospital systems would potentially give her center a bigger priority, and a few had expressed interest. Of course, potential increased institutional support—locally and elsewhere—remained a big unknown and would need due diligence. Would her big donors go with her? How much disruption would relocation cause to current care and research? Moreover, this approach could backfire if her bosses got wind of her strategy and started to rein her in. Also, Dr. Z recognized the dilemma of serving only her center's interests versus those of the institution.

Go It Alone: Dr. Z could explore becoming an independent nonprofit organization affiliated with multiple institutions. Her entrepreneurial streak got the center off the ground, and this trait appealed to many donors. "Going it alone" represented a high-risk/high-reward option. Freeing herself from a big institution would create flexibility, unleash her innovation, streamline her decision-making, and remove the drawbacks of a large bureaucratic system. Yet, Dr. Z would risk losing the safety net and prestige of the univer-

How Dr. Z Went Beyond a Yes/No Decision

Fight the Good Fight
Think strategically to grow the center, but challenging to get many new patients

Don't Rock the Boat
Modest expansion possible, strong growth unlikely

Dr. Z's Options

Joining Forces
Could be helpful whether she stays or leaves

Look For a Friend
Center would become a bigger priority, but risk of disruption and losing big donors

Go It Alone
High risk but potentially high reward

sity as well as its resources. The transition would be hard unless her donors stepped up substantially.

While she evaluated these options, another surfaced: an alliance with a competing organization. Joining forces could help, whether she stayed or moved, and thereby expand her set of considerations.

One unexpected benefit of these reflections was that Dr. Z expanded her prior decision frame of "stay or go." She started to approach her decision process as dynamically adjustable over time rather than as a fixed moment of choice between just two options, like a fork in the road. She decided to use the next few months to go down the decision path further. In uncertain times—reduced resources, changing funding priorities, increasing competition, and scarcity of talent—options thinking can be liberating.

Managers too often act as though they have to make a yes/no choice (as Hastings, Dr. Z, and Hernandes did at first). Just as with your personal financial planning, you can create a portfolio of alternatives and invest a little in each so that you can keep your options open as long as possible and adjust when necessary without betting the farm. Critical to options thinking is to take a long-term view.

Failing to adopt a portfolio perspective is a common framing bias in decision-making. When people examine an option without simultaneously considering all other available options, they fall victim to a bias known as the *isolation effect*.[15] Successful leaders, in contrast, know how to use a portfolio perspective in the stream of time. This mindset often encourages greater risk-taking, for two basic reasons. First, an options approach can help limit downside risk since you are not betting all on one option—you can pull the plug if your bet starts to sour. Second, when you pursue a portfolio approach, each individual move becomes less risky because of implicit hedges: if one option sours, another may sweeten beyond your expectation. Playing the long game means always keeping an eye on the future, beyond the current decision.

Actions to Explore Options

Here are some ways to create more options:

1. *Reframe yes/no decisions by explicitly asking for several other good alternatives. Always ask "What other options might we have?" when faced with a go/no-go or yes/no binary decision.* We saw how Golborne, Captain Ed, and Dr. Z benefited from exploring options. Netflix would have avoided a lot of grief if CEO Hastings had slowed down a tad to consider customers and other key stakeholders.

2. *Use impromptu meetings to generate additional options for the decision at hand.* This process need not be drawn out.

3. *List and review alternative options based on a clear set of criteria to weigh and rank the options.* Dr. Z made her top

decision factors explicit with the help of her advisers, as did Golborne.

4. *Divide big decisions into pieces so that you can understand component parts and better appreciate the risk of unintended consequences.* Dr. Z practiced this technique when she adopted a portfolio strategy that gave her approach flexibility.

5. *Involve others in your decision process to gain additional perspectives.* Marisol, Dr. Z, and Golborne all accepted that they couldn't succeed alone. Others helped them to step back and reframe their decisions.

SHOW COURAGE

The emotional and logistical pressure of a crisis situation can immobilize leaders. People postpone or avoid necessary decisions rather than subject them to rigorous reasoning. Too many decision-makers allow conditions such as lack of proof, conflicting data, or fear of failure to obstruct timely judgment. As a result, decision cycles slow to a deadly crawl, which is more harmful than rushing to imperfect solutions. As Winston Churchill warned, the maxim "Nothing but perfection" often translates into costly analysis-paralysis.

Courage, as we saw with Laurence Golborne, Ed Psaltis, and Reed Hastings, plays an important role in strategic decision-making. We argue that strategic leaders should pursue flexible options when uncertainty is high. But once a decision is made, they need to remain resolute and accept accountability for flexible execution.

Fear of Failure: Why Leaders Avoid Tough Choices

The best strategic leaders, like Golborne and Psaltis, find a middle ground between shooting from the hip and analyzing endlessly without pulling the trigger. It's the rare leader who is willing and able to assume real responsibility in a crisis situation. In today's uncertain economic climate, in which leaders face complex issues at every turn, the need for decisive, courageous leaders has become more acute. A survey conducted with managers at a financial services firm revealed high frustration with their leaders not being sufficiently decisive.[16] Their remarks illustrate the quintessential dilemma faced by most companies since the financial crisis of 2008:

> "Our leaders are often paralyzed. They fear taking and making decisions. They think problem, not solution, and feel their reputation is in jeopardy all the time."
> "A lot of our leaders are always asking for permission. There is a lack of capacity to take charge and assume personal accountability."
> "Leaders need more confidence and to have guts when dealing with uncomfortable situations; they must be more resilient."

Another firm used the term *walking wounded* to capture the reluctance of leaders to make bold decisions in the period following the financial crisis. A manager at a third company in the energy field described a similar phenomenon: "We tend to talk about decision rights and accountability the whole time instead of anyone stepping up to the plate. It is never clear who makes the decision, and it is also clear that a lot of leaders don't want to."[17]

What will it take to overcome the post-crisis baggage, or risk aversion, that has made many leaders so gun-shy? There is little argument that immense opportunity and competitive advantage await companies that can develop strategic decision-making capabilities.

Zappos: Courage at a Moment of Truth

Zappos faced a crisis in 1999 that could have put it out of business. At the time, selling shoes online was a novel concept. Most people

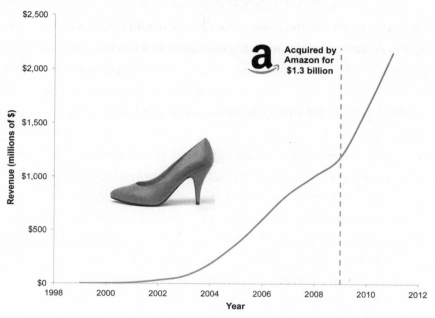

How Zappos Creatively Bounced Back

Acquired by Amazon for $1.3 billion

want to try shoes on before buying. Zappos's business model at the time charged customers for shipping, a cost above and beyond the price of the shoes. While Zappos had generated a niche following, it did not have a critical mass and was stuck. Venture funding by Tony Hsieh, who later became the CEO, was starting to trickle and new capital was sorely needed to pay the bills.

Founder Nick Swinmurn and executive Fred Mossler had a brainstorming session to generate new ideas. One outlandish idea, unprecedented at the time, was to provide free shipping. How it would make business sense was hard to see, but it surely was creative. The gambit would directly address the biggest customer complaints: not being able to try on shoes, yet having to pay for shipping when they didn't fit. Without worry over shipping or return costs, customers could order and try on as many shoes as they wanted to get the right fit—just as in a retail store. Without time to test or explore other ideas, Zappos's leaders concluded that it was their last and best option. They instituted this new policy for all customers. It worked.[18] Free shipping saved the company and unveiled an important insight: the customer experience and relationship mattered more than the size of the shoe selection. That first brave move led to other bold decisions that improved the customer experience.

The success of Zappos has been remarkable. It has set a new standard of service, much of it built on insights gleaned from the desperate experiment of free shipping. As it grew, Zappos took more control of the customer experience: the supply chain, logistics, inventory, and all other steps needed to ensure optimal customer care.

In 2009, Amazon acquired Zappos for $1.3 billion. According to Nick Swinmurn, the key lesson from the original gutsy call was "if you can take something standard and make it feel personalized, that is a great customer experience."[19]

Calculated Risk-Taking Versus Gambling

Were the Zappos leaders lucky or smart? As in most cases of success, the answer is "both." Many entrepreneurs—including Branson, Musk, and Hastings—reached moments where they had to make a high-stakes, risky bet. "I do a lot by gut feeling and a lot by personal experience," Branson says. "I mean, if I relied on accountants to make decisions, I most certainly would have never gone into the airline business. I most certainly would not have gone into the space business, and I certainly wouldn't have gone into most of the businesses that I'm in. So, in hindsight, it seems to have worked pretty well to my advantage."[20] The winners often feel they were taking a risk, but it was nearly always a well-thought-out decision. Also, they seem to have a knack for creating their own luck, recognizing that luck and skill often mingle in complex ways.

We distinguish *exercising courage*—making a bold decision after careful reflection—from the *overconfidence* that can lead to recklessness. We can see the distinction in Paul Reichmann, one of the most powerful real estate moguls of the modern era. Reichmann, an Orthodox Jew from Canada, was a devout and modest man in his personal life. Although he gave generously to charities and civic causes, he was a tough businessman at heart. He was considered a shrewd risk-taker in the high-stakes real estate business with its extreme boom and bust cycles. At the top of his game in the 1980s, he had assembled a personal net worth of over $10 billion. Years later in 1992, after one of the most astonishing financial collapses in the history of real estate development, his wealth had dwindled to less than $100 million.

Olympia & York, the Reichmann-family real estate development firm, owned forty major office towers in a dozen cities on both sides of the Atlantic and controlled $20 billion in assets. Its projects included the World Financial Center in Lower Manhattan and Canary Wharf in London's East End. At its peak in 1990, Olympia & York held about 8 percent of New York City's commercial office space, more than twice as much as that of its closest rival, the Rockefellers. But in 1992, the Reichmanns became overextended and their most ambitious project, Canary Wharf, failed to attract enough tenants, causing their real estate empire to quickly collapse.[21]

Paul Reichmann blamed his own overconfidence. Reflecting on his past big real estate decisions, he said in 1997: "The fact that I had never been wrong created character flaws that caused me to make mistakes."[22] Years earlier Andrew Sarlos, a prominent Toronto investment banker and Reichmann family friend, put his finger on part of the problem: "For Paul, it is like being a gambler, like being a heroin addict—he cannot stop." But as late as 2000, Reichmann scoffed at that sort of criticism. "You don't get the returns if you don't take the risk," he said in an interview.[23] For years, Reichmann's track record was so impressive that his creditors did not mind his high-roller approach. His sense of timing in the notoriously cyclical real estate market seemed infallible, and he was viewed as a master negotiator with an uncanny understanding of complex financing techniques. His overconfidence took him down.

Reichmann was by no means alone. Many entrepreneurs experience failure, even bankruptcy. Any leader in business worth his or her salt will have encountered numerous setbacks and losses; if not, they haven't taken enough risks. Risk-taking is an important skill; nothing ventured, nothing gained. But bold risk-taking by itself is seldom sufficient, and often disastrous. Consider the recent collapse of the empire of the Brazilian tycoon Eike Batista, who managed to lose $30 billion in a single year. Batista was brimming with confidence: he attracted well over $50 billion of investments by partners. His EBX Group consisted of large separate companies such as OGX in oil and gas, MMX in mining, OSX for the offshore industry, LLX in logistics, and MPX in energy.[24] Their names all ended with X to emphasize the multiplier effects he promised his investors. Unfortunately, the X factor turned out to be a small fraction, not a large multiple. Batista lost control of his business empire because a large offshore oil field in Brazil failed to produce oil. That failure put pressure on his related businesses.[25]

Batista preferred the fast lane. He was a playboy, a race-car driver with an expensive car parked in his living room, and the son of Brazil's minister of mining. In convincing others to invest, he fell for his own mythology. When asked about his goals in 2012, Batista answered "to become the richest man in the world," aiming to increase his $30 billion fortune to $100 billion. His choices were less driven by options or outside-in thinking than by an outsized ego, big dreams, seductive salesmanship, and outright superstition—lucky numbers, astrology, and voodoo economics. Not surprisingly, Batista's companies were poorly diversified and unprepared to withstand adverse conditions. Even so, before he crashed like Icarus from Greek mythology, many smart players had bought into Batista's Brazilian myth, among them Brazil's government leaders and a number of savvy Wall Street firms.[26]

The collapse of Reichmann's empire shows that courage is crucial to success in capital-intensive businesses, but a string of great successes can lead to overconfidence that may descend into hubris. The sudden failure of Eike Batista illustrates how risk-taking is influenced by hubris, to the detriment of the long game. Hubris can easily lead to reckless behavior, as when leaders pursue long shots without sufficient regard for failure. All leaders must learn to calibrate their courage to the task at hand. Apart from proper risk analysis, leaders need to keep their emotions in check. Reichmann failed to do so occasionally; and Batista, repeatedly.

Emotional Fortitude

Leadership requires strong emotional intelligence—the ability to read your own emotions accurately as well as those of others. Emotional intelligence insulates a leader from reacting to the emotions and demons of other people. It informs you of the time to cheer your team forward and the time to pull back. If the evidence starts to indicate that a project is flawed or doomed, the leader must be able to change course. In times of great success, she may need to embody a bucket of cold water, the one who awakens others to hard reality. This duty is very difficult, especially when people are intoxicated by undreamt-of fortune.

You may be tempted to let a team obscure the distinction between strategy and serendipity, between strong decision-making and sheer luck. Effective leaders clarify what the company must do to succeed in the short and long term. Without a beacon, people drift and lose control of their own destiny. You need people who will challenge your thinking and prevent rash decisions. Reichmann could have used fewer yes-men and more tough debate. The same is true for Batista: those who stood to gain from his investments urged him to fly closer to the sun. The most strategic leaders surround themselves with independent thinkers who have counterbalancing strengths and the courage to put contrarian ideas on the table, especially during periods of duress. Think of Ben Golub at BlackRock.

German Chancellor Angela Merkel, widely viewed as a level-headed political leader, led Germany and the European Union out of trouble during the recent global crisis. During the political elections in 2013, her campaign's central image, posted on billboards all across the country, was that of "safe hands." Earlier in her career, however, Merkel faced a personal and political choice that was anything but safe when she made a decision to denounce her political patron and boss. Merkel's intellect was never in doubt; among other achievements, she holds a doctorate in physics. But in 1999, a crisis demanded that she demonstrate emotional brilliance. Chancellor Helmut Kohl, Merkel's longtime mentor, was caught in a scandal over a political slush fund. The crisis tested Merkel's conscience, loyalty, and leadership. While other leaders in Kohl's party did not know how to respond, Merkel, his protégée, wrote a front-page article demanding his resignation in Germany's leading conservative paper.[27]

Hers was a brave and emotionally intelligent move, not to mention a breathtaking coup, marking her emergence from her carefully cultivated cloak of blandness. She drew on deep resources of emotional strength to chart her own course in the long game. "You could certainly say that I've never under-estimated myself," she later told an interviewer. "There's nothing wrong with being ambitious."[28] Although ambition is certainly part of her story, the capacity to separate herself from the crowd, step up, and challenge distinguished her from all the surrounding political cronies who kept their heads down when a tough call was needed. Merkel's emotional fortitude mattered as much as her intellectual savvy in making a gutsy decision.

There has been much focus on the German chancellor, especially following her huge political victory in September 2013. *Forbes* ranks her the most powerful woman in the world, and among the top five world leaders. She was at the center of the twenty-seven-member European Union as it determined the fate of the Eurozone and the euro itself. Although hardly flamboyant or charismatic, she is grounded, authentic, and tough. After Fukushima, she made a bold decision to move away from nuclear energy. Germany is a world leader in renewable energy, especially solar, which has been risky and controversial. Her stance on the euro crisis—that EU members need austerity plans, big budget cuts, and wide economic reform—is deeply unpopular in countries confronting harsh economic realities. But hers was a winning political position in Germany, where most people deeply resent the bailouts of undisciplined and free-spending countries with hard-earned German savings.[29]

Because of her long-game leadership and courage, Merkel has taken a lot of public abuse, some of it portraying her as the next Hitler. One especially ugly poster showed her foot on the neck of Greece. Despite the harsh reaction, she has not backed down. On the other hand, she tends to move cautiously once she has made a decision. According to *The Economist*, "She tries to break down problems into discrete units, observing and testing each solution separately before moving on to the next, as a good scientist would do."[30] Some leaders such as Branson, Musk, or Pope Francis have magnetic personalities. Others, like Merkel or Chile's Golborne, are less colorful but no less purposeful in making decisions. What they all have in common is emotional fortitude, conviction, guts, and an eye on the future.

It Takes Courage to Balance the Long and Short Term

Emotional fortitude is hardest to maintain when balancing short- and long-term pressures. Merkel, for example, is working hard to maintain the current strength of the German economy. If the weaker European counties do not turn around, Germany's long-term growth will ultimately be undermined. Reed Hastings was caught between the perceived need to move fast and the lack of proper due diligence to consider long-term consequences. Marisol Hernandes, with her instrumentalist mindset, got so stuck in the short term that she could not see larger industry changes. Balancing the short and the long was just as important for Dr. Z in the nonprofit world; her choices entailed both personal and institutional trade-offs.

In 1993, J. J. Irani, CEO of the Indian manufacturer Tata Steel, faced a unique leadership challenge. The Indian economy—along with Eastern Europe and Asia—was in the midst of a massive shift from a socialist to a capitalist model.

Since 1907, Tata had been immune to market forces. The government implicitly made many major decisions. Constraining its own production potential and meeting government quotas were in Tata's interest. Tata had no incentive to modernize. Then it all changed. Now a company that had never imagined the possibility of laying off a single worker would be forced by free markets to eliminate huge swaths of its labor force.[31]

Tata's protective and generous treatment of employees was a cut above other Indian companies. Over generations, Tata's founders and family leaders were among India's leading philanthropists, spearheading trusts and charities that benefited millions of Indian citizens. Helping people was Tata's legacy and its brand. To maintain the viability and competiveness of the steel business, Irani had to reduce labor without compromising Tata's values. That meant balancing the short-term need to cut head count with a longer-term plan for business sustainability, all the while maintaining a commitment to the vulnerable, loyal Tata employees.

Like Golborne, Psaltis, and other leaders we've profiled, Irani considered many options and engaged critical stakeholders—such as

Tata's union—to plumb their perspective. Irani understood that he needed to communicate to union representatives the dire nature of the situation and the need for radical steps.

The product of these conversations and Irani's reflections was the Tata Steel Early Separation Scheme (ESS). The plan was innovative as well as counterintuitive. Its main elements included a union-supported effort to identify and retain Tata's best employees and a one-time exceptionally generous offer to those who would be departing. Employees forty years of age or younger would receive full pay until age sixty-one. Older employees would receive pay that was between 20 and 50 percent above their current level. Benefits, healthcare, and housing offers were equally lavish. This generosity seemed absurd in the short term. Indeed, one Indian business leader suggested that Irani either had "too much money or not enough brains."[32]

But the plan worked. Over the next decade, Tata Steel reduced its workforce from 78,000 to 47,000.[33] Although departing workers did get full pay, pay levels were frozen, and Tata paid no payroll tax nor made retirement plan contributions. Extensive counseling helped people find other jobs and get them off the ESS program. Payroll costs actually declined from day one, and dramatically so before long. This approach to balancing short- and long-term perspectives actually led to twenty years of strong growth as Tata Steel transformed itself into a globally competitive industry player.

When faced with pressure to downsize, eliminate payroll, and slash costs, Irani made a gutsy, innovative decision: he looked past the immediate need to make drastic cuts that would harm people and brand. He figured out a way to sufficiently manage the short-term pressure while preserving core values that would sustain long-term growth. ESS's long-term play was so successful that Tata's leadership reinstituted it after the 2008 financial crisis.

Actions to Show Courage

Irani faced tough decisions when India moved to a more market-oriented economy and again during the downturn of 2008. He had the guts to balance long- and short-term interests rather than go for the quick cut. What are the practical ways to think through similar situations you face?

1. *Determine whether you own the decision in the given situation, and if you do, step up. If you don't, make sure someone does and see how you can help.* Golborne knew he had the decision power at the mines and so he stepped up and took control.

2. *In challenging times, have the courage to make tough decisions rather than following the tried-and-true course.* Merkel epitomized this type of guts in several moments of truth. Although she has taken heat, she has demonstrated the emotional fortitude to hold true to her convictions.

3. *Ask a colleague where you might be underestimating the decision consequences, missing risks, or overestimating the likely outcomes.* Batista and Reichmann needed this type of feedback to temper their overconfidence, and Hernandes benefited from it in her decision process.

4. *Form an interdisciplinary team whose members think creatively to consider breakthrough innovations in your business model, product mix, or customer experience.* Identify gaps in meeting new customer expectations, and inspire the team to be gutsy in finding innovative solutions to fill those gaps. Thinking outside the box has been a trademark of Zappos, which created a team-based, empowered culture to break from the pack and redefine the customer experience.

5. *Tailor your decision criteria to both long-term and short-term goals, in the proper balance.* Achieving balance takes guts

because it usually goes against company culture and will likely meet resistance. Irani struck the right balance when faced with pressure for an extremely short-term decision with lasting effects at Tata.

THE DISCIPLINE TO DECIDE: PULLING IT TOGETHER

Uncomfortable with ambiguity, Jane Wang frequently reacted to complex issues by imposing an artificial closure on open-ended situations. She described herself as "decisive" and couldn't tolerate "muddling around." In reality, the rush to decide proved as harmful as muddling. It wasn't true decisiveness but a form of avoiding uncomfortable feelings about ambiguity, ignorance, or chaos. The stories about the Chilean miners, the yacht race, and Dr. Z stuck with her. She made a mental note: get better at options thinking and taking the long view. Given her preference for structured approaches, she could start to insist on multiple alternatives in meetings with her team and avoid the rigidity of go/no-go decisions. She liked the idea that creating flexibility through staged decision-making had its own rewards, and she could design a clear process to conduct more options analysis and thus play the long game better.

Jane came to appreciate the difference between reacting and deliberating. She knew she had the *guts* to make tough calls on downsizing and cost cutting, both of which were important for the execution of her decisions. Now she needed the same courage to make bigger bets on surpassing the competition and *shaping the future* of her business. Importantly, Jane's view of risk and uncertainty was shifting from largely negative to more positive about the opportunities she could realize.

5 THIS MATRIX IS KILLING ME

The Discipline to Align:
Rally Key Players and Bridge Differences

WHAT COMES TO MIND WHEN SOMEONE MENTIONS "Whole Foods Market"? Bulk grains, beautiful fruit and veggies, and wild-caught salmon, perhaps? Or associates of diverse age, gender, and ethnicity? Perhaps it's the shopper reading labels or all those new mothers with babies lined up in Bugaboo Donkeys?

Wall Street sees the most profitable food retailer per square meter by a wide margin with revenues of $13 billion and a market capitalization of $19.44 billion.[1] Listed on NASDAQ, its share price has increased over *3,000* percent since the initial public offering in 1992. *Fast Company* dubbed it "the luxury brand of millennials." In 2013, the World Retail Congress named it "Retailer of the Year," *Fortune* magazine consistently ranks it among the "100 Best Companies to Work For," and the James Beard Foundation awarded its online magazine *Dark Rye* a James Beard award for best group food blog.

These accolades and the strong financial metrics of Whole Foods attest to the impressive journey of a company that markets itself as "the world's leading retailer of natural and organic foods

and America's first national 'Certified Organic' grocer."[2] Co-founded
in 1978 by John Mackey, Whole Foods has grown from a single store
in Austin, Texas, to 367 in North America and the United Kingdom,
employing some 78,400 people.[3] Although competition has stiffened
in recent years, the company is still remarkable for its consistent results and innovative approach to stakeholder alignment.

The premise is that there is an increasing demand for mouthwa-
tering, eye-popping, and organic food. And given Whole Foods'
growth trajectory, the evidence is clear: although it is working on
being more price competitive relative to mainstream food stores,
Whole Foods has shown that enough people will pay a premium for
products that taste good, are good for you, and sustain the environment. Walter Robb, John Mackey's co-CEO, sees two growth drivers
behind the Whole Foods story. One is a growing recognition, backed
by much scientific evidence and wide media coverage, of the intri-
cate connections between health and diet. The second is the in-
store experience, especially the exceptional personalized attention
Whole Foods provides its customers.[4]

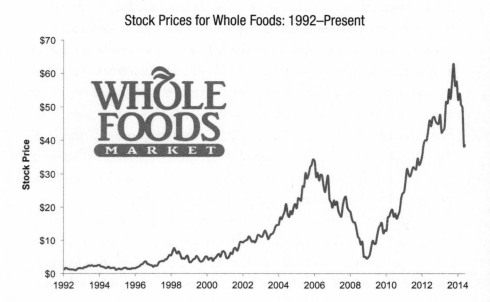

Stock Prices for Whole Foods: 1992–Present

Overall, Whole Foods has achieved remarkable internal organizational alignment. But critics have noted that its strategy is misaligned with its mission: "to promote the vitality and well-being of all individuals." Despite increased competitiveness with mainstream growers, its prices still say something else to low-income consumers. To the slogan "Whole Foods, Whole People, and Whole Planet," these critics add "Whole Paycheck."[5] "The perception that Whole Foods is too expensive and caters to a largely affluent demographic continues to be a challenge for the company," says Andrew Wolf, an analyst with BB&T Capital Markets.[6]

The misalignment between Mackey's founding vision and its current business model is not lost on Whole Foods' leadership. That's one reason why the board of directors appointed veteran retailer Walter Robb as co-CEO in 2010. Nor is it lost on US Secretary of Agriculture Tom Vilsack, who speaks bluntly of a conversation he had with Robb:

Walter, it's great that you have this wonderful grocery store, it's an experience to shop there, and the food's great. It's in suburbs, it's in university communities, . . . it's where people with money live. What are you doing about the folks who do not have as much money, who may not be able to afford to go into a Whole Foods? Do you think you have any responsibility to those people?[7]

Robb replied that he needed to think about the issue. He did, and then decided to do something about it.

Vilsack described Robb's visit to Detroit where he met with community leaders, subsequently sending his real estate team to investigate further. The property managers scoped out the inner city of Detroit. "This isn't going to work," they told Robb. Detroit ranks among the nation's poorest big cities, its residents among the most obese. Robb challenged them: "Change the model, make it work."

What if they designed a smaller store, canvassed the neighborhood to find out what people actually want to eat, and made deals with local farmers? What if they engaged public schools and showed kids how to grow vegetables on school property? What if Whole Foods sold those crops locally, too?

Robb went ahead and opened a store in midtown Detroit. Its lower prices serve its intention "to help heal America."[8] Within minutes of opening, newly employed workers and happy customers erupted into a chant: "Whole Foods! Whole Foods!"[9] Plans are under way for another store in an even more troubled neighborhood in Chicago—Englewood—at the corner of 63rd and Halsted, where violent crime is endemic.[10] The most recent census data peg Englewood's per capita annual income at $12,255.

This response to societal concerns is possible because the leaders of Whole Foods work at alignment on multiple levels. Whole Foods uses three operating principles it deems central to winning the long game—*shared purpose, stakeholder interdependence,* and *team ownership*. Each of these helps synchronize the expectations, interests, differences, and incentives of a wide array of stakeholders. These principles get all pieces of a plan working toward the same goal. Alignment is not a onetime event but an ongoing process, in which strategic leaders operate from shared organizational principles that drive change, as Robb illustrated in Detroit and Chicago.

Shared Purpose

Mackey considered Milton Friedman a hero. He was especially drawn to Friedman's ideas about the social benefits associated with profit-seeking behavior articulated in *Capitalism and Freedom*. As Mackey once told Friedman, "Making high profits is the means to the end of fulfilling Whole Foods' core business mission. We want to improve the health and well-being of everyone on the planet through higher-quality foods and better nutrition, and we can't fulfill this mission unless we are highly profitable."[11] Friedman would not likely have shared Mackey's personal social agenda if it had been pursued through his stewardship of a publicly traded company. But he would have admired Mackey's focus on profit maximization, since that's what Friedman believed public companies should do above all for their shareholders.

A shared purpose is a necessary condition for, but not a guarantee of, alignment. It is similar to a magnet pulling filings from different points in space toward a common location. Not all filings will align; some may be far removed from the magnet, encounter obstacles along the way, or have too much weight relative to the power of the magnet. Unlike filings, which respond to the laws of physics in predictable ways, humans are complex. They have free will, so the pull of a common vision may not be enough. People who are part of a team or community want to have influence, and leaders need their buy-in to sustain major change. That's why maintaining connectivity across stakeholders is critical when the success of an enterprise depends on many parties.

Stakeholder Interdependence

Mackey challenges the idea that different stakeholders (such as investors, employees, and customers) have such different agendas that alignment is always imperfect. Although no two people share identical needs and interests, Mackey argues that common pursuits can strongly bind them. The diversity of stakeholders is a central and necessary element in the Whole Foods business model: if one stakeholder suffers, Whole Foods will suffer in the long term. Conversely, if Whole Foods thrives, all stakeholders will thrive in the long term. As Mackey envisions it, stakeholders cross boundaries and play multiple roles. Employees, whom Whole Foods considers co-owners, are critical and must deeply understand the common vision. Leaders from the top down must help translate the overall mission so employees can bring it to life for customers. Additionally, many employees are shareholders, and most are customers as well—an arrangement that reinforces stakeholder interdependence.

Customers are an especially critical community group and often become team members and even shareholders. Suppliers are likewise crucial for Whole Foods' dynamic system, and they are screened to ensure that they share the same values as Whole Foods. These shared values are then reinforced through long-term contracts. As Errol Schweizer pointed out, "When we find a supplier that we want to work with, we share ideas and devote intellectual energy and time to help them innovate their products and bring them to market so they're not just out there on their own trying to figure out what's going to work."[12] Even competitors are critical in forcing Whole Foods from its occasional complacency, thus indirectly helping Whole Foods stir innovation in its operations. In addition, competitors help the organic and healthy-food markets gain size, which in turns helps bring down supply costs in the industry. Whole Foods recognizes that for it to grow, the entire ecosystem supporting organic food and other health products must grow and thrive as well. It is hard to reinvent and grow an industry all on your own.[13]

Autonomous Teams

Whole Foods' unique organization bolsters team members' sense of ownership and enables them to respond quickly to changing conditions and customer needs. Each store consists of about eight teams, each team acting as its own profit center. Managers run their teams as autonomous units with control over decisions such as pricing, in-store promotions, floor layouts, product selection, and inventory. As a result, teams solve problems more quickly than if decisions are highly centralized. Transparency is key: everyone has access to every team's performance data, salaries, and monthly bonuses awarded for profit per hour. Teams also have decision rights over hiring and firing team members. They give new hires a trial period, after which they vote them in or out. The votes usually align because the team's pay suffers when it keeps an underperformer.[14]

Autonomy and transparency go hand in hand at Whole Foods headquarters in Austin. For the past ten years, a team of five senior leaders has functioned as an office of the CEO, collectively making business decisions and sharing accountability. According to Mackey, this access to group wisdom accelerated Whole Foods' recovery from the recession.[15]

When we step back and look at Whole Foods from the outside in, we see aligned leadership and operations—just one example of an alignment approach whereby leaders have carefully integrated the firm's vision, strategy, structure, reward system, processes, culture, values, and purpose. This approach also reflects Mackey's strategic leadership in conceiving and orchestrating a distinct, nontraditional business based on core principles, each of which has evolved with time, experience, growth, and valuable lessons learned when they fell short of ideals.

Whole Foods epitomizes strategic alignment for the long run due to its ability to get all players pulling in the same direction. It also illustrates how difficult it can be to align a grand vision (healthy food for all) with a workable strategy that generates enough profit to ensure viability. In addition, the links between the business model and its day-to-day operations entail significant alignment challenges. Since leaders must manage all these moving parts, we focus on two key themes crucial to successful alignment. The first is *rallying key players* to a common purpose, vision, and strategy. Whole Foods does this with clear values, autonomous teams, and shared incentives; different solutions for rallying will be needed in other companies based on their context, culture, and business imperatives. The second major theme is *bridging differences* to resolve conflicts among stakeholders within the firm and its ecosystem.

As a way to assess how well you master the discipline of alignment, step back and think about how often you exhibit the following leadership behaviors.

Rally Key Players

1. *Do you rally your team around a compelling strategic vision that can win the long game?* Whole Foods' leaders hire people who have a passion for what they do, which is to lead the natural and organic foods movement "by supplying the highest quality, most wholesome foods available."[16] This takes patience, deep commitment, and staying power.

2. *Do you identify and reach out to those who have a significant stake in changing initiatives or strategies?* Stakeholder interdependence transcends competing agendas by elevating shared goals and common interests, and Whole Foods uses circle maps to visualize key interdependencies among different stakeholders.[17] These maps may change over time.

3. *Do you communicate intentions early, clearly, and continuously to all stakeholders?* Whole Foods leaders have created an open system with unparalleled levels of transparency and interaction. Their communications focus on both the short and long game, as needed.

Bridge Differences

4. *Do you pinpoint and address conflicting interests among stakeholders?* In Mackey's view, "Since everyone is aligned and moving in harmony, friction is minimal."[18] This aspirational belief guides team members' decision-making and action-taking at all levels.

5. *Do you understand the needs of key stakeholders and know how to build bridges across interests?* Whole Foods' autonomous teams are designed to minimize internal conflicts, and their shared purpose and transparency promote open dialogue.

6. *Do you actively seek to understand cultural differences and bridge cultural divides that could undermine collective action?* Building stores in inner-city neighborhoods like those in Detroit creates cultural sensitivities that will help Whole Foods expand into less affluent communities and less democratic societies.

RALLY KEY PLAYERS

Benjamin Franklin clearly articulated what was at stake for the American independence movement when he said at the signing of the Declaration of Independence, "Surely we must all hang together lest we all hang separately." Likewise, modern-day strategic leaders must be equally adept at finding common ground and achieving buy-in among diverse stakeholders who may have divergent agendas.

When launching new strategies, leaders must shepherd others along the desired path. The gap between *strategy* and execution remains devilishly hard to bridge. According to a survey published in *Fortune* magazine, only 30 percent of organizations execute their strategies effectively; 70 percent of strategic initiatives fail to reach their desired goal.[19] The key barriers to execution are the misalignment of vision, people, and resources. Among the organizations surveyed:

+ 95 percent of employees within an organization say they do not fully understand what the *strategy* is.[20]
+ 85 percent of leaders spend less than one hour a month talking about strategy and vision.[21]

In short, the inability to align stakeholders around a clear set of values and objectives diminishes efficiency, productivity, and team spirit.

Rallying Support for Strategic Change: How Kodak Missed the Middle

Lack of top team alignment was identified in one study as the most deadly of strategy killers, closely followed by poor coordination across functions, businesses, or national borders.[22] In another survey, 47 percent of leaders felt they were not appropriately involved in decisions that affected their role in implementation.[23] These findings are not surprising. The world is quite uncertain and organizations are messy, complex, loosely structured, horizontal, and globally dispersed systems. Many managers hate operating in a matrix with diverse stakeholders, competing interests, and opaque decision rights and incentives. However, when you fail to secure the buy-in of key stakeholders, particularly in the middle of the organization, you risk catastrophic outcomes.

Consider the Eastman Kodak Company, which accounted for 90 percent of film and 85 percent of camera sales in America in 1976. Until the 1990s, it regularly ranked among the world's five most valuable brands.[24] It is a tragic but common story that leaders were unable to keep with the long game when their business experienced a profound transformation. A common myth about Kodak's demise is that its engineers and management missed the digital revolution. In actuality, they invented the first digital camera and created the photo CD. Kodak spent billions for its R&D on digital and even formed a joint venture with Apple to marry digital photography with computing power. Recognizing the need for organizational change, Kodak's board hired George Fisher from Motorola in 1993. Fisher was a highly respected leader who would take Kodak through a digital transformation. As the new CEO, Fisher brought in a new top team, and Kodak rose to number two in digital camera sales in 2001. But the bump was fleeting.[25]

According to Fisher, the senior managers knew what they needed to do to transform to digital and stay in the game for the long run, as did the staff in Kodak's research labs.[26] But the real problem had to do with the multiple layers of middle management residing between researcher and senior leaders. Fisher struggled to get sufficient buy-in at the middle and prepare them for the long game. Kodak's middle managers were well-intentioned people, highly trained and skilled, but most felt deeply threatened by the long-term changes Fisher called for.[27] "Fear drove paralysis that manifested itself as time went on into just rigidity with respect to our strategy," Fisher reflected. "I did not see that at the start because Kodak is a very polite culture and people don't confront you generally."[28]

Passive resistance is another big killer of strategy alignment—in part, because it is so hard to see until it's too late. Frank Zaffino, former vice president and general manager of global equipment manufacturing at Kodak, said that "executives [there] abhorred anything that looked risky or too innovative, because a mistake in such a massive manufacturing process would cost thousands of dollars. So the company built itself up around procedures and policies intended to maintain the status quo."[29] This included organizational structure—strong, independent fiefdoms—that did not allow for strategic moves to be executed. Several CEOs came and went, but middle managers fighting the digital wave became increasingly calcified.

In general, few stakeholders truly embrace change, and many may not be in it for the long game. They might go along in public, only to hunker down in private and do more of the same. Their hidden stratagem is merely to outlast yet another CEO with cockamamy ideas. Major transformation initiatives unleash stress, instability, and uncertainty.[30] And fear of the unknown tends to intensify control over the known. By his own admission, Fisher underestimated these human and organizational tendencies: "[Kodak] regarded digital photography as the enemy, an evil juggernaut that would kill the chemical-based film and paper business that fueled Kodak's sales and profits for decades."[31] Another former

Kodak executive said, "I couldn't get anywhere without running into the consumer product or professional division selling film or paper—and every time I wanted to make a move, they would argue that I was destroying margin and destroying value."[32] Kodak needed more active engagement and challenge of the many managers who were still clinging to the past.

The *margin trap*, whereby managers treat their high margins as entitlements and their customers as chattel, has prevented many a company from changing course in time. The takeaway is clear: never underestimate the fears and countermeasures of stakeholders as you shape your strategic agenda. Engage them, rally them around your vision, and align their common interests with your change effort. Do not thrust it upon them; work diligently to maintain alignment, especially when people stumble and parts of the plan fail. Leaders must continuously advocate for their strategy, particularly when it requires many stakeholders to change.

Identify and Reach Out to Those with a Stake in Your Direction

Decision-making today is more diffuse and decision rights are more ambiguous, but you still have to rally the team. In a 2013 study, Jared Bleak and Tony O'Driscoll interviewed thirty-eight CEOs of global companies whose businesses were involved in ten industries around the world. They were examining how environmental shifts affected CEOs globally. A consistent theme was that, in less predictable business environments, most problems are no longer simple but become multidimensional. Effective problem solving requires connecting with more constituencies who have an array of different relationships that may be formal or informal, direct or indirect. Leaders must understand how to manage these different relationships both inside the company and outside their immediate orbit by aligning stakeholders across nontraditional boundaries.

One CEO in the study said, "There is an interconnectedness now in problems—and this changes the issues. You need to have more people involved with the decision making, leaving the leader less in control of the situation." A CEO from India elaborated: "Your direct influence on those variables [stakeholders] is much less. Increasingly, business is being done, not in terms of hierarchical structure, but more in terms of circles."[33] The ability to navigate this maze and come out the other side with strong alignment is a key component of the disciplines that strategic leaders have to master. It requires both patience and skill, as we will see shortly.[34]

How a New CEO Engaged Stakeholders to Own the Change Agenda

"KBWQ," a European engineering company with a long history of technological excellence and project execution, needed a leadership change badly. Its clients consisted of large international oil companies, and the company worked around the globe on complex projects to improve refining capacity.

At the beginning of this decade, KBWQ was not as well positioned as its competitors for growth in a vibrant energy market. A major reason was its narrow focus on historic services as well as its failure to adapt fast enough to new growth areas like shale gas. Additionally, the market had changed quickly, with larger global projects requiring the firm to work in a more integrated manner. A strategic transformation was necessary to play the long game well.

Even more challenging were the "sacred cows" deeply engrained in the leaders at both the headquarters and the operating companies. The most entrenched of these were the autonomous silos, fiefdoms with P&L responsibilities whose operating CEOs stockpiled resources for their own projects. They rarely collaborated well with their peers elsewhere. Mind you, this decentralized structure had worked extremely well in the past, when projects were more local and clients expected less global consistency. But in a globalized economy, with digital tools for overseeing projects anywhere in the world, the silos had become bottlenecks that were strangling value creation.

The board brought in Hans Wolker—known to both friends and colleagues as "HW"—to implement a new strategy and transform the organization model as well as its culture. New to this industry, HW had a lot to learn about the company. He knew he needed to shake up the organization without losing top talent or alarming critical stakeholders. But as he grew familiar with the business, he realized it needed more than a shake-up. A tectonic shift was in order and the silo structure had to go. Customers complained that working with different offices was like working with totally different companies, with no coordination between them. That wouldn't do: their clients, many of which were international giants, expected seamless, uniform, and transparent processes that didn't exist. Simply put, the company was structured for incremental growth at best, and it was falling behind.

HW explained the root of the problem to his top managers. These fiefdoms had become like the individual islands of the Maldives chain in the Indian Ocean, each one diminishing in size as the more integrated, open, and truly international competitors swallowed up pieces of their business. He argued that now was the time to change; otherwise, the competition would "eat their lunch." Growth required operating with more global consistency, increased firm-wide access to low-cost engineering resources, and new business lines such as shale gas and expansion in emerging markets. While straightforward, the plan required breaking down the silos, organizing around the customer, presenting a single face to customers, and deploying resources seamlessly around the globe. In short, HW would be killing many "sacred cows." But if the leaders were on board, and the change initiative succeeded, prosperity and recognition would be their reward.

In principle, the management team agreed on the need for these changes, but the company had failed previously at execution because not all key players were committed to following through. HW could not afford false starts and diversions on his first big initiative. He had the insights needed to reorganize the model, but he had to get even the most resistant players on board. Strong personalities in top positions were set in their ways, and HW needed their expertise and support. Somehow, he had to leverage the strengths of these fiefdoms and bridge the differences—but how?

First, HW formed a core team with "make-or-break-it" executives, those who were key influencers. He convened this team frequently to shape the change strategy and organization model. Second, with the core team, he identified a larger circle of about forty change champions who could fight legacy mentalities, provide diverse views, and garner legitimacy. This group represented the leaders of the operating companies as well as key function heads who needed to work across the businesses.

With the help of advisers, and a lot of input from firm leaders, the core team members articulated the structural barriers to growth. First, they questioned core assumptions about the existing mental model:

+ "What if we shared sales strategies and targets globally and focused on the best team for project execution regardless of location?"
+ "Can we get the best of both worlds by organizing with more alignment around growth markets, yet access expertise from all corners of the company?"
+ "Can we all use and co-own one low-cost engineering center?"

They agreed on criteria for success and shared aspirations for the future. They also created a range of organizational options to expand their thinking about how best to reorganize. In addition, they ana-lyzed the structures of competitors that outpaced them in organiz-ing for growth in emerging markets. This analysis served to *open the window* and bring in fresh perspectives.

HW organized a series of group workshops to bring stakeholders together for open discussion and debate with a constructive tone. He paid homage to the old model and explained why it had worked so well for so long. He also explained why the changes in the exter-nal environment called for a new strategy, necessitating a new struc-ture and a fresh mindset. In the workshops, people moved beyond their roles and self-interest and began to address a shared interest in enterprise growth. They began to look seriously at possible scenarios for the future.

Prior to each offsite, core team members met to identify issues they still needed to resolve. This forcing function enabled the top team to present a united view to the larger group. Debate and com-promise aligned those who disagreed. People felt heard, their ideas truly considered, and nobody paid lip service. HW did not ram his own ideas through. Instead, he held fast to a few critical principles, and the core team mapped out the details. They designed a new model combining existing operating units and changing leadership roles. In addition, they instituted global sales and project execution functions, key account strategies, and shared services. These moves would have been inconceivable in the past. The new approach earned the buy-in of key executives. As active contributors to the transformational plan, they took ownership of the implementation with the long view in mind.

To sustain this stakeholder alignment during execution, the core team expanded the stakeholder group and formed implementation teams. One team orchestrated a communications campaign to en-gage the rest of the organization. Although changes on this scale take time, the team's systematic work on broad and deep alignment expedited the transformation. Overall results suggest that the effort has paid off handsomely. A six-month post-reorganization survey showed that people could see real improvement in collaboration on sales and resourcing decisions plus more client focus. Business boomed as the company won more projects with key customers. A good part of this success can be attributed to the new structure and leadership changes, though external factors such as increased demand for projects and the shale-gas revolution also played a role.

Communicate Your Intent Early, Often, and Simply

Senior executives at KBWQ didn't just reach out to stakeholders; they maintained regular communication with them. Also, the CEO updated the board frequently, solicited input from key customers and joint venture partners, and encouraged team leaders to communicate using the guidelines provided by the steering team. The frequency of the message is as important as its clarity. What appears to be resistance at first is often fear and lack of understanding about the new direction. Therefore, you must not only be as clear as possible but also repeat your message as often as possible.[35] What may seem obvious to leaders can be incomprehensible to everyone else. The lack of clarity not only breeds doubt; it prevents cooperative people from participating. Transparency is a competitive advantage, as we saw with Whole Foods. Without abundantly clear explanations of where you are going and why, team members often revert to the familiar behaviors because these need no further explanation.

Communication is a great lubricant of change. Nobody knows that better than Olivia Lum; she grew up in Malaysia in a hut without running water or indoor sanitation and relied on her communication skills to change her life course. In 1989, Lum founded what would become Hyflux Ltd., a leading water-solutions company in Singapore with operations across Asia, the Middle East, and North Africa. "From a young age, I learned to value water," she says.[36] As

Hyflux's group president and chief executive officer, Lum spends a lot of time with her top team. "Fundamental to our mission is to deliver water that is clean, safe, affordable, and accessible to all," she says. "We . . . put in a lot of effort communicating with mid-level management and developing a system of mentoring the younger staff. With time, the communication avenues, common processes, and management systems . . . will be integral in transmit-ting our vision, mission, and shared beliefs and values to our entire staff across the different markets."[37]

Olivia promotes an entrepreneurial culture by engaging others: "We have the boldness to dream. We have a can-do spirit. Obstacles can be overcome; it's how we approach the challenges and solve the problems." Communicating across borders with cultural sensitivity and respect is one of her strengths. She has steadily grown Hyflux from a distributor of water treatment systems into an innovator in ultrafiltration membranes that facilitate large-scale wastewater recy-cling. In its 2011 *Entrepreneur of the Year* ranking, Ernst & Young ranked her among the most powerful leaders in Asia.

Action Plan to Rally Key Players

Although it seems self-evident that a leader should align key stake-holders in any change or strategy initiative, it is also clear that this is the exception rather than the norm. Simply put, pay significant and consistent attention to the continuous need to let people know where you are and where you are going:

1. *Set a clear and compelling strategic vision and follow through with a guide to action.* Learn from Whole Foods, Olivia Lum, and HW about articulating and communicating purpose or principles that guide decisions for the long game.
2. *Map the stakeholders most interested in and affected by the big decision.* Make clear, detailed notes on their level of interest

and influence, highlighting any interdependencies now or in the future.

3. *Identify whom to involve directly and who can influence others in implementing your decision.* After assessing the top influencers within the engineering firm KBWQ and canvassing opinion leaders, the new CEO created a core and extended team of key stakeholders.

4. *Carefully consider when to engage stakeholders in the process— from the outset, at key milestones, or around key decisions.* In general, sooner is better and setting up dialogues long before you choose is better than after.

5. *Check in on your stakeholders periodically even after you think you've achieved alignment.* Apply the wisdom of Colin Powell: stay close to your players in good and tough moments, and make sure you understand and address their issues. Consider conducting periodic pulse surveys to gauge team alignment.

BRIDGE DIFFERENCES

Thomas C. Schelling, the 2005 Nobel Laureate in Economics for his work on game theory in nuclear deterrence, arms control, and cooperation, highlighted the importance of focal points when people need to solve problems jointly.[38] Without common points of reference, he argued, people default to solutions that seem right to them personally but that do not necessarily yield the greatest value for the group. In organizations, these focal points can be the current plan or model, past success, or perhaps the status quo. Poor strategic alignment resulting from diverse focal points of key stakeholders produces low productivity, efficiency, innovation, energy, collaboration, external focus, and customer centricity.

On the other hand, when leaders align stakeholders around shared focal points, such as improved customer service, product innovation, or social change, the result is likely to be higher commitment and better implementation of the desired direction. With stakeholders who are external (i.e., outside your direct control) and many-sided (e.g., large global corporate clients with multiple strategic business units in many countries), a strategic leader's ability to align focal points, bridge differences, and resolve conflicting agendas is a competitive advantage. Nowhere is this truer than in public policy conflicts like healthcare reform or climate change.

Turning Opponents into Allies:
How the EDF Addresses Conflicting Interests

"We define success as partnerships that result in measurable environmental and business results and real industry-wide transformation," says Fred Krupp, president of the Environmental Defense Fund (EDF). "Our partnership with FedEx is one of those. Together we developed a next-generation hybrid truck that would have 90 percent fewer emissions and travel 50 percent farther on a gallon of fuel."[39] Another great success story comes from the EDF partnership with private equity firm KKR, "where we worked together to find over $900 million in cost savings and additional profit all by cutting back energy usage and waste production across their portfolio of companies."[40]

Krupp understands that to have a healthy environment, thriving ecosystems, and a thriving economy, his organization must engage energy producers, consumers, and polluters alike. In an interview, he articulated his views about alignment. "If you want to affect the global environment, it's tough to do that without understanding the multinational businesses that operate around the globe and without being able to talk to them. Being able to transcend [our own position] and see the world from their eyes, while maintaining a commitment to transformational environmental goals, has allowed us to define where there is common ground for real breakthroughs."[41]

How the Environmental Defense Fund Works

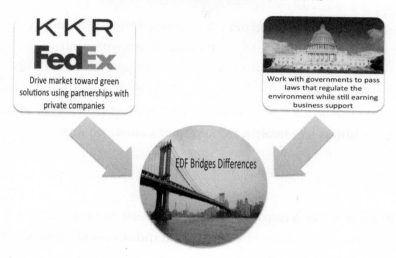

KKR
FedEx

Drive market toward green solutions using partnerships with private companies

Work with governments to pass laws that regulate the environment while still earning business support

EDF Bridges Differences

Krupp, unlike the leaders of most environmental organizations, sees business leaders as potential allies, not opponents. His central *modus operandi* is not one of protesting business polluters or harassing corporate leaders but more about reaching out to harness market forces for environmental ends. He did this very effectively in a campaign to reduce acid rain in the 1990s, cited by *The Economist* as "the greatest green success story of the past decade."[42] It set up a declining limit, or cap, on sulfur pollution, and a market in emission allowances to meet that cap, which created a powerful economic incentive to innovate to reduce pollution.

In his bridge building, Krupp's intent is to use carrots as well as sticks to help shape a greener future for all. With FedEx, for example,

[the EDF] set up a competition that encouraged vehicle producers to deliver the winning prototype. When we started, there were no hybrid trucks available on the commercial market. Within two years of our partnership [with FedEx], there wasn't a truck trade show in North America that didn't show hybrids. And at the 2013 leading truck industry trade show, there were 35 different hybrid truck options available and more than 100 different companies that were using them in their fleets. That's an example of industry-wide transformation.[43]

By relentlessly focusing his team on an important insight—that they can use economic incentives to align business interests with environmental progress—Krupp has made the EDF one of the most important power brokers in the environmental arena. His organization's budget has jumped from $3 million in the late 1980s to more than $125 million today, his staff has grown from 50 to 450, and EDF membership has expanded from 40,000 to more than 750,000. That's a lot of feet on the ground, working on behalf of the planet. Krupp is clearly in it for the long game and knows how to play it well by building unusual bridges.

Aspiring strategic leaders can learn from Krupp's transformation as he evolved from environmental crusader to mover and shaker with significant influence in political and business circles. Along his journey, he realized that taxation, command-and-control regulation, and litigation—though valid tools in general—could also lead to protracted battles. If he could enlist businesspeople, even those opposed to the environmental agenda, then he could unleash entrepreneurship and market forces as part of the solution. The challenge was to engage forward-looking leaders as powerful drivers of change.[44]

His approach has its critics, some of whom feel Krupp has betrayed the environmental movement by cooperating with the enemy. This criticism only sharpens his commitment to align capitalists and environmentalists in their respective pursuits of green. One of the most contentious issues today, illustrative of how Krupp and the EDF work, is the battle over hydraulic fracturing (i.e., "fracking"), an issue that has divided many communities.

Shale gas has the promise of both environmental benefits and massive economic revitalization, but it also poses potentially serious health and environmental risks. The EDF has worked with Southwestern Energy on model regulations to protect groundwater. EDF scientists have studied the problem with academics and concluded that if the leakage of methane can be contained below 1 percent, then gas can ease the transition to low-carbon energy. Despite the protests of many, natural gas is here to stay. The EDF accepts this reality and works with politicians and drillers to find common ground and safer practices for the future.[45]

Joe Nocera, reporting for the *New York Times*, commented on the EDF's bridge-building strategy in Colorado: "Here in the real world," he wrote, "new wells are being drilled every day, natural gas is becoming more abundant and the country is coming to depend on it. There is simply no way America is going to turn its back on natural gas. Which is why the EDF's approach makes so much sense: rather than calling for an end to fracking, EDF is working with states like Colorado to make it safer, more transparent and cleaner."[46]

Krupp is most proud that his team's efforts contributed to rules adopted by the administration of Governor John Hickenlooper of Colorado: "This is a first-ever rule at the state or federal level that would require companies to reduce their emissions of methane from natural gas operations, and it was supported by Noble, Encana and Anadarko [Colorado's three biggest oil-and-gas companies] because they understood what's in it for them and their producers—the social license to operate."[47] These efforts paid off in February 2014, when the Colorado Air Quality Control Commission adopted rules making Colorado the first US state to directly regulate methane pollution from oil and gas development. As reported by the *Denver Post*, "A unique piece of the process of creating the rules was a collaboration between the Environmental Defense Fund and Anadarko, Noble Energy and Encana."[48] And according to a *Washington Post* editorial, the EDF's "practical approach has done more to clean up fracking than the unsparing opposition of its more radical cousins."[49]

When we asked Krupp for his most enduring lessons for bridge builders, he cited several. First, hire the best people, not just in terms of academic and technical smarts but also in terms of open-mindedness and creativity. Second, leverage the power of your network and cultivate those connections as needed.

> I've begun to think of the world as a kind of electronic circuit board, and there is much strength in having the ability to connect those circuits. When one of my board members knows the board member at an energy company, there's the ability to pick up the phone, express a point of view, and have it listened to. There's a level of trust there that allows that circuit board to operate so that companies can really listen, understand and identify areas that serve their interest as well as a greater good.[50]

This lesson is relevant to any leader spearheading change—and one that can help us understand crucial misalignments, even in a highly public embarrassment.

The ObamaCare Website Fiasco: Failure to Surface and Bridge Differences

Few issues in recent political history have been as contentious as those surrounding the 2010 Affordable Care Act (ACA), also known as ObamaCare. The Obama team strongly believed in its social and economic value and worked to anticipate and bridge the ideological differences between Republicans and Democrats. In fact, the principles of the ACA are the brainchild of the Heritage Foundation, a conservative think tank in Washington, DC, and its architect designed the model implemented by then–Massachusetts governor Mitt Romney, a Republican. Despite efforts to bridge policy differences, the job required a high-touch, hands-on approach on both sides of the aisle, and that's not Obama's strength.

It also required large-scale outreach to diverse stakeholders with competing interests across the complex US healthcare system. Too many compromises could complicate the program or even undermine its integrity. The politics leading up to passage of the Act were divided and partisan. No Republican voted for it. Not even one single vote. Contrast that with the vote on the Civil Rights Act of 1964: it passed with "ayes" from 152 Democrats and 138 Republicans in the House, and 46 Democrats and 27 Republicans in the Senate.[51] Obama's signature legislation has been embattled from the very beginning, reaching a crescendo when the enrollment website got seriously off track. Let's see what we can learn from the widely reported alignment fiasco.

From the evidence available, the initial launch of healthcare.gov reflected a failure to align major stakeholders on this ambitious project. Key agencies—the Centers for Medicare and Medicaid Services (CMS), the IT firm hired to lead the effort, and various Consultants to Government and Industry (CGI)—didn't trust each other. According to Harvard Business School professor Amy C. Edmondson, "The two major players didn't share priorities: CMS prioritized the October 1st deadline above operability."[52]

In addition, there were early signs of trouble with the portal, including budget and time constraints due to lack of funding from Congress and lack of cooperation by many Republican state governors. There was also a serious organizational design problem from the start. For example, the CMS "assumed the role of project quarterback, responsible for making sure each separately designed database and piece of software worked with the others, instead of assigning that task to a lead contractor." An internal government progress report in September 2011 identified the inability of employees steering the project "to manage the multiple activities and contractors happening concurrently" as a "major risk" to this very complex project. Those working on the web project expressed concerns, such as not stress-testing the system before launch, but people at senior levels, it seems, didn't get the memo.

People inside and outside the federal bureaucracies were raising numerous red flags. "We foresee a train wreck," said an insurance executive working on IT in February 2013. "The level of angst in health plans is growing by leaps and bounds. The political people in the administration do not understand how far behind they are." Medicare officials "began to suspect that staff members at CGI were intentionally trying to hide flaws in the system to cover up for their inability to meet production deadlines." Only months before the launch, both Marilyn B. Tavenner, the administrator of the CMS, and Kathleen Sebelius, the secretary of health and human services, insisted that "the project was not in trouble."[53]

The ObamaCare rollout strategy entailed extraordinarily high stakes, lots of pressure, and public scrutiny. Under these circumstances, only the most stalwart would publicly voice their concerns. But this case highlights the absence of internal alignment among the different groups coordinating this very complex project. With no strong, independent central team or leader, the parties resorted to finger pointing rather than working to solve problems jointly.

Strategic leaders nip such dysfunctional dynamics early and directly. For example, a leader might say, "I hate getting bad news unless I am the first to know it." In complex change initiatives with many moving parts, repeating such messages is very crucial. Healthcare.gov lacked clear strategic leadership from the start.

What happened with the website launch is not unusual per se. In many complex, multifaceted large projects, such as the design, installation, and rollout of a new enterprise resource planning system in a large company, people make mistakes—and everybody can learn from them. So why did the ObamaCare implementation team fail to study and apply the hard-won lessons from other large systems-integration projects? Why did they underestimate the importance of alignment? Why did they not involve the right technical experts?

For most leaders, the integration challenges will not be as grand, political, or public. But they can still lose their job by failing to align their stakeholders. Since the launch, Kathleen Sebelius and several project leaders have resigned. They did get their act together, align the team, fix the problems, and achieve their original enrollment targets—an outcome that underscores the power of good leadership and strong strategic alignment when these are in place. But the lack of teamwork in the beginning undermined the healthcare reform that the Obama administration considers one of its seminal achievements.

Help, This Matrix Is Killing Me!

Dr. Vanda Mirash, the head of R&D at a life sciences company, shared this e-mail from a senior manager: "The organization has become stifling. I have to talk with six different people from different departments with different bosses, who have different priorities, to get everyone on the same page to move forward. It's impossible to get things done to support the strategy. This matrix is killing me."

Juan, the president of the South American division of a chemical company, learned his lesson about matrix management and cross-divisional cooperation the hard way. He worked tirelessly to expand market opportunities but couldn't get support from colleagues located in different regions of this global business. The old-world curmudgeons at European headquarters didn't share his urgency or enthusiasm for opportunities, particularly in Brazil, and so he plowed forward alone, alienating them further. "I'll grow despite them," he thought. At the same time, Juan was in a succession leadership program for executives with C-suite potential. He received feedback indicating that his colleagues didn't fully understand his strategy, didn't know what he was up to, and thus hesitated to invest at the requested levels. This hit Juan hard. His boss agreed and criticized Juan for operating remotely, not reaching out, and not making time for open communication.

"Where do you currently stand with the people you need to influence?" Juan's boss asked. "Do you understand the position of each key player relative to your growth plans? Do they understand what support you need and why?" These questions, which served as a type of "stakeholder mapping," helped Juan work through his issues systematically and highlighted his need for a deeper dialogue with his colleagues.

This assessment requires analyzing whether key relationships are feeble, failing, or frozen, each representing a different barrier to open dialogue. When key relationships are *feeble*, there are minimal levels of information exchange, openness, or just plain listening to other people. When they are *failing*, there is diminishing trust and respect, limited bonding, and a fixation on insurmountable differences. And stalemate is the main characteristic of *frozen* relationships, in which no bridging of fixed positions seems possible.[54]

Drawing on the work of the late Wharton professor Howard Perlmutter, we tailored a plan for Juan to enlist these critical collaborators and build a mindset and skill set for strategic alignment. Juan realized his relationships were failing and on the verge of freezing. With guidance, he initiated regular face-to-face meetings with stakeholders to understand their priorities and constraints and to detail his growth plans. He solicited feedback and shared his rationale. These straightforward actions began to thaw his relationships. Gradually, his colleagues became more open-minded and saw the opportunities in Brazil. As they got past the freeze, they understood how Juan's strategy would benefit their own growth objectives. He helped them overcome their fear about the risks and unstable demand as he explained what was changing in the chemical sector of Brazil's economy.

Thanks to increased collaboration, Juan came to view these colleagues as indispensable strategic partners, not obstacles to his growth plans. In particular, he realized he needed to develop skills to *bridge differences* constructively and spend more time bonding to build closer, more intimate connections. Since he was seeking to align with colleagues from a different part of the world, Juan had to bridge time, language, culture, and geography so that communication could flow more freely. He also had to build relationships with his colleagues to overcome misunderstandings and highlight their shared interests in the long game.

Deep Dialogue

Strategic leaders who master the art of alignment use structured dialogue explicitly to expose areas of misunderstanding or resistance. It's an iterative process that requires continual monitoring of the positions of your stakeholders, to stay in synch as needs or positions evolve.

The art of constructive dialogue was one of the great skills of Sir Alex Ferguson, the legendary UK football (soccer to Americans) coach of Manchester United. Considered the greatest football manager of his era, he had a reputation as a tough guy but invested time and energy in understanding all stakeholders, especially his players. He understood that open and honest conversations with deep dialogue were a critical part of his job. Football stars have big egos and the vulnerabilities of youth. Few fully appreciate Sir Alex's ability to give these young stars his full attention. "For a player and for any human being there is nothing better than hearing 'well done,'" he was known to say.[55]

David Gill, CEO of Manchester United, recounted his relation-ship with Ferguson: "Sometimes we disagree, but we respect each other, and know that arguments are just arguments. He is very fair. He moves on quickly." Ferguson's longtime secretary said, "If some-one knocks on his door, and they have a problem, the first thing he does is turn around his chair and say, 'Sit down, let's talk.'" Despite how busy and pressured he was, Sir Alex always made time for deep dialogue—and his players prospered from it. When he needed to tell a player "You're not starting in this game," he sat down and ex-plained why, one on one. "Some players like to have the coach's shoulder," explained Ferguson, a need even more pronounced today with players imported from all over the world to play on teams in a culture foreign to them.[56]

Building Bridges Across Cultural Divides

Strategic leaders appreciate the extent to which culture can influ-ence strategic alignment and mutual understanding. Geert Hof-stede's seminal study of IBM managers across countries underscores the important dimensions for understanding organizational cul-ture.[57] In particular, comprehending the role of power distance, individual versus team orientation, future orientation, and uncer-tainty avoidance enables a strategic leader to align and build bridges without offending stakeholders from different backgrounds. A more recent study called GLOBE, which examined many differ-ent cultures, further highlighted the importance of gender equality and assertiveness in explaining how leadership effectiveness differs across countries.[58]

In a globally connected world, strategic thinkers are leaders that have to be especially sensitive to cultural differences when they devise alignment strategies. They can frame ethnic or reli-gious differences, for example, as a set of constraints within which to operate, or as touch points to connect more deeply with people to generate diverse, robust solutions.

Lenovo, a Chinese company and the world's biggest seller of personal computers, views cultural alignment as a central part of its success story.[59] It ranks number one in five of the seven biggest PC markets, including Japan and Germany. Its mobile division is poised to leapfrog Samsung into the top spot in China, the world's biggest smartphone market.[60] It has been a remarkable run ever since Yang Yuanqing was brought in as CEO in 2009.

When Lenovo founder Liu Chuanzhi bought IBM's personal computer division in 2005 for $1.75 billion, he initially relied heavily on Western managers to run the new acquisition. There was simply a shortage of Chinese leaders with sufficient English-language skills and cross-cultural experience.

William Amelio, a former IBM executive who led Lenovo following the acquisition, faced the complex challenge of managing change in a business that had one foot in China and the other in America. As Lenovo's president and CEO, he oversaw the integration of IBM's PC Division, some thirty thousand employees in total. Amelio was able to increase annual revenue from $13 billion in 2005 to $15 billion by 2008. During that period, the company grew its brand internationally and, for seven successive quarters, had sales profits exceeding the growth of the overall market. But then Lenovo posted a 2008 fourth-quarter loss of $97 million.

This financial loss, combined with a culture clash, led Lenovo to bring in senior Chinese leaders with a deeper understanding of the country and its culture. IBMers had bristled at Chinese practices such as mandatory exercise breaks, public shaming of latecomers to meetings, overanalyzing past decisions whether they worked or not, and creating three- to five-year plans rather than the typical annual, quarterly, or sometimes monthly targets.[61] As a Chinese Lenovo executive explained: "Americans like to talk; Chinese people like to listen. At first we wondered why they kept talking when they had nothing to say."[62]

Lenovo needed to develop a uniquely Chinese management model and cultivate local talent to grow its business in and outside China. Hence the appointment of Yang Yuanqing as CEO. Yang spoke little English when Lenovo acquired IBM's PC unit. So he quickly moved his family to North Carolina and immersed himself in the American way. His experience in the United States paid off. Whereas foreigners at Chinese firms often stick out culturally, at Lenovo they appear to belong. One American executive praised Yang for instilling a bottom-up "performance culture" instead of playing the traditional Chinese corporate game of "waiting to see what the emperor wants."[63] In short, Yang understood the need to align a Chinese company culturally with its global imperative. This deliberate intent to build cultural bridges is paying off, as Lenovo is well on its way to becoming one of China's first global brands.

Action Plan to Bridge Differences

Whether the divides are cultural (Lenovo) or political (ObamaCare), or between business and environmental priorities (as adroitly addressed by Fred Krupp at the EDF), strategic leaders pay a disproportionate amount of attention to the right attitudes, outreach efforts, and techniques necessary to reach across the aisle. Here are some ideas to enhance your own bridge-building disciplines:

1. *Reframe the problem from win-lose to a search for mutual interest.* Seek to understand the motivations of those you wish to influence as well as the relevant market drivers, as Fred Krupp did when he redefined his orientation to business partners.
2. *Seek out sources of resistance, make them visible, and facilitate a structured dialogue to openly discuss differences and ways to*

bridge them. This technique worked for Juan and has been instrumental to the strategy and evident sucess of the EDF.

3. *Look for and approach signs of resistance, including passive aggression.* Don't make the mistake that senior leaders made at Kodak; attend to managers in the middle of the organization, understand their concerns, dig deeper for passive resistance, and appreciate the natural forces opposing change.

4. *Understand and diagram matrix relationships and weak links that are likely to result in conflict.* Ask probing questions, as Juan did, to see the issue from the perspective of his matrix partners.

5. *Listen more than you talk, and ask questions to pinpoint differences.* Understand the issue by listening carefully before trying to solve it based on surface knowledge. Change-leaders should spend half of their time getting input and gaining buy-in.

6. *Promote deep dialogue within your team, across teams, and with matrix partners.* Make time for deeper, more intimate connections with your team members (as we saw with Sir Alex Ferguson) or with collaborators (as Juan learned to do).

7. *Become a student of cross-cultural dynamics.* Read up on cultures and the GLOBE study; inquire about how others approach cultural issues, and make these insights an imperative in your business and alignment strategies.

THE DISCIPLINE TO ALIGN: PULLING IT TOGETHER

Jane Wang had always excelled at building a team. As she took on larger roles, she continued to *rally key players*. She discovered early in her career that alignment was a key success factor for project execution—her core strength. The biggest idea she took from the story of Whole Foods was the importance of repeatedly communicating a shared purpose and vision to her team. She simply had not thought enough about her role in *shaping the future* by articulating a clear, compelling, and empowering vision. In particular, Jane needed to act more boldly and persuasively when talking about where she wanted to take the business. Taking the long view was not one of her strengths and she resolved to work on that.

Bridging differences came naturally to Jane, perhaps because she did not like conflict and was adept at finding common ground. To her, conflict meant distraction and inefficiency. Even in bigger roles and within a matrix structure, she was confident in her ability to navigate, collaborate, and minimize such conflict when necessary. However, she acknowledged that she preferred to head off or avoid conflict because she struggled to see it as constructive and mutually beneficial. She could work harder to surface competing views when tension was high or resistance strong. Doing so might actually release tension. She thought back to some of the voices on her team, those who raised concerns about changing customer preferences. Perhaps she tuned them out? Perhaps she torpedoed rather than surfaced issues that might have increased awareness? Was she just too task- and deadline-oriented?

As Jane reflected on her strengths at aligning, she determined to push beyond her comfort zone, to be bolder about her vision, and to embrace resistance. She accepted the insight that conflict among ideas is necessary to find the best course, and that people can disagree with each other without becoming disagreeable. Most important, she started building on her alignment skill to reach out to others, expand her network, and rally others to her view. This also meant that she would have to work on her weaker side where necessary, such as positioning for the long game.

6 MY GIFT WAS NOT KNOWING

The Discipline to Learn:
Experiment Widely and Delve Deeply

"ELON MUSK IS ONE OF THE MOST CREATIVE BUSINESSPEOPLE I know," said CNN's Fareed Zakaria, alluding to Musk's electric carmaker Tesla and his spacecraft manufacturer SpaceX. He added that people think of Musk as "something of a dreamer." Where does all this creativity come from? he asked Musk in a recent interview. "Just trying really hard—the first order of business is to try," Musk replied. Most people do not really try, he believes; they are generally not focused on being creative. "You must try until your brain hurts."[1] What's not acceptable, Musk added, is senior engineers or executives not attempting radical innovation. When asked about sources of ideas, Musk mentioned that science and technology are key in his business, but also said that he drew much inspiration from history and literature. Underlying Musk's responses was a deep desire to learn, fueled by boundless curiosity and energy. When hiring people at his companies, Musk looks for evidence of exceptional ability. This means not just good grades, as those can be subject to gaming, but also special achievements in school, sports, or previous jobs that offer clear evidence of creativity, ambition, and tenacity.

Later that day on CBS, 60 Minutes ran "The Cleantech Crash," a segment critical of the failures in clean technology. Vinod Khosla, a legendary venture capitalist in Silicon Valley and a prominent advocate of cleantech, was candid on camera: "Sure, we've done lots of things that failed in energy. But every time, we learned, picked ourselves up, and tried something new." TV reporter Lesley Stahl persisted: "Some people call you a dreamer, and I don't think they mean it in a positive way." Khosla replied, "You need dreamers to stretch. I probably have failed more times in my life than almost anybody I know. But that's because I've tried more things. And I'm not afraid to fail because the consequences of avoiding failure are doing nothing." Stahl accused Khosla of "downplaying the glitches," and called upon a chemical engineer to say that Khosla had received federal subsidies and then "set up a system where he over-promised and under-delivered, and so the public and the politicians all developed unreasonable expectations."[2]

A week after the segment aired, Khosla sent CBS an open letter stating that 60 Minutes "grossly misrepresented the state of the sustainable energy industry." He wrote, "You fundamentally do not understand how innovation works," and quoted Robert F. Kennedy, "Only those who dare to fail greatly can ever achieve greatly."[3] That is the first lesson in Venture Capital 101: nothing ventured, nothing gained. Or as Albert Einstein put it, "Anyone who has never made a mistake has never tried anything new." Khosla more than earned his credentials in the venture world, first as an early backer of Sun MicroSystems and later as a senior partner at Kleiner Perkins. Even after some notable venture flameouts, he remains a long-standing member of the billionaires' club and knows how to play the long game.[4]

To be a strategic leader, you must abandon any pursuit of perfection or a meticulously weeded career path. No one would expect a child to learn how to walk without falling, or an adult to master skiing without taking numerous tumbles. The more mistakes you make, the faster you learn. Any leader who takes a team or organization into new territory is bound to stumble. What matters is how well everyone learns from these setbacks. The mantra of Procter & Gamble is to fail fast, cheap, and often. Tom Watson, founder of IBM, told his people: if you want to succeed faster, make more mistakes.[5]

Few leaders take the advice to heart, and understandably so: media, markets, and most organizational cultures view missteps as crippling rather than as a way of finding firmer footing. Trip up and your share price plummets, you get criticized, and people may lose faith in you. In fact, the "blame" culture that permeates so many organizations paralyzes the natural desire strategic thinkers have to take chances and experiment. The consequence is a culture that abhors mistakes and creates incentives that punish failure. Strategic leaders try hard to reframe this warped view for their people, since zero mistakes mean zero learning. Just ask Sara Blakely.

Keep Trying and Don't Give Up: From Spanx to Riches

Blakely's father would often ask her and her brother, "What have you failed at this week?" Like Vinod Khosla, he reinforced the message that the essence of failure is *not trying*, as opposed to *getting a bad outcome*. His view, said Blakely, "really allowed me to be much freer in trying things and spreading my wings in life."[6]

Try she did. The Florida native flunked the law school admissions test (LSAT) twice, braved stand-up comedy, formed an ill-fated venture with Disney World, and sold fax machines door to door, cold-calling businesses for seven years. All this effort informed her eventual success. Spanx was born out of an everyday frustration: what to wear under a pair of white pants? "I cut the feet off my pantyhose and wore them underneath," she recently told *Forbes*. "But they rolled up my legs all night. I remember thinking, 'I've got to figure out how to make this.' I'd never worked in fashion or retail. I just needed an undergarment that didn't exist."[7]

To succeed, Blakely had to convince people to manufacture and sell this unprecedented intimate. Easy, right? No. "I must have heard the word 'no' a thousand times," Sara said. "It didn't faze me. I didn't have any special abilities. It was sheer drive and telling myself to keep going." Blakely became a one-woman show. She made her own samples, cut feet from panty hose, and went on the Internet to find out who made the stuff. To save legal fees, she wrote her own patent from a textbook purchased at Barnes & Noble and set aside $100 to incorporate her company. But she couldn't decide on a name. After a succession of uninspiring ideas, she settled on Spanks, which seemed a contraction of *Spandex* and elicited giggles, some of them uncomfortable. She substituted an *x* for the *ks* at the last minute after reading that made-up names sold better. "The word *Spanx* was funny. "It made people laugh. No one ever forgot it."[8] Blakely put her entire savings of $5,000 into launching the product without giving up her full-time job.

Not going by the book is a great approach to discovery. "My greatest gift was not knowing the rules. I called Neiman Marcus by phone. I just rang them, which shocked others when they heard I did not go to trade shows. I did not know about trade shows and just tried things." Blakely's most important tip: "Believe in your idea, trust your instincts, and don't be afraid to fail. It took me two years from the time I had the idea for Spanx until the time I had a product in hand ready to sell into stores. If you believe in your idea 100 percent, don't let anyone stop you! Not being afraid to fail is a key part of the success of Spanx."[9]

Blakely's embrace of failure earned her the title of youngest self-made female billionaire in America. Spanx, the body-shaping undergarments, have become a global sensation for women and now men. In an interview on CNBC, Warren Buffet said, "[Blakely] is the reason we need to be bullish about America. She saw a need and a way . . . to make women's lives better."[10] And she seized it. In a VUCA world—volatile, uncertain, complex, and ambiguous—Buffet values the ability to learn from everything you do and then adjust your plan accordingly. "I feel that failure is life's way of nudging you and letting you know you're off course," Sara said at a Women in the World Summit. "And boy, are women glad she didn't pass the law boards. Think of the world without Spanx, ladies! So many panty lines!"[11]

Sara Blakely's key message for strategic leaders is that failure is about trying, not giving up, and learning. "It changed my mindset at an early age that failure is not the outcome, failure is not trying. Don't be afraid to fail," she said. "What are you most afraid of failing at? Will you get in the cage with your fears and take a step toward

Spanx's Remarkable Growth

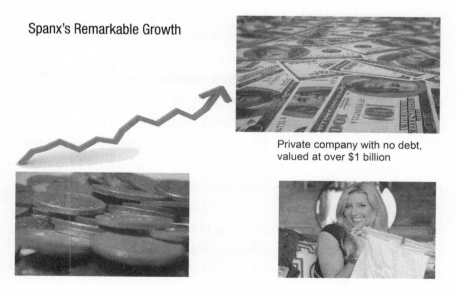

Private company with no debt, valued at over $1 billion

your dream today?"[12] Or, as Sir Richard Branson frames it, "The challenge is to follow through on a great idea. I think if [you've] got a great idea, you need to just give it a try. . . . And if you fall flat on your face, pick yourself up and try again. Learn from your mistakes. And, remember, you've got to go make a real difference in people's lives if you're going to be successful."[13]

Strategic leaders face their fears and promote an organizational culture of inquiry and discovery. They encourage people to try new things and share what they learn. They harvest the data of failure and success—their own and that of their teams, their competitors, and industry leaders across the market—and discuss their missteps openly, constructively, and without ego. They pursue new ideas with the understanding that surprises present learning opportunities. Such strategic leaders excel because they *experiment widely* and *delve deep* to improve their business model. What is your own attitude toward learning? Consider the following.

Experiment Widely

1. *Do you encourage experiments and "failing fast" as a source of innovation and learning?* Blakely's experimentation, resilience, and fast recovery from mistakes constitute a model for all strategic leaders. Many leaders talk this talk, but few walk it as she does.

2. *Do you learn from the outside in instead of through internal or industry conventions?* To what extent do you seek novel ideas from beyond the boundaries of your own business? Sara Blakely's good fortune was her ignorance of the rules, which gave her freedom to experiment.

3. *Do you expose yourself to a range of different models and cultures?* Blakely learned about the culture of retail by going to fabric makers in North Carolina and cold-calling Neiman Marcus. She then applied what she learned in a different market, the United Kingdom— only to discover that the Brits use different terminology.

Delve Deeply

4. Do you establish regular checkpoints and after-action briefs as early indicators of success and failure? The ability to pause and peruse outcomes and pass on lessons is the essence of Procter & Gamble's fail-fast-cheap-and-often culture.

5. Do you correct your course when receiving disconfirming evidence or surprises about the current direction, even after you committed to that direction? The toughest act of strategic leadership is to reverse course if a decision proves to be off track, as when Netflix pulled back and refined its plan to raise prices and split into two companies.

6. Do you share stories about success and failure to promote institutional learning and foster collective intelligence? Sara Blakely is a storyteller who honed her skills doing stand-up routines, and her honesty in talking about how she's failed and what she's learned has nurtured a culture within Spanx that celebrates learning.

EXPERIMENT WIDELY

In his classic book *The Fifth Discipline: The Art and Practice of the Learning Organization*, Peter Senge assigned leaders the special role of cultivating new patterns of thinking, personal mastery, shared vision, and team learning within organizations.[14] Senge advocated systems thinking so companies can anticipate, adapt, and respond faster to change. A quarter of a century later, the learning organization still doesn't have much of a foothold in the business world, despite skyrocketing uncertainty. There are countless examples of organizations whose failure to learn fast enough led to disaster. Consider the fate of the BlackBerry device marketed by the Canadian company BlackBerry Ltd., owned by RIM.[15] Only a few years ago, the BlackBerry smartphone was king of the hand-held world with its dominant technology and high market share of mobile devices.

How did BlackBerry's leaders miss their learning opportunities when they still had time to act?

Is Your Head in the Sand? The Inability to Try New Things at BlackBerry

When Apple introduced the iPhone in 2007, BlackBerry's co-CEOs Mike Lazaridis and Jim Balsillie continued to invest in mass production of its existing products rather than experimenting with far more consumer-friendly touch-screen options. Like Steve Ballmer of Microsoft, BlackBerry's leaders didn't see the iPhone as a threat. They underestimated the Apple device because it consumed too much bandwidth, lacked a physical keyboard and adequate security, and didn't support e-mail, and because consumers complained about its short battery life.[16] In 2012, the board replaced Lazaridis and Balsillie with Thorsten Heins. After assessing the situation, Heins claimed there was "nothing wrong" with the company, even as BlackBerry shipments plummeted 37 percent.[17] Heins left his CEO position a year later.

BlackBerry's leaders failed to learn from numerous other firms that fell victim to market disruptions of their business models. As Clayton Christensen notes in his best-selling book *The Innovator's Dilemma,* technological disruption often comes from new entrants who offer cheaper or easier solutions, rather than from firms offering yet more bells and whistles.[18] If RIM's founders had paused to consider what their competitor Steve Jobs did in 1979 with Xerox's prototype of the mouse—seeing it as a breakthrough in personal computing, much to Microsoft's consternation—they might have learned from a much younger Jobs how to compete against him in 2007.

So what really happened? "Simply put, BlackBerry's leaders didn't see the iPhone as a threat to their business, and their mental models prevented them from seeing it as anything but a very limited

phone."[19] They couldn't imagine the iPhone as a miniature computer that would grow ever more powerful in consumers' hands.
Ironic, wouldn't you say, for a company originally named Research
in Motion (RIM)?

This denial by leaders proved far more dangerous to BlackBerry's
health than experimenting with a fail-fast way of thinking and acting. No technology company is "too big to fail" when failure is an
industry norm.[20] This is a profound point for anyone striving to be
more strategic. It reminds us of the Encyclopedia Britannica and
Kodak. In contrast, Ursula Burns, prior to becoming CEO of Xerox,
saw her company's leaders engineer a major corporate transformation by learning from a near-death experience. They refocused the
business from a product company in the machine-selling business to
a services company in the document-outsourcing business.[21] Burns
observed:

> One of the things I characterize as fearlessness is seeing an op-
> portunity even though things are not broken. Someone will say
> things are good, but I am going to destabilize them because they
> can be much better and should be much better. . . . You have to be
> a little bit ahead of it well before you have to. Companies get into
> trouble when they get really complacent, when they settle in and
> say, O.K., we're doing O.K. now.[22]

In *The Corner Office*, journalist Adam Bryant of the *New York
Times* notes how Burns and other CEOs reward people who have
the guts to experiment, uncover hidden opportunities, and make
decisions that might shake up the status quo.[23] Amid great uncertainty, strategic leaders who want to sustain their organizations
across generations offer incentives for experimenting and learning
from mistakes. The reason is simple: by the time everyone clearly
understands why you need to change course, your ship has already

hit the iceberg. Leaders must make their moves when the future is still ambiguous. That's why learning is so critical to winning the long game. By definition, learning is a form of change. If an organization is continually learning, then everyone is primed to change and ready to move in a different direction each day. The courage to move and the timing of the movement are what differentiate strategic leaders from the rest.

Experiment Small and Learn Fast

Arie de Geus, former head of strategic planning at Royal Dutch Shell, studied what companies must do to survive for two hundred years or more.[24] He found that long-lived companies stand out in four ways:

1. They cultivate an *external focus* to countervail large navel-gazing bureaucracies.
2. They conduct many small experiments at the fringes of their business to learn faster.
3. They define themselves more by their *core values* and less in terms of their frequently changing product lines, customer groups, or technology platforms.
4. They practice *conservative finance*; that is, they limit their debt and fly below the radar rather than close to the sun.

De Geus concluded: *"The ability to learn faster than your competitors may be the only sustainable competitive advantage."*[25]

A Passion for Experimentation and Learning at Google

Sara Blakely experimented with abandon because she did not know the rules. In 2011, Richard Branson's Virgin Media partnered with THECUBE, a collaborative workspace to support aspiring entrepreneurs.[26] Their aim is to form an "innovation zone" to brainstorm, stress-test, and develop new product ideas that would be suited for the next generation of digital entertainment. Bringing together entrepreneurs, tech start-ups, and experts from across the Virgin Media group, the collaboration aims to push superfast connectivity to its limits with new applications and services. The aim is to "develop ground-breaking consumer mobile platforms and new propositions that will enable organizations across the UK to innovate and grow." The partnership was initiated to infuse fresh thinking into Virgin Media and stimulate experimentation for the benefit of Virgin as well as the broader entrepreneurial hi-tech community in East London's "Silicon Roundabout."[27]

Google Inc. has been a learning-culture pioneer. "Experimentation is practically a mantra; we evaluate almost every change that potentially affects what our users experience," said Diane Tang, who works on data mining at Google. Tang and her team have created an environment where there is an insatiable appetite to try new things and growing skills in the experimental process.[28] In a research presentation, "Overlapping Experiment Infrastructure: More, Better, Faster Experimentation," Tang's team broke down Google's framework into three parts:

+ *More* means "more simultaneous experiments" and greater "variety in the types of experiments supported,"
+ *Better* means "valid experiments" and "robust experiment design," and
+ *Faster* means "easy and quick experiment set-up," "experimental data available quickly and automatically," and "quick iteration."[29]

Why run more experiments, you ask? "To remain innovative while growing," Tang's team answers. They underscore the need for more than a framework: "Googlers" have access to tools for designing, configuring, and analyzing each experiment, and ongoing education in the form of experiment councils and expert forums that guide design and interpretation.[30]

The leaders at Google take pride in their ability to push beyond conventional boundaries of experimentation and in their openness to failure. Google X, which they refer to as their "moonshot factory," is a lab where engineers collaborate on audacious ideas. Teams are encouraged to think big, focus on society's toughest problems, and use "science fiction–sounding solutions" in search of novel, breakthrough ideas. They are rewarded for bold thinking even if they fail, since Google knows that failure is valuable when innovating.[31]

Steven Levy—author of *In the Plex: How Google Thinks, Works, and Shapes Our Lives*—explains that CEO Larry Page and co-founder Sergey Brin modeled Google after Stanford University and borrowed from the Montessori schools they had both attended. "It's really, really ingrained in their personalities," former Google vice president Marissa Mayer, now Yahoo CEO, told Levy. They always "ask their own questions, do their own things. Do something because it makes sense, not because some authority figure told you."[32]

Google promotes its culture of learning through Google University and peer-to-peer teaching. Google's core curriculum goes beyond basic orientation: it includes courses on management and skills such as public speaking. Its "Googler to Googler" program assigns teaching roles to employees across departments rather than just to the HR staff to reinforce the point that teaching and continuous learning is everyone's job. Googlers have initiated such popular courses as "Search Inside Yourself" on mindfulness and "Creative Skills for Innovation" on design thinking. About 5 percent of Googlers have volunteered to teach more than half of Google's official classes.[33]

At Google, the obsession with learning extends to hiring talent as well. Laszlo Bock, senior vice president of people operations (hiring) at Google, emphasized that "[t]he No. 1 thing we look for is . . . learning ability . . . the ability to process on the fly." In Google's view, "somebody who has high cognitive ability, is innately curious, is willing to learn and has emergent leadership skills . . . [and] no content knowledge" is more attractive than "someone who's been doing just one thing and is a world expert." Bock makes it clear that Google prioritizes learning aptitude over functional expertise (excluding, of course, technical coding skills) due to the value of flexible thinking and new ways of approaching challenges.[34]

Strategic leaders are best positioned to champion learning because they can foster a culture that values learning, applauds experiments, and takes the long view. They can also shine a spotlight on both success and failure as a basis for learning. Although spotlighting success is easier and more welcome in most companies, untangling its causes is still difficult since skill, design, and luck are often intermingled. Diagnosing failure is even harder due to the added complexity of discomfort, finger pointing, and possible legal exposure. Nonetheless, learning can become contagious when leaders delight in it. Think about your own team or organization. How can you infuse greater entrepreneurial spirit? What experiments can you try? How can you engage others in testing limits and learning from pilots?

Learn from the Outside: How CTCA Invented a Patient-Centric Model

Being curious and open to input from outside the four walls of the business are important traits for strategic leaders to cultivate. Seeking out mavericks, challenging conventional wisdom, and sourcing new ideas from diverse teams will change both you and the world around you.

Consider how Richard J Stephenson, a businessman and a Freemason with a strong moral code, brought change to the healthcare industry. In 1975, his company bought an Illinois hospital situated halfway between Milwaukee and Chicago. This hospital, which served as a general medical-surgical facility, including cardiac and podiatry care for the community of Zion, had been struggling, so Stephenson focused for well over a decade on improving operations and the introduction of truly patient-centered care.

Then his mother was diagnosed with bladder cancer. The Stephenson family searched far and wide for the best cancer treatment available. They found it in the expertise of world-renowned cancer hospitals, all staffed by specialists in their fields. But what these experts saw was a tumor, not a mother—*his mother*—and that really troubled him. What's more, these leading hospitals—with their high demand—were organized to maximize staff effectiveness rather than to minimize patient suffering. That troubled him too, especially since that's how he ran his own hospital. When Mary Brown Stephenson passed away in 1982, her son vowed to change cancer care. Never again would his hospital put diseases, processes, or payments before the people in pain.

Stephenson worked with his team to develop what he calls the "Mother Standard®" of care, an integrated and holistic approach that combines clinical treatments with pain management and therapies focused on mind-body, nutrition, and psychological support. They reoriented the relationship between patients and physicians, placing the latter on salary and freeing them from marketing, billing, and collecting for their services so that they could fully focus on their patients. They upended the process so that the entire medical team, not just one doctor, met with the patient wherever the patient waited. They retooled the environment so that it signaled hope at every turn and ensured that all patients and their families or care givers were always treated with great dignity, respect, and compassion.

In 1988, Stephenson re-launched his Illinois hospital as a cancer treatment center dedicated to wellness and well-being. He defined value in terms of consumers' perception of quality and results, and marketed the center directly to consumers rather than relying on doctor referrals. People responded favorably. Two years later,

Stephenson opened a second center in Oklahoma, rebranding the pair as the Cancer Treatment Centers of America (CTCA). As CTCA grew, Stephenson's little network soon bumped up against regulators and health maintenance organizations that controlled costs by limiting their members' choices.

How could CTCA scale operations in this environment without sacrificing its patient-centric care and its innovative delivery model? To answer that question, Stephenson sought outside expertise. He hired Steve Bonner to replace him as CEO in 1999. Bonner was a lawyer and had been in private industry for decades. He introduced disciplined decision-making processes and more structured strategic planning to ensure cohesion, innovation, and learning across CTCA's locations. He improved infrastructure and set high growth goals that mobilized the team. CTCA has grown about 20 percent per year under Bonner and now has five cancer treatment centers around the country.[35]

Realizing that major provisions of the Patient Protection and Affordable Care Act would take effect in January 2014, CTCA leaders wondered how that would change healthcare in practical terms. What should CTCA do next? Stephenson and Bonner agreed that they needed another injection of visionary thinking and deeper learning to take patient care to yet a higher level. This time they focused on a related but much larger service industry: worldwide hospitality with a special focus on the best hotels around the globe.

CTCA's board found its answer in Gerard van Grinsven, a Dutchman who operated and managed Ritz-Carlton hotels in a dozen countries across different continents. Before joining CTCA as CEO, van Grinsven had applied the Ritz-Carlton approach to the Henry Ford West Bloomfield Hospital in Michigan. He was convinced that most hospital administrators didn't understand their customers, especially those from culturally diverse backgrounds. At Bloomfield, van Grinsven set out to understand the community by visiting patients and their families at their homes on Sundays. And at the hospital, van Grinsven asked patients how Bloomfield could improve. He discovered that cancer patients enjoy walking the grounds but tire quickly, and so he added more outdoor benches. To reinforce healthy eating habits, Bloomfield offered cooking classes and introduced an organic café.[36]

As the CEO of CTCA, van Grinsven holds out a tall challenge for the organization overall: how to re-imagine cancer care? He encourages the members of his staff to view patients as guests worthy of five-star-hotel treatment, to try whatever enhances patient care, and to share what they learn across the CTCA system. He wants them to excel at compassion and personal care. CTCA continues to staff its hospitals not just with technical wizards but with professionals who care deeply about their patients and who work exceptionally well in teams. Prima donnas need not apply.

Van Grinsven urges all participants in the debate to "start by reshaping the conversation in health care based on questions that explore connectivity to our patients."[37] To take CTCA to the next level, he recognizes his role in shaping the larger context of cancer care. He also realizes that he needs to change the thinking of his leaders and transform the culture. This new CEO is spearheading an organizational re-imagination effort to ensure that his team has the capacity to learn and adapt as fast as the patients and healthcare environment require. Van Grinsven is positioning CTCA to win in the long run while recognizing that the healthcare game is drastically changing in America due to Obamacare, an aging population, technological advances, and new business models for cancer care.

How Samsung Spread the Seeds for Global Growth: Cross-Cultural Learning

Today's manager has to be globally literate and culturally sensitive— well-versed in international trends, aware of innovations from other regions and industries, and always abreast of changes with customers and rivals. Perhaps no company has made a greater leap in achieving global sensitivity and in developing the skills to be an international competitor of the first rank than Samsung.

Korea was long known as the hermit kingdom. The overall mindset was xenophobic and the country was largely closed to outsiders. It did not do much business internationally, and the people running its companies were not particularly curious about the world outside. Samsung, founded by Lee Byung-chul in 1938, was no different.

Lee's son Kun-Hee Lee stepped into the CEO role after his father's death in 1987. The company was stable and solid, but the prodding of the South Korean government, eager to transform the country into a manufacturing giant that could compete with Japan, provided the impetus for change. Kun-Hee Lee became determined to transform Samsung from a South Korean success story into an international business force. In 1993, "Lee famously told his employees to 'change everything but your wife and kids.' True to his word, Lee attempted to reform Samsung's profoundly Korean culture. Foreign employees were brought in and local employees were shipped out as Lee tried to foster a more international attitude to doing business."[38]

During the same year, Kun-Hee Lee went on a world tour to figure out how his company was doing internationally. He was not happy with what he saw and vowed to become a globally recognized player by 2000. In a famous speech, which became known inside Samsung as the "Frankfurt Declaration of 1993," Lee laid out a blueprint to learn from the outside world. This radically transformed the company to succeed in the long run.[39]

Twenty years later, Samsung ranks fourteenth on Fortune's global 500 and first in revenues in the electronics industry. It is Apple's principal rival in mobile electronics. One of Lee's key learning initiatives was the "regional specialist program." Samsung took the best and brightest talent and sprinkled these people around the world to promote global awareness and outside-in thinking—a radical move for a Korean company at the time. Dr. Sea-Jin Chang, who is an authority on the management of diversified multinational firms and chairman of the National University of Singapore Business School, sees the program as "pivotal in the transformation of Samsung into a global powerhouse."[40]

Since 1993, over fifty thousand Samsung employees have participated in year-long assignments in more than eighty countries. "They don't work," says Tae Gyun Shin, president of Samsung's Human Resources Center. "They are given three missions: Learn the local language, learn the local culture, and become an expert in their specialty."[41] Samsung's chairman told every employee who participated in The Wharton School's executive development program to travel throughout the States by land after the program. Over time, the program became a vehicle to generate fresh ideas. Participants foster personal connections to key figures in various countries and share information about other markets, cultures, and business practices.[42] It was the "company's most important globalization effort" and nurtured

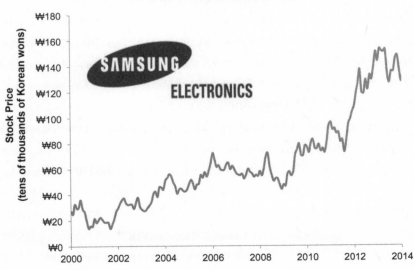

Samsung Electronics: 2000–2014

a generation of managers ready to pursue Samsung's worldwide ambitions.[43] Many of the regional specialists were later assigned to senior positions at Samsung's offices in the areas they studied.[44] The connections and cultural insights that came from the people who participated in the program ultimately paid off in countries such as Russia, where Samsung is now the best-selling brand in consumer electronics.

Learn From Competitors, Pioneers, and Innovators

"Competition is needed in the electronic vehicle market," according to BMW CEO Norbert Reithofer. At the premier of the i3, BMW's new electric car, Reithofer said that the electric carmaker Tesla was important to BMW and he "wanted Tesla to do well." In industry after industry, competition fuels innovation. It advances design, delivers greater customer value, and creates new markets. "As a competitor," Reithofer added, Tesla serves as "an example that electro-mobility will be important in the future."[45]

The initial success of the Tesla Model S "means that the market for electric vehicles in the world is growing." Reithofer used Tesla as a benchmark for BMW's long-term electric strategy. He said that, by 2025, 30 percent of BMW's catalogue will be electric or hybrid cars. BMW also plans to follow Tesla's approach of by-passing dealers, selling the i3 over the Internet and offering test drives through a new mobile sales force that will meet potential buyers at their homes. Sales head Roland Krueger said, "We can well imagine that internet sales could be expanded for all models."[46]

Rather than tether BMW to twentieth-century technology, its leaders decided to learn from Tesla and bet on the technology of a new century. The i3 is essentially a strategic option for BMW, a viable alternative to the internal combustion engine in case it is needed. If Tesla's Model S ultimately fails, then BMW will have learned a lot and still have time to rethink its plans in the electric-cars market. And if Tesla succeeds, BMW will have a leg up on its traditional rivals.

Action Plan to Experiment Widely

Although trying something new and taking chances seems easy enough, it is still more the exception than the rule. The fear of mistakes trumps an experimental mentality for far too many managers. Use some of these ideas to initiate a passion for learning on your team:

1. *Make a personal and public commitment to explore outside your comfort zone.* For Samsung, that meant moving beyond Korea in terms of business customs, languages, and methods of educating leaders. Samsung's executives traveled by ground, not by air. Imagine doing that across India, Africa, and South America. Investigate other industries, markets, and cultures from within.

2. *Take chances, try things, and worry less about protocol.* Sometimes ignorance works in your favor: Sara Blakely cold-called Neiman Marcus because she didn't know enough to go through distributors, buyers, or trade shows.

3. *Consider pilot programs or experiments rather than big bets, and build in checkpoints to determine whether you should continue, expand, or close the experiment.* Draw from the lessons of Procter & Gamble, Google, and Spanx; experiment, fail fast and cheap, and extract lessons.

4. *Include qualitative, longer-term, and quantitative measures of both process and outcome to evaluate projects, investments, or decisions.* Measure such soft dimensions as improved strategic thinking, globalization, collaboration, innovation, and customer experience as well as other less tangible strategic qualities. If Samsung had measured only financial return on investment, it would likely have cut the regional specialist program. For CTCA, the feedback and reactions of patients is at the top of the evaluation scorecard.

5. *Pull the plug on initiatives that are not producing as expected.* Encourage a healthy level of detachment so that your people can readily kill off their pet projects. Follow Google's lead in designing, monitoring, and analyzing experiments and then acting fast on results.

6. *Schedule time to study other companies and leaders from outside your industry.* Read, take executive courses, and visit other companies as Steve Jobs did with Xerox and as Samsung has done around the world. Immerse yourself in the processes, tools, products, and business models of other organizations and industries.

7. *Study your competitors with an open mind, and without a defensive posture.* Examine their moves and strategies as a source of new insight, as BMW's CEO did: perhaps your rivals are smarter than you. Use scenarios and war-gaming techniques.

DELVE DEEPLY

Many of the people we've discussed in this chapter are well known and have learned from both successes and failures. A word of caution: learning from experience requires the courage to look squarely, honestly, and impartially at your own performance, similar to "looking in the mirror." Sometimes the lessons are obvious; only people in deep denial fail to grasp them. More often, though, the lessons are elusive and require both digging below the surface and systematically creating tools for surfacing insights.

Conduct After-Action Reviews and Pre-Mortems

The US Army institutionalized after-action reviews (AARs) in the 1980s in order to make every mission an opportunity to learn. These are "conducted during or immediately after each event; focus on intended training objectives; focus on soldier, leader, and unit performance; involve all participants in the discussion; use open-ended questions; are related to specific standards; determine strengths and weaknesses; [and] link performance to subsequent training."[47] The AAR is a highly structured process for analyzing what happened, why it happened, and how to do it better next time. It involves those responsible for the overall mission. All speak frankly and freely, without fear of rank or retaliation. So illuminating are these reviews, and so unconventional is warfare today, that all branches of the US armed forces have integrated the AAR into operations.

The Israeli army has a similar process, and it is particularly intense in the more elite units. "Each day is an experiment. And each day ends with a grueling session whereby everyone in the unit—of all ranks—sits down to deconstruct the day."[48] In an interview captured in *Start-Up Nation*, Harvard Business School graduate Tal Keinan, who flew F-16 fighter jets in the Israel Defense Forces (IDF), explains: "The debrief is as important as the drill or live battle. . . . Each flight exercise, simulation, and real operation is treated like laboratory work to be examined and reexamined, and reexamined again, open to new information, and subjected to rich—and heated—debate. That's how we are trained."[49]

Keinan goes on to say that the art of debriefing is so highly valued that everyone in the unit is graded on this skill: "[T]here are numerous questions regarding a person's ability to debrief himself and to debrief others. . . . If you screwed up, your job is to show the lessons you've learned. Nobody learns from someone who is being defensive." The intent is not to point out mistakes and punish but, rather, to create a mindset that accepts mistakes as natural and normal as long as they are a source for learning. According to *Start-Up Nation*, with nearly everyone serving in the Israeli military, the culture and skill of debriefing have been major contributors to the success of Israeli start-ups in the private sector. Similar to Pixar's morning-after meetings, this approach is relevant for every business that wants to be a learning organization.

Ultimately, the purpose behind extracting lessons from mistakes is to transfer and apply insights to new situations, thus preventing future problems.[50] The US and Israeli military forces are obsessed with such reviews because the stakes are too high to keep making the same mistakes. One approach is to apply the learnings from an after-action review as a type of pre-mortem to the next project of that kind. When starting a new project, ask what lessons from previous projects might apply to this new case. Then brainstorm how the new project might die. Once you have listed the various pathways leading to ruin, make the current plan more robust, identify early warning signs of trouble, and develop contingency plans so that you can mitigate risks.

Why Scientists Love a Surprise, Good or Bad

Over a century ago, the biologist Max Delbruck, a Nobel laureate, advocated strongly for "the principle of limited sloppiness." He advised his students to be sloppy enough in their lab experiments to allow for the unexpected, but not so sloppy that they could not identify the reasons for their anomalous results.[51] Case in point: the eccentric Scottish scientist Alexander Fleming. His peers considered him a brilliant but somewhat sloppy researcher. In 1928, after a long summer holiday, Fleming returned to his laboratory and began gathering up the contaminated petri dishes for a good scrubbing. Then he noticed something different about one of them: there was a halo where a blue-green mold appeared to have dissolved the bacteria.[52] Scientists live for such anomalies. An ordinary biologist might have missed the small irregularities in the contours that caught Fleming's eye. But Fleming knew bacterial growths as an artist knows his medium, because he occasionally shaped colonies of staphylococcus into portraits of his co-workers.

Where did this fungus come from? Fleming had neglected to close a window in the lab before he left on holiday. He deduced that the wind had carried tiny spores through the window, and some ended up in his petri dishes among the staph bacteria that grew uncovered there for weeks. The spores happened to possess un-known properties that inhibited the growth of certain bacteria around them. Perhaps these properties killed staph infections? If so, that would mean a cure for sore throats, boils, and abscesses! Flem-ing cultivated the fungus in a separate culture and then created a filtrate or "mold juice" that he called penicillin. He tested the mold juice on a range of bacteria and found that it killed streptococcus, meningococcus, and diphtheria. But he couldn't produce a pure enough filtrate to show antibiotic effects in the human body. So he published his findings and set the mold juice aside.[53]

It took another ten years before two other scientists, the Austra-lian Howard Walter Florey and Ernst Chain, a gifted German scien-tist, managed to purify and scale the process. Chain's accurate mapping of the mold's structure enabled the Oxford team to isolate and concentrate the drug. Soon they were processing some 500 li-ters of the mold juice a week. With this supply of the purer filtrate, Florey began a series of experiments with animals and learned that his drug protected mice against the deadly streptococcal bacteria.[54] In 1941, doctors injected the drug into a police officer who had pricked his mouth and developed huge abscesses around his face and lungs. Within days, he started to recover but the supply ran out and he didn't survive.

As the two scientists worked to increase supply, Florey met with the US pharmaceutical companies Eli Lilly, Merck, Pfizer, and Squibb. Their response was so lukewarm that Florey enlisted various government agencies to drum up support. By 1944, Florey and Chain were ready to commercialize the drug. During World War II, penicillin saved an estimated 15 to 20 percent of the millions of injured soldiers who would otherwise have died from infections. Fleming's original discovery helped create the field of modern anti-biotics. He was knighted in 1944 and shared the Nobel Prize in Medicine with Florey and Chain in 1945.

Scientists realize that like big data, nature cannot speak for itself, and that it takes hard work to extract new insights. It requires dogged pursuit, painstaking analyses, and crowdsourcing samples. Scientists generally use follow-up experiments, in which they change only one variable at a time, to untangle the multiple causes at work. And when they cannot do such controlled variations, as in large field studies, they use statistical techniques to control for multiple factors. Typically, every answer leads to another question—and that is the essence of the scientific process, which is a long game par excellence. This kind of disciplined learning is the essence of what we refer to as delving *deeply*.

Failure as a Source of Innovation

Your organization can't learn unless you've primed the minds of your team members. Swiftly sweeping mistakes under the rug to minimize reputational damage will not encourage a culture of learning. Strategic leaders surface all hidden information—a form of "dark data"—and look for valuable takeaways. They show everyone how to make hay when things go haywire.

Create a mistake bank. Set up an internal website where people can deposit their mistakes, anonymously if they wish, so that others don't repeat them. One hospital looking into medical errors realized that its nurses were most likely to make drug mistakes—about the type, dosage, timing, and side effects of drugs—when they got interrupted. Now, when nurses at this hospital administer medicines, they wear a cap or other garment that signals clearly "Do not disturb." This simple technique reduces errors daily. Make sure to include near misses in your mistake bank since these often hold important lessons. The Federal Aviation Administration records and studies all close calls involving airplanes. The Danish company Grundfoss, the world's leading pump manufacturer, asked its assembly-line workers to record things that almost went wrong. They learn as much from these near misses as from actual screw-ups.

Run a competition. When one of us published a book in 2011 provocatively titled *Brilliant Mistakes*,[55] the publisher decided to run an open competition with a jury and prizes. It invited people to describe mistakes from which they learned a great deal, exceeding the cost of the mistake itself. Many submissions were received, and the top ones ranged from a physician who stumbled upon new medical insights to a children's entertainer who used balloons very creatively after she had forgotten to bring her other props.[56] The top prize went to Dr. Stephen Salzman of Olive View–UCLA Medical Center, who proved by mistake that his hypothesis on why athletes have low heart rates was completely off the mark.

Make deliberate mistakes. David Ogilvy, the advertising genius, ran ads that he and his team did not believe would work as a way to test their theories.[57] They knew that they would waste half of their investment but they didn't know which half. So they experimented widely, including the famous Hathaway shirt advertisement to which Ogilvy added a man with an eye patch at the last minute.[58] The ad was a brilliant success, ran for a long time, and received several industry prizes. Consider a more extreme example: a twenty-year-old New York University drama student, after many fruitless forays into the New York City dating scene, decided to try a bold and outrageous experiment—letting go of her selection criteria. She resolved to say yes to anyone who asked her out on a date (with the exception of those she suspected might be murderers and rapists). After a series of interesting and excruciating dates, described in her book

The Year of Yes, she finally married a divorced playwright whom she would not have given a second glance before her experiment.[59]

Training and learning. If you want to help your team get better, first teach them how to frame any mistake as a learning opportunity. Second, build on principles of positive psychology and deal with each setback or failure as something temporary, isolated, nonpersonal, and valuable.[60] Third, emphasize that learning something new is the goal. A British girls school declared a Failure Week because the headmistress, Heather Hanbury, wanted to impress upon the students that "it is completely acceptable and completely normal not to succeed at times in life."[61]

Strategic leaders can adapt the US Army's after-action review and Pixar's *plussing* technique (where you build on ideas rather than critique and subtract) to show their teams how to learn from mistakes. The Israeli culture promotes an appreciation for what it calls "constructive or intelligent failures." Seasoned leaders know that, without a large number of failures, you can't innovate. In the military, they tend to view performance or results as value neutral. "So long as the risk was taken intelligently, and not recklessly, there is something to be learned."[62]

Mid-Course Corrections Are Key

In industries where failure is common—such as oil and gas where most holes drilled remain dry, or venture capital where only one of five investments scores big—managing failure well is key. Start-up investor Whitney Johnson points out that all entrepreneurs make mistakes, and most face bankruptcy along the way. Resilience and recovery time matter. "You need to move fast, be agile and flexible, and learn from your mistakes, get your head back in the game rather than waste precious time bemoaning what is and was. Don't let your mistakes define you, but use them to create your new success."[63]

Jesse Treu is a senior partner with Domain Associates, a successful venture capital firm based in Princeton, New Jersey. Domain specializes in pharmaceuticals, medical devices, and diagnostics. When Treu examined Domain's successes and failures, he noticed that most of the successful ventures had changed their business plan and even their business model. In contrast, the unsuccessful ones stuck with the wrong strategy for too long, hampering their chances of success.[64] This finding highlights an important truism: *the ability to revise a plan when needed is more valuable than the ability to draft a plan.* That's why venture capitalists bet on people rather than on projects or business plans.

The new division president of manufacturing at a pharmaceutical company discovered that division managers tended to punish mistakes rather than learning from them. Many leaders went to great lengths to cover up things that went wrong. The manager and his team realized that they had to change the culture to one that encouraged learning from poor outcomes. They launched three initiatives:

+ Cross-divisional teams conducted novel experiments to solve tough customer problems—and reported the results regardless of outcomes.
+ An innovation tournament generated new ideas from across the organization.
+ A program publicized stories about projects that initially failed but eventually led to innovative solutions.

Ultimately, the pharmaceutical company shifted toward more shared learning and bolder innovation. Executives there are listening better to customer complaints, learning sooner about festering issues, and addressing the issues rather than sweeping them aside. Also, the senior team is regularly praising managers who share what they learn from their missteps.

Brad Smith, CEO of Intuit, recounted a story about how he learned to "fail forward."[65] He described how he made a big bet involving e-commerce. "I convinced the board to give us $40 million to sign two e-commerce deals, telling them that we could sell more things online than our sales force could sell. I told them we wouldn't even need a sales force. After $40 million, we sold just 15 units." Preparing for a board meeting, he assumed he would get grilled and fired. He decided to tell it straight and brace himself for the worst. He explained: "Here's what I thought. Here's what happened. Here's where I was wrong, and here's what I would do differently." He was shocked when one board member started clapping and said, "You know what? You are more valuable to us now. The first reason is that you won't make that mistake again, so we want you to go and make a bunch of new mistakes." They also saw potential in the new product, sales strategy, and enhanced competitive positioning, but the moral of the story was: Be open to learning and resilient in the face of failure.

When interviewing new hires, Smith probes to see if the person has the learning orientation central to his company's culture and success. One of the key questions he asks is "What is the single biggest professional business mistake you've made, and what was the lesson you took from that?"

Communicate Stories About Success and Failure

The president of an Ann Arbor, Michigan, business instituted what he called the Golden Egg Award to make sure his organization would extract as much learning as possible when people laid an egg on the job.[66] He figured that these eggs, so to speak, were really valuable assets the company had already paid for but hadn't benefited from. He asked managers to share their units' misadventures at the monthly meeting. After much apprehension, these confessions eventually became a favorite part of the session. The president decided to give a symbolic award to those managers who had the most egg on their faces and were courageous enough to deconstruct the experience. He concocted a simple and modest trophy—a L'eggs pantyhose plastic egg sprayed with gold paint—that signified the best mistake of the month.

At first, the lucky winners stashed their trophies in desk drawers and filing cabinets. Over time, however, winners began proudly displaying the trophies on their desks for an entire month. This sparked many opportunities to transfer knowledge whenever someone visited the office and wondered about that odd-looking trophy. Over time, the company president managed to change the organizational culture by celebrating eggs laid and hatched.

Strategic leaders must be mindful and relentless in creating a learning culture.[67] In entrepreneurial circles, talking about one's failure is a rite of passage, a necessary aspect of innovation. Sara Blakely, Elon Musk, Richard Branson, Larry Page, and countless others convey a consistent message: fail fast, learn deep, and move on. There are many ways to apply this valuable mindset in your own settings and teams, as follows.

Action Plan to Delve Deeply

Digging deep takes discipline, curiosity, and toughness. The ability to diagnose mistakes is rare and countercultural in most cases. Here are ideas you can try:

1. *Begin new projects by acknowledging what is difficult or unprecedented.* Conduct a *pre-mortem:* "How might this project or decision go wrong, or what would we do if we wanted to kill or reverse it?" This is a good way to anticipate why this project might fail.
2. *Conduct after-action reviews to extract insights.* Make the AAR a standard practice, as the US Army and many companies

do. Define mistakes and successes in terms of process more than outcomes, and *focus on process* to account for luck, timing, treatment effects, and other contextual influences.

3. *Shine a light on mistakes as sources of new learning.* Sara Blakely grew up in a home where her parents admired her for trying and failing, and she has incorporated this view into her leadership philosophy.

4. *Communicate lessons learned from mistakes so that your people can share, internalize, and apply these to future initiatives.* Think like Googlers and view setbacks as temporary, akin to a process of "time-released successes."

5. *Reach out to others at the first sign of trouble.* Don't hide or try to figure things out yourself: share your situation with those who can help. Be proud of trying. It shows that you can handle failure. Heed the advice of start-up investors Brad Smith and Whitney Johnson about rebounding quickly after a setback: just get up and try again.

6. *Publicize stories about failed projects that led to innovative solutions.* Praise those who learned from their errors and try to extract insights from near misses. Create your own version of the Golden Egg Award to help foster a genuine learning culture.

7. *Once your people appreciate the value of mistakes, elevate your game by making some mistakes on purpose.* You may be pleasantly surprised, just as David Ogilvy was when he ran ads that he and other thought wouldn't work. Consider opening a mistake bank.

THE DISCIPLINE TO LEARN: PULLING IT TOGETHER

Jane Wang always got excellent grades in school and was a conscientious student. That's why she couldn't believe she needed to improve her ability to learn. In reading about Sara Blakely, Elon Musk, and Google, she came to understand the difference between "learning" and "avoiding failure." Yes, she had tried things in the past, but only after she was pretty sure she would do well and had prepared sufficiently. She really did not like to fail, and this aversion ran deep in her family and culture. Could she change centuries of mental, cultural, and emotional programming aimed at avoiding mistakes? Based on the feedback from her manager, she had a choice: take a different approach to learning and move up in the company, or keep playing it safe and remain where she was now—or worse. She needed to upend how she felt about failure: instead of worrying about mistakes, she had to learn from them. She increasingly appreciated, having read a month earlier, that Procter & Gambles' CEO views mistakes as gifts.

The question now was how and where to start taking more chances, where to experiment without fretting over protocol. Just as hoping never moved a project forward, idle worrying never prevented setbacks. Like the employees of Samsung, Jane wanted greater exposure to the world and jotted down steps she could take that would expand her horizons culturally so she would be truly ready for the long game. Participation in the high-potential program seemed increasingly attractive. Another idea was to make a little bet on a new product introduction in one of the growth markets where her team needed to out-maneuver competition.

Certainly, learning could be fun, and she felt liberated by not having to be perfect all the time. She was getting excited about the opportunity she now had to put these ideas and initial actions together into her own strategic leadership plan. She was ready and eager to start *shaping her own future*, realizing that it would entail a few missteps here or there.

7 TWO VISIONARY LEADERS

Mandela and Barnes—Combining It All

IN THE VERNACULAR OF THE XHOSA LANGUAGE, *ROLIHAHLA* means "troublemaker." That is the name Hendry Mandela, a Thembu chief in South Africa, gave his newborn son in 1918. Hendry served as a senior adviser to the tribe's royal family. Whereas Hendry was illiterate and practiced his tribe's traditional religion, Rolihahla's mother was drawn to Methodism, an eighteenth-century religious movement that had splintered from the Church of England. When Rolihahla turned seven, she enrolled him in the local mission school, where he learned to read and write English and received the English name of Nelson.

Nelson Mandela became one of the most influential strategic leaders of the twentieth century. He developed a full range of cognitive, emotional, and behavioral abilities as well as organizational and strategic competencies that served him well over a long life. His achievements required not just an enthusiasm for *learning* but a capacity to *anticipate* outcomes and to *interpret* even the most subtle statements and events. While much of Mandela's greatness came from within, he needed the skills of making tough *decisions* under uncertainty, *aligning* people, and speaking truth to power. Further, without the ability and the courage to *challenge* long-standing rituals and beliefs, no man or woman could have accomplished what Mandela and his contemporaries—Mahatma Gandhi and Martin Luther King Jr.—did in their lifetimes.

This chapter looks at how effective leaders exercise all six disciplines systematically to advance their strategic agenda amid escalating volatility, uncertainty, complexity, and ambiguity—the world of VUCA. Conversely, failure to master all six disciplines often results in flawed or disappointing strategic leadership. To make the point, we profile two different leaders to contrast how they deployed the strategic leadership elements in concert. Although we describe each leader in terms of the six disciplines, the reality of leadership requires blending them together, much like a well-trained orchestra produces great music. We show how the exercise of these disciplines can either yield a greater overall effect (as in the first case) or limit success when any of the parts is out of synch (as in the second case).

The first profile is of Nelson Mandela, whose strategic leadership freed South Africa from apartheid and white minority rule. The second profile is of Dr. Albert C. Barnes, a gifted innovator who amassed a world-class collection of paintings from 1912 to 1951 and founded an educational institution whose mission was to cultivate a more intelligent and informed citizenry. Though Barnes's vision and accomplishments were truly remarkable, he undermined his own impact and legacy through leadership behaviors that proved detrimental to his long-term vision. His story holds important lessons for strong-willed leaders whose personalities or eccentricities may at times get in the way of achieving their aspirations. Mandela was largely a humble leader who managed to win the long game, in part due to his iron resolve. Dr. Barnes was equally strong-willed but often confrontational to a fault, which really hurt him in the long run. His intolerance of others and unwillingness to compromise diminished his ability to rally enough support around his ultimate educational goal.

NELSON MANDELA: A TALE OF UNCOMMON COURAGE AND VISION

On his deathbed, Hendry asked the regent of the Thembu tribe to educate his son beyond the academics of the Methodist school. So when Rolihahla was twelve, his mother walked with him on the five-mile journey from their village of Qunu to the Great Place of Mqhekezweni where he would henceforth live with the royal family. At the elbow of the eminent regent, Rolihahla witnessed tribal politics firsthand. The debates among leaders of the various tribes within the Xhosa nation awakened his interest in the discourse of justice. When Rolihahla turned sixteen he passed, as was the custom, into manhood through a painful circumcision ritual, during which he received small water rations and stayed isolated in a small hut for weeks to strengthen his character. Mandela continued his studies at Clarkebury Boarding Institute in Engcobo and the Wesleyan College at Fort Beaufort. He enrolled in the University of Fort Hare, where he encountered Marxist ideas, engaged in student politics, and was expelled with fellow student Oliver Tambo for participating in a student strike. He finished his degree by correspondence and enrolled in law school.

In 1942, Mandela began attending meetings of the African National Congress (ANC). The ANC had formed in 1912 to unite Africans in preserving their freedoms amid European imperialism, much as Gandhi organized the Natal Indian Congress in South Africa two decades earlier to assert the rights of Indians there. Mandela knew of *satyagraha*, Gandhi's policy of passive political resistance against British rule in India. Nonviolent protest appealed to the principled and cerebral Mandela as a long-term strategy.

With his schoolmate Oliver Tambo, Mandela helped to found the ANC Youth League (ANCYL) and was elected its national secretary in 1948—the same year Gandhi was assassinated in Delhi, and the year the National Party (NP), composed largely of Dutch-descended Afrikaners, came to power in Johannesburg. The NP promptly installed *apartheid*, which means "separateness" in Afrikaans. Apartheid was a policy of strict racial segregation that affected all nonwhite South Africans.[1] Enforcement was harsh and unrelenting. In 1953, the ANCYL worked with the Indian Congress to lead a nonviolent Defiance Campaign, the largest of its kind, against apartheid. Mandela was arrested, convicted, and sentenced to nine months of hard labor. The campaign got the United Nations' attention, and ANCYL membership skyrocketed. Despite the jail term and his commitment to political protest, Mandela still managed to pass the bar that year and, with Tambo, opened South Africa's first all-black law firm.

For the next eight years, Mandela advocated peaceful noncompliance and was frequently arrested and then acquitted for his nonviolent political protests. Then came the infamous Sharpeville Massacre, in which white police opened fire on some 20,000 mostly black unarmed protesters, killing or wounding 250.[2] The UN Security Council passed Resolution 134 condemning the NP's policies and enforcement, years after the NP had outlawed the ANC.[3]

How could a just man live by such unjust laws except by breaking them? Mandela changed his approach. He went underground to form *Umkhonto we Sizwe*, or "Spear of the Nation." This guerrilla wing of the ANC used various forms of targeted sabotage against the NP's harsh measures. Its bombings were aimed at government property, not people, and designed to limit collateral damage. The South African police state branded Mandela a communist terrorist, hunted him down, and convicted him of treason in 1964.[4] The judge spared him death but condemned him to life in prison on Robben Island, a penal colony reachable only by a long sea-ferry ride from Cape Town.

Nonetheless, Mandela managed to remain active in the underground resistance, passing messages through guards. Over time as his circumstances allowed, he honed the six leadership disciplines. We illustrate below how each element factored into Mandela's evolution as a leader, and we emphasize their functioning as a system.

Anticipate: The Force of Freedom

In 1985, with the South African state under continued threat of violence, global censure, and economic sanctions, the hard-line white president P. W. Botha publicly offered Mandela freedom if Mandela renounced violence and abided by apartheid. Mandela clearly saw that Botha sought to shift the blame for injustice from the government to Mandela himself. He did not fall for this transparent ploy. As a man, he very much desired to end decades of hard labor and isolation. As a leader, he saw clearly that freedom on Botha's terms would betray his followers and sabotage the ANC's long struggle for equality. Like the Reverend Martin Luther King Jr., Mandela scanned wide and saw that South Africa's system of social injustice and brutality could not survive. Apartheid's small-minded proponents could not hold their flawed positions against a global force favoring freedom, he felt, and so he continued to focus on the long game.

From Robben Island, he thought ahead and considered strategic consequences: his public rebuke of Botha's offer would embolden ANC members and his personal sacrifice would draw international attention as it had several times before. Mandela publicly replied to Botha: "What freedom am I being offered while the organization of the people remains banned? . . . What freedom am I being offered if I must ask permission to live in an urban area? . . . Only free men can negotiate. Prisoners cannot enter into contracts." Mandela decided to serve out his sentence in a cold, dark cell rather than exchange it for the larger political prison in which black South Africans de facto lived. As he anticipated, the world recoiled against the National Party's brutal police-state tactics and the global media portrayed the unyielding hard-nosed Botha as a pariah. Inside South Africa, business leaders increasingly challenged P. W. Botha and his successor F. W. de Klerk to change course.[5] Young whites voiced opposition to apartheid and racism in churches, schools, social clubs, markets, and places of work. Even the Dutch Reformed Church, whose Calvinist interpretations of the Bible had initially rationalized racial segregation, changed its views.[6]

Challenge: The Fall of Apartheid

Mandela stood out as a man of principle and dignity, willing to sacrifice his life for his beliefs. Prison life was harsh: bad food, worse bedding, a cold cell in the winter, and wall-to-wall loneliness. Despite these conditions, Mandela mustered energy to challenge his keepers. His very presence on Robben Island served to hold a mirror to the face of apartheid's leaders, and they could no longer look away from their failing strategy. Their hope had been to contain the black population in townships and to isolate them ethnically in newly created homelands such as Transkei, Bophutatswana, Venda, and Ciskei.[7] However, during the 1980s, black townships became better organized to protest and revolt against forced relocation. Mandela understood that his own plight symbolized that of his people and that his imprisonment propped open a window through which the rest of the world could view the evils of apartheid.[8] By word and deed, Mandela challenged the system that denied him liberty and would eventually cost South Africa's economy its commercial riches and freedom. Over time, business executives insisted upon change; the global boycotts of the apartheid regime during the 1980s hurt South Africa greatly, well beyond the decline in exports and GDP growth.

Botha's successor, F. W. de Klerk, realized that his party had painted itself into a corner. The Berlin Wall crumbled in 1989 and the Cold War was ending. South Africa had to change, too. In a seminal speech to Parliament in Cape Town in February 1990, de Klerk announced:

> Only a negotiated understanding among the representative leaders of the entire population is able to ensure lasting peace. . . . The season of violence is over. The time for reconstruction and reconciliation has arrived. . . . In this connection Mr Nelson Mandela could play an important part. . . . I wish to put it plainly that the Government has taken a firm decision to release Mr Mandela unconditionally.[9]

President de Klerk had called for democratic elections in 1994 (one man, one vote), which effectively meant that his white government would lose and become a minority party. While naively hoping that he could share power with the ANC's majority, de Klerk and his party accepted the results of the 1994 election: Mandela would become president of South Africa. And so, a remarkably peaceful and orderly transition took place in which the black majority held most political power. Mandela and de Klerk shared the Nobel Peace Prize in 1993 "for their work for the peaceful termination of the apartheid regime, and for laying the foundations for a new democratic South Africa."[10]

Interpret: Connecting Through Diversity and Forgiveness

Mandela studied what Robert Mugabe wrought in bordering Zimbabwe, a rich country known as Rhodesia when under British colonial

rule. Zimbabwe had become a failing nation under brutal dictator-
ship, and its lessons amplified what South Africa needed to avoid
if it did not want to wind up an economic basket case. Like Mandela, Mugabe had embraced Marxist ideologies at the University of
Fort Hare, had founded a resistance movement against white minority rulers, and had fought for black liberation in the 1960s. In
1980, once British rule had ended, the black population elected
Mugabe prime minister.[11] Mugabe's reign descended over time into
despotism. His grievances against the white minority played out in
his politics over several decades. Many white Zimbabweans fled the
country. Those who stayed lost their farms. When a fellow freedom
fighter challenged his leadership, Mugabe was brutal. As a consequence of Mugabe's internecine revenge, an estimated 20,000 to
30,000 people were murdered during the 1980s in Zimbabwe.[12]

Mandela recognized that South Africa could easily follow in
Zimbabwe's footsteps, unless he himself practiced racial harmony.
He realized he had to bring people together. That meant forgiving
without forgetting and sharing power with minorities in the population. "We have to surprise [the white minority] with restraints
and generosity," he said. A master of symbolism, Mandela invited
his prison guards to his presidential swearing-in ceremony. He
traveled to Orania, a small gated community of Afrikaners, to visit
the widow of Henrik F. Verwoerd, the primary architect of apartheid and South Africa's seventh prime minister until his assassination in office in 1966.[13] Mandela worked daily to raise all South
Africans above past injustices. He called on the best talent, black
and white, for his government; embraced Archbishop Desmond
Tutu's call for truth and reconciliation; and focused on a shared,
democratic future. Mandela truly envisioned a future resembling a
rainbow nation in which different ethnic groups would blend together as one.[14]

Mandela's interpretation of history, and how to shape the future, was on track. South Africa could prosper as a multiracial society only if its leaders mutually forgave each other. "I am working now with the same people who threw me into jail, persecuted my wife, hounded my children from one school to the other . . . and I am one of those who are saying: Let us forget the past, and think of the present."[15] We shall see whether, in the wake of Mandela's death in 2013, South Africa's new leaders can similarly rise to the occasion and reject the kind of destructive paths chosen by Mugabe. The former reign of Thabo Mbeki (who denied that AIDS was caused by HIV) and the current presidency of Jacob Zuma (who has faced many criminal charges) are not promising starts. The state remains at risk of failing but could recover from its current malaise if honest new leaders aspire to Mandela's vision of inclusion.

Decide: Calling for Calm, Calling for Unity

In 1993 Thembisile "Chris" Hani, a leader of the South African Communist Party, was assassinated by an anti-Communist Polish refugee in a racially mixed suburb of Johannesburg. Clive Derby-Lewis, a member of the South African Parliament, was given a life sentence for involvement in the assassination. Black South Africans cried "Murder most horrible" and accused Afrikaners and Mugabe-fearing Rhodesians (Zimbabweans) of importing skinheads and fascists from states of the former Soviet Union to do their dirty work.[16] Hani's assassination triggered a widespread demonstration against de Klerk's administration.

Mandela, released from prison in 1990, understood how precarious the situation was. He himself was still being called a Marxist because of his prior association with Hani. Chris Hani was charismatic and influential among the radical township self-defense groups that had splintered off from the ANC. Hani's South African Communist Party presented the only serious threat to Mandela's own party in the 1994 presidential elections. There would be rumblings that the ANC also had a hand in Hani's death.[17] Amid the risk of civil unrest and continued violence, Mandela rose to the occasion. He did not want ethnic or political warfare but a nation that could heal. He had the courage to call for peace when people wanted revenge. At the risk of losing political support, he made a bold decision and went on television to appeal for calm.

> Tonight I am reaching out to every single South African, black and white, from the very depths of my being. . . . The cold-blooded murder of Chris Hani has sent shock waves throughout the country and the world. . . . Now is the time for all South Africans to stand together against those who, from any quarter, wish to destroy what Chris Hani gave his life for—the freedom of all of us.[18]

Even though whites dominated top-level sports in South Africa, Mandela made a courageous decision to use sport as a means of healing: "Sport has the power to change the world. It has the power to inspire, it has the power to unite people in a way that little else does."[19] Just before the 1992 Olympics in Barcelona, the International Olympic Committee lifted its ban on South Africa's participation. At long last, South African athletes would compete. After questioning the initial decision to participate, Mandela reconsidered and explored his options, finally deciding to attend and support the mostly white athletes during the opening ceremony. "There is no doubt in my mind this is the correct decision," Mandela said. Of the ninety-five-person delegation, only eight were black. "I would have liked [the team] to be a reflection of our population, but there has to be a starting point."[20]

Mandela proudly wearing a Springbok jersey

In 1995, Johannesburg hosted rugby's biggest game, the Rugby World Cup. To black South Africans, rugby had come to represent racial discrimination—nearly all players were white—and while the Joburg Springboks were a world-class rugby team, the club had not been welcomed to compete on the world stage during apartheid, which was a deep blow to the white ruling class.

Black sports officials wanted to change the team's logo and jerseys to root out any association with apartheid. Not Mandela; he anticipated how uprooting such cherished symbols would alienate whites in the now black-led South Africa. He had the guts to tell his comrades, "That is selfish thinking. It does not serve the national interest."[21] Instead, he decided to challenge his own base and don a Springbok jersey for the final match. "Not in my wildest dreams did I think that Nelson Mandela would pitch up at the final wearing a Springbok on his heart," said Francois Pienaar,

South Africa's captain at the time. "When he walked into our changing room to say good luck to us, he turned around and my number was on his back. It was just an amazing feeling." As Mandela stepped out onto the field in the long-sleeved green and gold of the Springboks, 65,000 white rugby fans in Ellis Park erupted into a chant, "Nelson! Nelson! Nelson!"[22] It was another defining moment of his strategic leadership.

Align: Co-Creating the New South Africa

Elected South Africa's first black president in 1994, Mandela announced that he would serve only one term, even though two were permissible under the constitution. On the African continent, he was surrounded by post-colonial despots—not just Mugabe in Zimbabwe but also Kenneth Kaunda in Zambia, Yoweri Kaguta Museveni in Uganda, and Idriss Déby in Chad, to name just a few.[23] Clutching power to their breasts, these leaders were anything but inclusive: in several cases, whites and blacks outside the ruling ethnicity stayed in their own countries at great personal risk.

Mandela understood that rallying key players and bridging diverse interests in this complex country meant making room for others. Black supremacy was as depraved as white supremacy, in his view. Mandela knew that more than a billion people around the world would watch his inaugural presidential address on television and he used this speech—emphasizing the plural pronouns *we, us,* and *our*—to build bridges and align a deeply divided nation around a common vision:

> We have, at last, achieved our political emancipation. We pledge ourselves to liberate all our people from the continuing bondage of poverty, deprivation, suffering, gender and other discrimination. . . . We understand it still that there is no easy road to freedom. We

know it well that none of us acting alone can achieve success. We must therefore act together as a united people, for national reconciliation, for nation building, for the birth of a new world.[24]

By the time Mandela took office in 1994, he had met many high-profile business leaders from South Africa and around the world. To help win over former enemies and align them around Mandela's rainbow vision of South Africa, he would invite white leaders to help him with civic projects. After a devastating flood in the Eastern Cape, for example, Mandela called upon a prominent business leader to accompany him to the region. The executive expressed his regrets: an important prior appointment, he claimed, clashed with Mandela's request. Mandela's office assured the businessman that he would not miss his appointment. The executive had little choice but to accede to the president's call. Knowing that Mandela frequently used these occasions to request donations for public works, he quickly consulted with his financial director to determine a reasonable sum: 500,000 rand.

The South African Air Force flew the president and the executive to the East Cape. From there a military helicopter whisked the two from the airport to a large football stadium. As the helicopter descended onto the field, about 80,000 black schoolchildren—all adorned in crisp white shirts—simultaneously bowed to acknowledge Mandela's arrival. At that moment, Mandela planted his hand firmly on his guest's back and said rhetorically, "Now, I hope you are not going to disappoint me?" Instantaneously, the business leader decided to double his company's donation to 1 million rand (about $100,000 in those days).[25] That was how Mandela reached out to white leaders to co-create a new South Africa. He tried to allay their fears and change their attitude by getting them involved. By asking them to share in rebuilding the country, Mandela started to build bridges with his former enemies and fashioned a new inclusive vision for South Africa.

Learn: From Marxist Maxims to Capitalist Markets

Mandela, like his father Hendry, was both stubborn and quick to learn. He tried different tactics to survive in prison. It was there that he rose to prominence as a political leader, and where government officials would visit him. Sometimes, they flew him out to meet in secret with President Botha, and later with F. W. de Klerk, in Pretoria. In these situations, Mandela had to leverage complex political agendas to advance his cause. He befriended white guards who passed secret messages to the ANC, including drafts of his autobiography, which became an international best seller upon its release.[26] Mandela deliberately probed for information from the outside. He wanted to know what was going on politically. Each meeting provided a new piece of the puzzle: How far could he push? What were the real agendas? Who truly held the power?

Mandela faced a big challenge after his release from Robben Island: What should he do about the faltering economy? For most of his life, Mandela operated at the socialist and even the Marxist end of the political spectrum, while South Africa's white business community favored a privileged form of capitalism that benefited from apartheid.[27] Only when the international boycotts started to hurt their bottom lines did South African business leaders push for the abolishment of apartheid. Given the abuses he had witnessed, Mandela was suspicious of free markets and private ownership. So after his release from prison, he said, "The nationalization of the mines, banks and monopoly industries is the policy of the ANC, and a change or modification of our views in this regard is inconceivable."[28]

But he came to learn what decades of socialism had done to the states of the former Soviet Union. His thinking took a sharp turn in Davos, Switzerland. Professor Klaus Schwab, the founder of the World Economic Forum (WEF), had invited Mandela to speak to

WEF members in January 1992. There in Davos, Mandela met with leaders of the Communist parties of China and Vietnam. They told him: "We are currently striving to privatize state enterprises and invite private enterprise into our economies. . . . We are Communist Party governments, and you are a leader of a national liberation movement. Why are *you* talking about nationalization?"[29] Mandela learned that his peers viewed socialism as passé and communism as a discredited ideology. The key to growth was to unleash people's entrepreneurial desire to better themselves. A fairly regulated free market was a better mechanism to prosperity than a state-run economy. Considering its economic decline, South Africa needed a robust private sector.

Democracy and open markets did appeal to Mandela conceptually. Mandela's life struggle had been about personal freedom, which he came to realize required economic freedom. And so he was willing to experiment with a different economic model. "They changed my views altogether," Mandela told his biographer, Anthony Sampson. "We either keep nationalization and get no investment, or we modify our own attitude and get investment."[30] Some investors viewed Mandela's change of mind with skepticism. Was it just a ploy to attract foreign investment? But Mandela's transformation was genuine. He listened to the leaders of other countries and learned how the world had changed during his term in prison.

Shaping the Future in Service of a Vision

Mandela exemplifies how a strategic leader adjusts strategy and execution amid complex social, political, legal, and economic forces without compromising deeply held values. He never wavered on deep principles related to fairness, freedom, and human dignity, even though he did change his views about use of violence early in life and about economic systems later in life. Strategic leadership is not just about motivating people and creating political support to execute an initial strategy, but also about maintaining broad support through successive adjustments to the strategy.[31] That is why Mandela played the long game so well: he started by fighting for the freedom of his people and evolved into fighting for the human rights of *all* people, including Afrikaners. The implementation of this strategy required an unprecedented level of support from both blacks and whites at every phase. Nelson Mandela, affectionately known by his clan name *Madiba*, exercised all six disciplines of strategic leadership with great purpose, humility, and effect.

We next contrast Mandela's inspired use of the six disciplines with the case of Dr. Albert C. Barnes. Both were determined, controversial leaders with far-reaching visions. Mandela left a lasting, positive legacy. Although his successors thus far have not filled his shoes, during his lifetime he modeled the strategic leadership needed for South Africa's future.

Dr. Barnes died in a car accident in 1951. His legacy endures through the foundation that bears his name. In fact, the Barnes Foundation has become a premier tourist attraction since its move to Philadelphia in 2012. However, this move was controversial, the outcome of a protracted legal battle and in clear opposition to Dr. Barnes's written instructions.

Barnes had stipulated that everything in his collection be left exactly where it was at the moment of his death. His art could not be moved, lent to other institutions, or sold. The collection's stewards were to maintain the art in the Merion gallery, just outside of Philadelphia, in perpetuity precisely as he had designed and left it.

But other decisions he made throughout his lifetime and in his will would lead to mismanagement of the foundation's resources some fifty years later. We touch on the brilliance of Barnes, the choices he made, and the roots of this controversy to provide valuable insights for strategic leaders who have grand aspirations for the long game, yet little capacity to compromise, respect, and align others who don't buy in completely.

DR. ALBERT BARNES:
BOLD VISION AND TOUGH PERSONALITY

No one had an eye for Impressionist, Post-Impressionist, and Early Modern paintings quite like Dr. Albert C. Barnes. The art world has long known of Dr. Barnes's remarkable collection, a must-see for art lovers and students of art housed in a limestone gallery in Merion, a suburb of Philadelphia. He designed this gallery for educational purposes, not as a museum, having formed his foundation to serve as a school where students would study and view art using what he called the "objective method." This approach was radically different from the mainstream models then holding sway in the art world.

In some ways, Barnes was the "Warren Buffett of the art world," picking pieces according to his assessment of their fundamental artistic value, not according to market trends. Leading critics of his day had ridiculed Barnes's artistic judgment, but he proved to be ahead of his time. Barnes intended that his methods would teach ordinary people to think critically about art. More importantly, he saw this objective method as a means of educating people to function more intelligently in their lives. He believed that cultivating critical-thinking skills would lead to the greater actualization of the individual and greater potential for a more upwardly mobile, democratic society. That had been his own trajectory, and he wanted to share that opportunity broadly.[32]

Barnes had grown up in a poor working-class family in a rough Philadelphia neighborhood. He and his brother learned boxing to defend themselves. Barnes's mother recognized her son's gifts and hoped Albert would become a doctor. She valued education as a means of transcending their humble circumstances. When he was eight, she began taking him to Methodist church camp meetings. There he was exposed to the sights, sounds, rhythms, music, and dance of this branch of the Methodist church led by African-American ministers. Even though black and white congregants sat separately, they still shared a common experience—only seventeen years after the emancipation of slaves. Barnes said of these early experiences: "[The camp meetings] influenced my whole life, not only in learning much about the Negro, but in extending the esthetic phase of that experience to an extensive study of art."[33]

Barnes was a brilliant student. He graduated at the top of his class at Central High School, the premier public school in Philadelphia, and received a scholarship to the University of Pennsylvania, earning his medical degree by the age of twenty. He soon realized that his true passion was not clinical medicine but chemistry. He trained and worked as a chemist and pharmacologist in Germany before returning to Philadelphia to seek his fortune. His scientific background became an approach to life and would inform the questions he would pose about the essence of the artistic, creative experience. He came to see art as reflective of an adaptable intelligent human mind.[34]

Although Barnes was an acknowledged genius in art and business, few have examined him through the lens of strategic leadership for the long haul. From the vantage point of our six disciplines, we see towering strengths that led to innovative breakthroughs. We also note his inability to leverage all six disciplines, underscoring the importance of working toward a balanced and integrated leadership style.

Anticipate: An Eye for Intellectual Property

One important insight of Barnes as he pursued his first career in pharmacology was that he had more passion for inventing medical products than for practicing medicine. The use of silver in drugs especially captured his imagination. How could he create a silver compound that could be used as an antiseptic but wouldn't burn like silver nitrate? The answer came to him in a flash as he was drinking with a fellow graduate student in a beer garden in Germany. But the practical aspects of how to mix and commercialize his breakthrough solution had to wait until he finished graduate school.

To support himself in those years, Barnes offered his consulting services to the Mulford Chemical Company (which became part of Merck & Co.), spending all his spare time working on his pet project. He sought his client's permission to hire a special chemist, Hermann Hille from Germany, to develop a method for producing a silver compound that could be easily absorbed by humans. Once Barnes and Hille hit upon a technique that worked, they presented their findings at an academic conference, thereby establishing credibility. In 1902, they left Mulford Chemical to form Barnes & Hille, a commercial partnership that manufactured and marketed the compound that Barnes called Argyrol, after the Greek word for silver.[35]

Barnes trademarked Argyrol but chose not to patent it because the formula would be in the public domain once approved and could be freely copied once the patent would have expired (about 17+ years after issuance). He made this decision to protect the long-term secrecy of the compound so that other chemical companies could not produce Argyrol. He also maintained control of the manufacturing process rather than outsourcing production to third parties. This was novel, strategic thinking and showed a keen insight into the growth possibilities of the business.

To drum up interest in Argyrol, Barnes sent a sample to Dr. Edward Martin, a well-known surgeon and his former professor in medical school. Martin tested it and confirmed its efficacy over other antiseptics. Barnes implored Martin to write down his endorsement, which Barnes then copied and mailed to thousands of physicians—an unprecedented business move. In so doing, Barnes saw sooner than his competitors that soliciting expert testimonials and marketing directly to the prescribers themselves could yield great rewards, a move that made him millions.[36]

His business continued to prosper. When the stock market hit an all-time high in the summer of 1929, Barnes decided to cash out and devote all his resources to collecting art, which he had started doing years before. In July of that year, he sold his company to the Zonite Products Corporation for stock that he converted to cash. With uncanny timing, he earmarked the money for investing in art, not the stock market, so that when the Great Depression hit, he had plenty of cash on hand. The long global depression also meant that the art market was severely depressed, such that cash-rich Barnes in a cash-strapped world could acquire treasures at bargain prices.[37]

When he started collecting, Barnes focused on the work of artists he loved and considered to be high caliber, ignoring conventional opinions. The art he exhibited at the Pennsylvania Academy of Fine Arts, as a preview to the new Barnes Foundation's art collection, was received with derision by the art establishment. Barnes himself was publicly lampooned; the press depicted him as deranged.[38] But, like many strategic leaders who anticipate ahead of the pack, Barnes had the conviction to stay the course despite criticisms. He used his own criteria to evaluate what was distinctive in art, based on the objective method he developed and taught at his school. Clearly he was seeing sooner what the art world would later deem to be some of the most valuable works of this era.[39] Confident of his judgment, Barnes once said to a young Joseph Alsop, a Harvard student at the time and later an influential journalist, syndicated columnist, and art connoisseur, "Just remember, young man, these pictures you are going to see are the old masters of the future, *the old masters of the future!*"[40]

Barnes scanned wide to discover and promote new artists like Chaim Soutine, a Russian émigré working in Paris; Horace Pippen, an African-American painter who was then a student at the Barnes Foundation; and many lesser-known American artists like Alfred Maurer, Marsden Hartley, and Maurice Prendergast, before their work was recognized. He collected a variety of decorative, functional, and domestic art works as well as African sculptures imported from the west coast of Africa—art that others at times used as ballast for ships.[41]

There is no question that Barnes was prescient about what was important in art, and he mastered the long game of amassing an invaluable collection. However, he failed to adequately anticipate the future strategic peril his foundation would face long after his death. Considering his keen ability to anticipate future changes in the worlds of pharmaceuticals, business, and art, it is puzzling that he fell so short in this arena despite giving it much attention. Barnes wrote a very detailed will and testament including specific, but shortsighted and narrow, guidelines on all aspects of the foundation: "He gave people life-time jobs and capped their pay at 1951 levels. Investments could not be changed and many organizational policies were frozen. He could not see how this limited the growth potential

Dr. Barnes at home with his art

or choices for the Barnes."[42] The foundation honored his directives and stayed intact for thirty-seven years following his death. It was run by his educational director, co-author, and chosen successor Violette de Mazia.

However, following de Mazia's death in 1988, Barnes's vision began to fade. Under the stewardship of Lincoln University and Richard Glanton, who became president of the foundation, funds were squandered in legal battles with the residents of Merion and various other parties.[43] Despite Barnes's clear intent to preserve the foundation as it was in perpetuity, the courts concluded in 2004 that financial problems threatened the very existence of the collection. Moving the foundation just five miles into the cultural heart of Philadelphia, with the collection intact just as Barnes had designed it, was considered acceptable by the courts. The foundation would garner the financial support of the city's political and cultural power brokers who helped orchestrate the move. Since its opening in 2012, it has become the crown jewel of Philadelphia's center-city museums. But Barnes would have fought tooth and nail against the move, just as many of his followers battled to prevent it, as documented in the 2009 film *The Art of the Steal*.[44] That his beloved foundation might become a popular tourist stop open to any casual visitor was a detestable idea to Barnes. He was committed to serious students of art and abhorred any indiscriminate display of his paintings to the public.

Challenge: Disagreeing and Being Disagreeable

For many of Barnes's wealthy contemporaries, art served mostly as evidence of their social status and financial means. But for Barnes, art was a means to an end: it could be used to promote social emancipation through educating the practiced observer. He wanted to use art to open windows of learning. Few understood that Barnes curated his art and founded his school primarily to teach others how to think critically, systematically, and objectively. In so doing, he hoped to cultivate a more democratic society in which people from all social strata could participate fully and equally.[45] To Barnes, actualization of an individual's potential through education was the key to a better functioning society and a happier, more gratifying life for all. Like John Dewey, America's preeminent philosopher of education, Barnes embraced "the belief that there are no foregone conclusions in life. Destiny isn't written in the stars, or proscribed by class or race. People are the agents of their own fate."[46]

In what Barnes would call his educational experiment, he hung works of art on the walls of his Argyrol factory for his employees to enjoy and study. He held classes in philosophy and aesthetics, and freely discussed racial issues with the factory's African-American workers. Here is how factory administrator Mary Mullen explained the intent behind Barnes's experiments: "The object of education is to find one's self in the world and to make one's self at home there."[47]

Barnes challenged the traditional values of the art community. The exterior design of the original Barnes Foundation in Merion combined a strong African motif and Cubist bas-reliefs by Jacques Lipchitz on the façade of the Beaux Arts building—choices antithetical to the classicism more conventionally appreciated at the time. In this way, Western and non-Western art traditions were united and prized as equally important expressions of the human aesthetic experience.

But Barnes sometimes went too far in the way he challenged convention, providing an important lesson for strategic leaders with strong contrarian views. He believed he had to fight hard to break existing mental models that he considered inadequate but in doing so he could be adversarial to a fault. For example, Sidney Fiske Kimball, a pioneer in architectural preservation, admired Barnes and toured his collection from time to time. When the Philadelphia Museum of Art board appointed Kimball director, he reached out to his old friend Barnes and started to bring various guests to tour Barnes's collection. But Barnes reacted badly. He felt that Kimball was exploiting their friendship because he and his peers failed to understand what the art meant to Barnes; they failed to see its educational and social mission. Barnes had little respect for people who merely gazed casually at museum art collections or used them for amusement or social-climbing. Kimball apologized profusely, but Barnes rebuffed him and would never forgive what he saw as a betrayal of his values. When Kimball invited Barnes to show some of his paintings in the Philadelphia Museum of Art, Barnes wrote a letter in which he replied viciously that the invitation "would make a horse laugh" and "would be offensive to the intelligence," were it not "so provincial and embedded in the matrix of the stereotyped blah which comes to us so often from performers who would like to annex us as a sideshow to their circuses."[48]

Although this diatribe clearly reflects Barnes's strong views about his mission, and his disrespect for patrons of museums for whom art is merely another form of entertainment, such an aggressive response was counterproductive to his strategic leadership. Whatever the validity of Barnes's point, it got lost in the style of his attack. An effective act of challenge pinpoints areas of difference without mocking the individual. Barnes contrasts strongly in this regard with how Nelson Mandela spoke to P. W. Botha or F. W. de Klerk during their negotiations. Mandela was as tough as Barnes but showed far more respect for his opponents overall. Mandela understood that blacks and whites would have to live together if South Africa was to prosper, whereas Barnes was unable to find a middle ground with those who did not appreciate his view for the proper role of art in society.

The letter Barnes wrote to Kimball was not an anomaly; there were other similarly nasty, condescending letters and poison-pen newspaper articles aimed at those he considered too academic or closed-minded. His contempt blinded him to the consequences of these acts and, even worse, blinded others to the potential greatness of his contribution. In this regard, he played the long game very poorly, with low strategic acumen and far too much emotion.

His friend and educational partner John Dewey, who greatly admired Barnes's vision, intelligence, and courage, foresaw the risk he was taking—that Barnes could be his own worst enemy—and cautioned him accordingly. In a letter, Dewey warned Barnes: "A policy of even ten percent vituperation, to say nothing of fifty percent, will gradually and surely alienate, or render access difficult to, the persons whom you are concerned to reach. One group after another will fall away, and you will [be] left with simply a few courses at the foundation itself attended by a comparatively small number of persons."[49] Like other strong-willed entrepreneurs and geniuses who were ahead of their times, such as the brilliant architect Frank Lloyd Wright or the incomparable Steve Jobs who built Apple, Barnes could not control his compulsion to challenge aggressively. In his case, this ultimately undermined the full realization of his grand vision.

Interpret: Plastic Means and the Wall Ensemble

An integral part of Barnes's genius was his approach to interpreting art differently, using an objective method rather than a subjective approach of conjecture and personal opinion. Ross Mitchell, former gallery director of the Barnes Foundation and now executive director of the Violette de Mazia Foundation, explained in an interview that Dr. Barnes's objective method reflected his scientific background. In an era of science and rationality, he created a rational, logical approach to defining what makes a successful painting.[50] Barnes wanted viewers to concentrate on the universal visual qualities expressed within the two-dimensional world of paint and canvas, rather than on *its subject* or the storyline beyond the canvas such as the artist's biography or the symbolisms of the time period.

He taught people to look at what he labeled the "plastic means"—namely color, light, line, and space—to appreciate broad human qualities or "aesthetic aspects." Barnes believed that "a painter's worth is determined precisely by his ability to make the fusion of plastic means forceful, individual, characteristic of his own personality."[51] With this focus, he amplified aspects of paintings that others overlooked in order to get to the artists' intent and technique.[52] Barnes was not just a collector; he had an insatiable intellectual curiosity. He went deep in his pursuit, becoming a world-class expert on Renoir, Matisse, Cezanne, and other Impressionist, Post-Impressionist, and Early Modern artists, writing definitive books about them based on his theories.

Barnes read widely, discovering deep connections between his own views and those of philosophers like William James, John Dewey, and Bertrand Russell.[53] At age forty-six, Barnes started attending Dewey's seminars at Columbia University. He formed a deep friendship and intellectual partnership with Dewey that lasted for the rest of their lives. Dewey served as the first educational director of the Barnes Foundation.

Barnes devised an often misunderstood pedagogy, the "Wall Ensemble," based on his unique interpretation of the aesthetic linkages between very different forms of art. By juxtaposing art from different periods in wall compositions of paintings, sculpture, metal works, furniture, textiles, and other crafts, he connected the aesthetic dots across traditions, mediums, and cultures to help others gain insight and make their own thoughtful interpretations. Barnes offered these novel perspectives so that his students would come to understand art by applying the objective method. It was about discovering patterns of universal qualities rather than reading expert opinion or being told what to see. Violette de Mazia, lifelong director of education at the Barnes Foundation and his frequent co-author, once wrote:

In our gallery this material is purposely arranged to excite the student's curiosity as to why these apparently disparate objects are placed in the same room, even, at times, on the same wall. . . . The student, at first disconcerted by the break with the conventional, seeks a new orientation. . . . [H]e discovers their common denominator of human values and meanings and their common source in human nature.[54]

Decide: Easier to Choose Painters Than Partners

Barnes made many consequential personal and business decisions: he chose chemistry over clinical medicine, entrepreneurship over corporate life, direct marketing and manufacturing over patenting. He collected art for its aesthetic qualities and preferred investments in art over those in the stock market. Once Argyrol was a success and selling well, he made a gutsy call not to patent the drug so as to keep it secret. He bought out his partner Hermann Hille to secure complete control of the enterprise. He commissioned his high school classmate, the painter William Glackens, to scout Europe and acquire pieces for his art collection. His first purchase of a Picasso cost only $100, a hefty sum compared to the $50 spent on his first Matisse.[55] He purchased paintings he loved—paintings that dealers regarded as secondary—and at times paid higher prices at auctions than anyone expected. Many in the art world regarded him as insane: "[T]here was derisive laughter from some of the worthy dealers and others. . . . As the sale proceeded, their derision turned to indignation, for they saw all their standards of value shattered."[56] But Barnes held firm and had the courage to buy art that he valued, at prices that later turned out to be exceptional bargains.

Facing the reality of his own mortality, Barnes grappled with the weighty decision of choosing a worthy institutional partner that would continue the mission of the Barnes Foundation after his death. The many options he explored included overtures to his alma mater, the University of Pennsylvania; the Philadelphia Museum of Art; and the Pennsylvania Academy of the Fine Arts. But the gap in philosophy and vision between Barnes and these institutions was too wide. He refused to compromise his ideals. It is ironic that the fiercely independent Barnes, who railed against academia and the art establishment, felt compelled to seek out an academic partner rather than keep the Barnes Foundation independent.[57]

Barnes finally selected Lincoln University, the country's oldest black university, located forty miles from Barnes's country estate. Lincoln University resonated deeply with Barnes given his lifelong connection to African-American culture. Lincoln's outsider status appealed to Barnes's anti-establishment bent. Aligning his foundation with Lincoln University during a time of racial segregation took real guts. But Barnes was fearless in the pursuit of his educational principles and had the emotional fortitude to hold up under pressure and derision.

Align: The Cost of Alienation

Barnes was a bold man with an audacious plan for a better, stronger, truly democratic society that he felt could be achieved only by educating those most often overlooked. He educated his students not by asking them to memorize information but by cultivating their creativity and independent thinking skills. Barnes used art as a tool to expand strategic and critical-thinking capacity. He employed art as a means of teaching people how to observe, analyze, and understand their own experiences in the world. To take this mission to the larger society, however, he would need others beyond his inner circle to join his cause. This proved an obstacle too great for him to overcome—and therein lies a profound lesson for strategic leaders who have great vision and strong will. His inability to collaborate, rally others to the cause, and build bridges to his adversaries was his great blind spot. Barnes was unable to align broader groups of the key stakeholders he needed—from the worlds of art, education, and society—in order to make his dream a reality beyond the walls of his foundation.

Barnes did build a strong, loyal team of advisers and artists. He rallied key players and great minds in psychology, education, and philosophy such as Bertrand Russell and John Dewey. Dewey considered the Barnes Foundation's educational program to be "the most thorough-going embodiment of what I have tried to say about education"[58]—incredible praise and validation from "the Father of American Education." Barnes collaborated with Dewey so that his curriculum and approach would succeed in lifting people up from poverty and obscurity.

Richard Wattenmaker, former director of the Archives of American Art at the Smithsonian Institution and a former instructor at the Barnes Foundation, wrote:

> Dewey saw in Barnes a man who was willing to put to a practical test many of the philosopher's social and educational ideas and the values animating them . . . [but someone who] . . . could not be toned down, intimidated, or forced to "behave" for convention's sake. Over the years Dewey winced at some of his friend's blunt tactics and exasperating proclivities for provocation, but although he sometimes urged Barnes to handle people more gently and even to hire a press agent to put across his plans, he not-so-secretly admired him as an individual who could not be daunted.[59]

Ironically, Barnes mistook Dewey's support as a justification to disregard others. "Given Dewey's sanction for his ideas, Barnes saw no need to bow or to be diplomatic to 'lesser authorities' such as professors, administrators, museum directors and others he regarded as mere functionaries."[60] This was a mistake. Barnes alienated too many key players. He verbally boxed with social elites who did not understand or agree with his views. Rather than finding ways to engage and build bridges with adversaries, as we saw in the Mandela profile, he fought with them. Barnes's own alma mater, the University of Pennsylvania, ignored his overtures about administering the foundation after Barnes's death because he had offended too many Penn officials. In his follow-up "poison pen" letters to those who rejected him, Barnes castigated them rather than simply reiterating his deep commitment to social and educational values.[60] He lacked the patience or willingness to find common ground with those he considered lesser minds or who did not appreciate his grand design. His uncompromising standards and innate stubbornness burned many bridges and irrevocably damaged essential relationships with powerful people, many of whom just did not want to deal with him anymore.

In short, whether out of purity of purpose or pride, intolerance, and self-sabotage, Barnes was his own worst enemy. He had a transcendent vision and great financial means but too few allies. In the end, despite the Barnes Foundation's success as a popular first-class art museum to visit, it has failed to achieve Barnes's grander mission. This sentiment was expressed well by Edward Sozanski, the principal art critic for the *Philadelphia Inquirer*, at the time of the foundation's move to the city.

The closing of Merion not only marks the end of an era, it also represents a radical transformation in the nature of the institution. . . . [T]he essential spirit of the place—its genius loci—and a good deal of Albert C. Barnes as well, will be left behind. Barnes Parkway will resemble Barnes Merion in some respects. . . . But the Replica (or, if you prefer, the Faux Barnes) will be a different institution, a museum with members instead of a school. No more strolls through the Merion arboretum . . . and, most important, no more historical context. . . . Why is this important? Because

Barnes Merion is not only one of the world's greatest private art collections, it's also a *Gesamtkunstwerk,* a comprehensive artwork in itself. Besides painting, sculpture, and decorative arts galore, Merion also embodies and evokes architecture, horticulture, educational philosophy, American social history, and the personality and taste of the founder.[62]

Learn: A Pioneer in Peer Learning, Training, and Development

By nature, Barnes was curious, smart, and disciplined. He was his own first pupil, having taught himself boxing, foreign languages, science, marketing, philosophy, and art. He applied his deep understanding of the scientific method to fields of art and education. He instinctively delved beneath the surface of these subjects and directly tapped authorities such as painters Glackens and Matisse, philosophers Dewey and Russell, and art connoisseurs Leo Stein and Paul Guillaume. In the process, he became a world-class art scholar, which is to say that he cultivated a keen eye for talent—much like what every CEO needs to do. He articulated his thought leadership in books and in essays such as "The Art in Painting."[63] He was also willing to take risks by hiring and cultivating talented people in his foundation even though they may have lacked traditional training in the arts. One notable case was Violette de Mazia, his educational director, whom Barnes hired just ten days after she arrived in Philadelphia from England. She came to Barnes through an employment agency. He also put workers from his factory in prominent roles at the foundation, mostly with great and enduring success.[64] Thanks to this approach, his former bookkeeper Mary Mullen would write a scholarly article, "An Approach to Art," that is still used to illustrate the objective method.[65]

Trained as a scientist, Barnes continually experimented, tried unusual things, and refined his ideas. He traveled to Europe to learn from artists and art critics like the Steins. In a letter to Gertrude Stein, Barnes explained how his analytical method evolved over time so that what he once valued no longer appealed to him, even though he had paid good money for those pieces. Barnes developed an especially close relationship with Leo Stein, an influential critic and promoter of twentieth-century art who became his mentor. As Wattenmaker points out, "The notion of a disciplined, scientific approach to art appealed to Barnes, and Stein had the experience and knowledge to provide the theoretical underpinnings and insights Barnes sought."[66]

Barnes especially experimented in his gallery. During classes, teachers took paintings off the walls, compared them to others, and even held them upside down to see the paintings' aesthetic qualities more clearly than its subject. Moreover, Barnes kept moving pieces around, testing different ensembles, tirelessly seeking the optimal conditions for learning.

Barnes's pursuit of knowledge also infused his corporation's culture. His company's development programs for employees were far ahead of the times; they were learning-centered and truly diverse, covering life issues meaningful to the employees such as gender-based violence and racial discrimination. The program's curriculum looked more like Google University today than anything corporations typically provided factory workers then or since. Barnes's female and African-American employees enjoyed equal opportunities at a time when this was certainly not the norm. Employee Mary Mullen spoke of the voluntary nature of factory classes and the *esprit de corps* that propelled workers— black and white, male and female, young and old—to study and discuss aesthetics as well as psychology together. Dewey encouraged Barnes to start his foundation based on Barnes's learning experiments with his workforce. As Barnes wrote, "I never intended to start a foundation until Dewey urged me to after he saw for himself our experiment with a group of mixed white and black people."[67]

Group learning was a unifying and democratizing force. "We never needed a boss," Barnes told *The Saturday Evening Post* in 1942. "We had a common respect for the personality of each employee. Each participant evolved his or her own method of doing a particular job in a way that fitted into the common needs."[68] These examples reflect a progressive visionary who was experimenting with many elements to expand creative and critical-thinking processes.

An Aspirational Vision for Shaping the Future

Barnes's personal journey molded a belief system that was a powerful driving force, as explained by one of his many biographers, Henry Hart:

> The key to Dr. Barnes' personality was that he believed in human perfectibility and was messianic about it. He believed in it because he was convinced he had proved its feasibility in his own life. . . . All, he never tired of saying, because he had embraced, and utilized, ideas that have validity in the real world. . . . Had he embraced other ideas, he believed, he would not have been the man he was.[69]

Barnes did indeed shape his own future for better and for worse. Although he did not achieve all his transformative goals, his successes and shortcomings illustrate the power of the six disciplines of strategic leadership. He mastered some to a great degree but was never able to embrace other key disciplines such as alignment or learning from his interpersonal mistakes. His life provides useful lessons for those who aspire to lead more strategically and shows that leaders must continuously address their gaps while playing to their strengths.

ENVISION: THE COHESIVE POWER
OF STRATEGIC VISIONS

Barnes and Mandela were stubborn and feisty outsiders. The status quo didn't just frustrate them; it offended their sense of justice and possibility. Transformational leaders such as Pope Francis and Richard Stephenson, founder of the Cancer Treatment Centers of America, develop powerful strategic agendas to reimagine worlds they consider intolerable. Their strategic visions provide an organizing framework to blend multiple disciplines into a coherent path forward. Without this capacity to *envision and architect* their own change plan, leaders are vulnerable to management fads, stock market twitchiness, or other biases that can pull them right and left.

Organizational life is complex. We think of a leader's vision less as a magnetic pole that pulls everyone in one direction than as a surgeon in the operating room adapting his or her decisions, and the actions of staff, to deal with the unexpected within a broader context. The intentions and visions of leaders, like those of artists engaged in the act of creation, are continually influenced by myriad factors encountered along the way.

Mandela and Barnes did not have strong visions early in their lives; at first, they sought only to right perceived wrongs. Over time, however, their skirmishes with the world sharpened their sense of timing and strategic choice. Our six disciplines represent a systems view of leadership. Each discipline works with the others, sometimes complementing, sometimes supplementing, and often interwoven. Leaders who start with a strong sense of direction can use the six disciplines to reach their destination. Leaders without a well-formed vision can call on their abilities to anticipate, challenge, and interpret the world around them to envision a different future. Strategic leaders have the courage to make strong commitments once they have a clear destination in mind. But they also adjust their visions, as we saw with Mandela and Barnes, in response to a continual flow of inputs. Then they re-align the people around them and jointly learn whatever they need to know next in the world of VUCA.

The envisioning process is goal-directed but subject to the vagaries of context: where stakeholders are pushing, what customers are demanding, what competitors are doing, how regulations are changing, what crises are lingering or looming. Such sensitivities to circumstance make strategy very path-dependent and explain why the best-laid plans often go astray. This view does not deny that leaders must set explicit strategies; rather, it emphasizes that they must also accept that few strategies survive contact with the real world.

In most cases, strategy emerges when bottom-up forces influence top-down plans, and we can often fully understand its realization only in hindsight. Our view of strategic leadership highlights its dynamic and iterative nature. Strategic leaders learn from mistakes, experiment, develop options, and continually evolve. In pursuit of a vision, successful strategies are highly adaptive, and over time the use of the six disciplines becomes nuanced, synergistic, and purposeful.

Consider Mandela and Barnes. Whereas Mandela reached out and embraced those who scorned him, Barnes pushed back and engaged in unproductive conflict. Whereas Mandela's humility opened his detractors' hearts and minds, Barnes's stubbornness closed them, just as John Dewey had cautioned him. Mandela learned early that "resentment is like drinking poison and then hoping it will kill your enemies." He asked, "Do not judge me by my successes, judge me by how many times I fell down and got back up again." When Mandela passed away, people around the world expressed their gratitude for the moral force of his vision and work and celebrated his achievements.[70]

Barnes's is a tale of extraordinary accomplishment, but ultimately he was not able to achieve his most far-reaching aspirations. He anticipated almost everything except the fate of his own institution. His anti-establishment challenges served an important purpose and created breakthroughs in art appreciation and education, yet his rigidity in relationships was counterproductive. He did not have the wisdom or temperament to forge alliances with his detractors or those who didn't understand his mission. Instead, he burned bridges. When his foundation fell upon hard times because of mismanagement, the protests against relocation of the Barnes collection were too little too late. The cantankerous Dr. Barnes was a genius in business and art but not in diplomacy. In striving toward his perhaps utopian vision for social change, he was a flawed leader.

Both Mandela and Barnes were determined outsiders, operating for long stretches of time at the edges of their respective societies in an attempt to inspire transformational change. We leave it to historians to judge their legacies and long-term impact. Their acts of strategic leadership are much clearer: they provide valuable insights about the differing approaches and styles of leveraging our six disciplines.

EPILOGUE:
BE MORE STRATEGIC
Your Personal Plan

W E'VE FOLLOWED JANE WANG THROUGHOUT THE BOOK, since her boss Lee Azner gave her some tough feedback: "You're a great operational leader, Jane—but Brazelton Global needs you to be more strategic." She wouldn't advance unless she *demonstrated* increased strategic leadership ability. Like thousands of managers, Jane had only a vague idea about what "being more strategic" meant, and she lacked the specifics needed to translate this into action. Unlike Azner, Jane's vice president and director of Asia Pacific operations at Brazelton, we've thought a lot about the Wayne Gretzkys of the world who "skate to where the puck is going."

Every profession has people who not only think and act strategically but also inspire others to join them in doing what needs to be done in a world of volatility, uncertainty, complexity, and ambiguity—even when what needs to be done is unclear. That is what strategic leadership is all about.

We've studied what sets strategic leaders apart from those who merely excel at operations or execution under normal conditions. Strategic leaders don't necessarily do any one thing superbly all the time. They just apply our six disciplines consistently well when they need to: anticipate, challenge, interpret, decide, align, and learn. There are times when strategic leaders are required to anticipate events and interpret data to excel; other times, they need to decide what to do, align people around that decision, and manage blowback. Still other times, they must challenge the interpretation of evidence and learn from failure. At all times, they need to reward these behaviors in others. Our point is that the best strategic leaders are ready and able to call on any or all of the six disciplines as needed to envision, shape, or execute a strategic direction.

These six disciplines are grounded in research, reflect best practice, entail tools and methods, require skill building, and, above all, take resolve and dedication to develop. In the first six chapters, we isolated and broke down each of the disciplines into discrete parts and concrete actions, just as athletic trainers do for every set of muscles in the body. In Chapter 7, using the profiles of two powerful leaders, we showed how the six disciplines work as a system. Now, as we wrap up our book, we want to inspire you to customize a strategic leadership plan that fits your own aspirations, so you can shape your own future. We shall explain how to use our framework and tools to diagnose patterns, strengths, and gaps in your own capabilities. Ideally, you should do the same assessment for your team, individually and collectively, to create your skill-building agenda.

AN AGENDA FOR STRATEGIC LEADERSHIP

While creating a game plan is straightforward, developing new habits will take you outside your comfort zone. If that's not the case, then you're not stretching or looking in the mirror hard enough.

246

Traversing this agenda requires dedication, patience, and tenacity. Just as you don't learn to speak a foreign language overnight, you don't become a better strategic leader instantly. Paraphrasing the old adage: It is not your will to win but your will to *practice* that matters most. You need both honesty and humility in your self-assessment, courage in confronting your weaknesses, and openness in reaching out to others for help. As we emphasized in Chapter 2, on the discipline to challenge, you must *open the window* to take in fresh perspectives and frank input from colleagues. You must also *look in the mirror* to address the biases and fears that hold you back.

The action plans for developing each discipline will take time because of the simple reality that a large part of your day involves short-term firefighting. But we have seen strategic leaders transcend short-term pressures by reprioritizing various tasks, delegating or postponing less critical ones, taking the long view, learning from role models, and bringing closure to lingering decisions. In due time, such leaders become learning fanatics. Steadily, they reawaken their curiosity and begin thinking from the outside in, and develop an acuity for the future. Here is how to get ready for the long game:

1. Assess how well you now master each of our six leadership disciplines.
2. Continue to play to your strengths by building on what comes most naturally to you.
3. Focus deeply on the big gaps and address those most critical for your situation.
4. Select the right tools and methods from each chapter to bridge the most crucial gaps.
5. Create a team plan in order to nurture strategic leadership in yourself and others.
6. Leverage support from others in your organization and beyond to hone your skill set.

As an illustration, let's look at what Jane should do overall, building on the preliminary plans she already has for each discipline as summarized at the end of each previous chapter.

Mapping Jane's Profile

To assess the extent to which Jane practices the six leadership disciplines, she conducted an honest self-assessment using the Strategic Leadership Assessment survey below. For each item, Jane rated her behavior on a Likert scale from "rarely" does (1) to "almost always" does (7) the action described.

STRATEGIC LEADERSHIP ASSESSMENT				
	How strongly do these statements describe your behavior? Rate yourself from 1 to 7, where 1 is "rarely" and 7 is "almost always."	*Self-rating*	*Others' ratings (rounded to nearest whole number)*	*What instances come to mind?*
1	**Anticipate**			
a	*Scan wider, from the outside in:* See market uncertainty as a source of potential advantage; gather information from a wide network of experts; study innovators inside and outside your industry.	2	2	
b	*See sooner, from the future back:* Track industry trends and uncertainties; foresee the changing needs of customers; predict competitors' likely moves and reactions.	2	1	
	Average	**2.0**	**1.5**	
2	**Challenge**			
a	*Open the window:* Seek out diverse views to see multiple sides of an issue; challenge long-standing assumptions and conventional wisdom.	3	2	
b	*Look in the mirror:* Reframe an important problem from several angles to understand root causes; encourage both constructive criticism and creative thinking to surface new perspectives.	4	3	
	Average	**3.5**	**2.5**	

3	Interpret		
a	*Amplify weak signals:* Develop deep insights; move fluidly between details and the big picture; leverage both analytic reasoning and intuition.	2	2
b	*Connect the dots:* Explore multiple working hypotheses before jumping to conclusions; demonstrate curiosity and an open mind.	4	3
	Average	*3*	*2.5*
4	**Decide**		
a	*Explore options:* Evaluate multiple options; determine trade-offs, risks, and unintended consequences; balance speed and rigor when making complex decisions.	2	3
b	*Show courage:* Show the courage to make tough choices; champion innovative solutions and risk-taking; balance long-term investment for growth with short-term pressure for results.	3	5
	Average	*2.5*	*4*
5	**Align**		
a	*Rally key players:* Rally your team around a compelling strategic vision; reach out to those with a stake in your initiatives; communicate intentions early, clearly, and continuously.	6	6
b	*Bridge differences:* Pinpoint and address conflicting interests among stakeholders; seek to understand and bridge cultural differences.	6	6
	Average	*6*	*6*
6	**Learn**		
a	*Experiment widely:* Encourage experiments and failing fast; expose yourself to models and cultures outside your own.	2	2
b	*Delve deeper:* Establish regular checkpoints and after-action briefs; course-correct on the basis of disconfirming evidence; extract and communicate lessons regularly.	4	5
	Average	*3*	*3.5*

* A version of this condensed survey was completed by more than twenty-two thousand global executives and published in "Strategic Leadership: The Essential Elements," *Harvard Business Review*, January 2013. An even more comprehensive Strategic Aptitude Survey is available at www.decisionstrat.com.

To make sure she wasn't in denial, or blind to her shortcomings, Jane asked some colleagues to evaluate her as well. They independently confirmed that her self-ratings lined up reasonably well with their observations and experiences of her. Using this assessment, we can construct a strategic leadership profile for Jane that visualizes her performance on all six elements. The solid lines show Jane's own scores; the dashed lines are the mean scores her colleagues gave her.

Jane's Current Strategic Leadership Scores

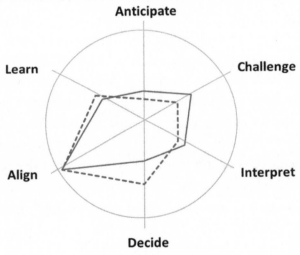

Jane is weakest in *Anticipate* and strongest in *Align*.

Interpreting Jane's Score and Crafting a Plan

The chart shows Jane's biggest weakness, *anticipating what's to come*. That fits with Lee's performance review: he criticized her for not keeping abreast of market changes, such as being surprised by competitors' moves and missing important shifts in customer needs. Although there are several aspects to the discipline of anticipating, the survey revealed Jane's biggest gap to be *seeing sooner*. Because of her weakness here, Brazelton's market share was declining, along with Jane's upward mobility and personal development.

A good starting point for Jane is the *Action Plan to See Sooner* detailed in Chapter 1, which lists practical suggestions for setting priorities that she then discussed with Lee, her team, and colleagues who were participating with her in Brazelton's high-potential program. Jane selected a few actions that would address the feedback she received and be relatively easy for her to implement. Rather than just catch up with the competition, her team needs to leapfrog and stay ahead of competitor moves and changing customer preferences:

+ *List important threats and opportunities that you recently missed. Be honest with yourself. Why did you miss them?*

Jane was careful not to blame others. If people weren't telling her what she needed to know, it was because she hadn't asked them to and hadn't set up a channel or expectation to ensure communications. She realized that she spent her time on what she could control, on operations under way; the more she did that, the more she placed her group in a reactionary mode to changing markets and competitive dynamics.

+ *Talk to your customers, suppliers, and other partners regularly to understand their challenges. Block out at least an hour each week and make an initial list of people or organizations to contact. List and discuss the key uncertainties in their industry.*

Jane was surprised when she discovered that a number of Chinese customers were tweeting about Brazelton on Weibo, China's equivalent of Twitter. She planned to talk with Brazelton's marketing and customer service department to identify all the other customer touch points in social media.

✦ *Analyze fast-growing rivals, especially nontraditional ones, and examine which moves puzzle you and why. Use this analysis to form the basis of competitive briefing books that allow you to anticipate and counter competitor moves.*

Jane realized she was not sufficiently well informed to anticipate the moves of her main rivals. She assigned teams of two to do a deep analysis of the top three competitors gaining the most market share. One was a newcomer, another was a growing threat, and a third was Brazelton's long-standing, traditional competitor in the market. Jane decided to develop short profiles that would capture each rival's strategic intent and business model. This would allow her and her team to do a better job of predicting competitive moves.

Next, Jane and her boss performed a similar analysis for each of the other disciplines where there was also a large gap. She developed a concrete plan to strengthen her abilities to *Challenge, Interpret,* and *Learn.* She was also determined to build on her strong ability to *Align.*

First, she leveraged her alignment skills by actively rallying her team to help implement her new change initiatives. This reinforced her image as a leader who can get things done.

Second, she reached out to new stakeholders who could provide more insight about the market, customers, or competition. She connected with a coach who helped address her largest gaps in the other skill sets—particularly *Challenge* and *Learn,* as these required her to take more risk. When she *looked in the mirror* she had to admit that risk-taking and stepping out of the known, were areas in which she needed to improve.

Third, she volunteered to mentor another Brazelton manager—one who rated high on anticipating and challenging—on his weak ability to align. Apart from the positive halo that such coaching generosity radiates, it actually improved her ability to *Learn*. The best way to learn, after all, is to teach.

HOW TO BUILD YOUR OWN PLAN

Jane wrestled with a deeper question: how best to take advantage of her strengths while tackling weaknesses. There is no one-size-fits-all answer here, except "it depends." It depends on your role, your career expectations, and industry dynamics. If it's still early in your career, then you are still adaptive enough to correct major deficiencies, addressing each in turn so that they will not handicap your growth potential. Also, you may wish to adjust your career path so that you can build on your innate talents to make an impact as a strategic leader. If *anticipating* is your strength, and you have mastered the associated technical skills, then roles in strategic planning, consumer research, or financial projections should come naturally. In the short run, shore up your weaknesses so that you progress toward goals and maneuver into positions where your strengths match the success factors of the organization or industry. In the long run, relying on any single strength at the expense of others is akin to placing all your leadership eggs into one basket. We recommend a portfolio approach, where you reduce your risk of leadership irrelevance by training for multiple skills rather than reinforcing any one particular talent. We can't stress it enough: strategic leadership skills are at a premium in a VUCA world. Exercising our six disciplines effectively will set your apart from other leaders.

Step 1: Assess Your Current Capabilities

Start with general questions: Do you think long term and see the big picture? Do you have and communicate a vision? How well do you handle surprise and failure? How well do you learn from your mistakes and show resilience?

To accelerate your development, you should isolate specific skills, break down your habits, and build up new ones. Assess yourself, as Jane did, based on the Strategic Leader Assessment survey above. Also, ask your peers, managers, those reporting to you, and even customers or suppliers for their assessment so that you can compare how people in these different groups perceive you.

Step 2: Play to Your Strengths

Second, recognize and play to your strengths. *Align* was Jane's strong suit. She used it to rally key players to her cause. Jane was less forward looking than some of her colleagues and poorly attuned to competitors, so she engaged her team and others to brainstorm about the future and to study customers and competitors using scenario planning. Thanks to her alignment talents, Jane leveraged the strengths of colleagues in her network to fortify her weaknesses.

Let's imagine that your two top strengths are *explore options for Decide* and *experiment widely under Learn*. We'd say you have an experimental mindset vital for coming up with new ideas, solutions, products, or proposals. You are probably a lateral thinker—that is, someone who can reframe issues and see multiple alternatives and connections left and right before locking in on a choice. Both are creative roles needed when problems are complex and the team must consider a wide range of options. Seek a role or get on projects where these assets can shine. Share these skills, or propose options thinking, with colleagues who resist trying new things or rush to judgment. Revise your LinkedIn profile to highlight these skills and their benefits to organizations. Remind your colleagues, team, and manager that you have these talents. Offer to leverage them more fully and teach others.

How you apply these strengths day to day depends greatly on the needs of your current role. Is your profile a good fit for your current situation? Does your manager value your strengths? Are these skills

Your Roadmap to Strategic Leadership

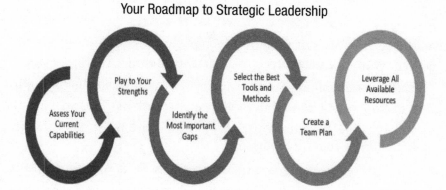

mission-critical? If not, then you might seek opportunities that better fit your skill set. Do your strengths counterbalance weaknesses? It's important to note that your relative score matters as much as your absolute score on the six dimensions. Nearly always, you face competition for choice promotions or special assignments. How can you play up these strengths to differentiate yourself from others?

Step 3: Identify the Most Important Gaps

Use the survey scores to identify the gaps between where you are and where you need to be. Doing so may seem obvious, since the survey yields scores for each of six dimensions and thus indicates gaps relative to the maximum scores attainable. However, a gap that is twice as large as another does not necessarily deserve twice as much attention. In some situations, the biggest gap may not be the most important. It depends on your business context and the fit between your role and your capabilities. You need to think strategically about the internal competition and to keep an eye on the outside demands on your team or organization. If new talent joins the organization, your relative scores may shift, and thus much depends on your circumstances when prioritizing gaps.

Jane was criticized for *anticipating* poorly—specifically, for not *seeing sooner* what competitors were doing or how customers were changing. The company was losing market share rather than realizing its strategic priority: growth in the Asia Pacific emerging markets. In effect, her weakness jeopardized the business plan that was mission-critical. In other cases, the threat may not be obvious. Talk with your manager, other leaders, or mentors to get insight into the changing dynamics of your environment. This will allow you to become crystal clear on what skills are most essential to enhance.

So what is your weak area? Let's assume you score low in *Challenge*. The feedback you receive indicates you don't sufficiently *open the window* for new, outside-in perspectives and that you tend to settle into the status quo. Further, you rarely *look into the mirror*, question conventional thinking, or fight to change course. Perhaps these habits served you when you were supervising a small-project team charged with improving quality. But suppose the management team promoted you to lead the quality unit. Now you are responsible for setting goals for higher quality standards and generating customer interest in better solutions. Your score implies that you must both take and shape marching orders, including evaluating whether the current course supports a new corporate priority. This will require bolder thinking that challenges conventional wisdom and action in the face of resistance. You may have to align better to *rally key players* and *bridge differences* for such a change agenda.

Step 4: Select the Best Tools and Methods

The actions needed to improve one skill are different from the actions required to enhance another. To garner new insights about changes in the marketplace, and to see customers and competitors in a new light, Jane committed to building networks inside and outside the organization. She held internal team meetings to debate current projections. She planned a war-game to map potential competitor moves and developed strategies to anticipate and counter them.

If you need to *Challenge* more, look back at the *Action Plan to Open the Window* in Chapter 2. Here are three of the specific ideas listed there:

+ *Engage mavericks and respect contrarians.* Seek out those who truly see the world differently from you and try hard to understand why they do so.
+ *Surface long-standing assumptions.* Ask a diverse group to come up with the general assumptions of your team, organization, or industry.
+ *Challenge dubious assumptions and outdated mental models from the outside in.* Form counter-teams (i.e., "red teams") that collect data and argue why current strategies must be adjusted. Have the teams ask: "Which assumptions are potentially vulnerable and need to be tested?"

Assess which actions would work best in your current situation or whether other items, perhaps from the *Action Plan to Look in the Mirror* (also in Chapter 2), are more on target. Whatever focus you choose, how far can you push yourself? How much can you shake convention and try new things? Set an ambitious but achievable plan. Put points on the board and get wins to create momentum. Remember that Dr. Barnes built his art collection a few paintings at a time, with a keen eye for *avant-garde* painters. This approach helped educate him about art and built his confidence such that he could challenge the entire art world. Involve your manager in crafting your plan. That's what Jane did. She got feedback, drafted a plan for becoming more strategic, and then met with Lee to get his input and endorsement. He applauded her efforts and made resources available for external training and a new mentor.

Although your career will benefit from improving your aptitude in any of the six disciplines, at some point you'll get diminishing returns. No dancer would work on improving only her flexibility if the precision of her movements were below par for a new dance in rehearsal. So tailor your personal growth plan to your current profile and then adjust it over time. Consider your organization's broader strategy, especially the extent of change envisioned for the future. Leaders in gradually changing environments, for example, may need profiles different from those experiencing jolts of disruption or total chaos.

Step 5: Create a Team Plan

Your strategic leadership can flourish only if you have support from other people. This means that your team and organization will need to increase their strategic capabilities as well. You can easily adapt our Strategic Leadership Assessment survey to diagnose patterns and gaps in your leadership team or across an entire organization. In Jane's case, we looked at the collective management team results and found that *Anticipate* and *Learn* represented the weakest areas of strategic leadership in the senior ranks. In a feedback session with the top leaders, we used these results to discuss candidly what inhibited entrepreneurial risk-taking across the organization.

The tendency to punish rather than learn from mistakes surfaced as a key cultural issue. The potential for rebuke caused people to keep their heads down, focus narrowly on the task at hand, and play it safe. Rather than work in a novel way, the norm was to do what worked before. To foster adaptive learning, the CEO and top executives agreed to address this head-on. They did not intend to hold leaders back individually or collectively, yet that's what they were doing. Inadvertently, they had conditioned people to dread the kind of messiness that characterized Alexander Fleming's laboratory or the painful but valuable mistakes that catapulted Sara Blakely to entrepreneurial success. The CEO and top executives committed to addressing the underlying cultural issues through open dialogue, training sessions on fostering a culture of learning, and new incentives to reward experimentation. Above all, they started to celebrate the act of *experimentation* regardless of outcome.

Step 6: Leverage All Available Resources

Strategic leaders don't survive in a vacuum. They build support systems that help them become more strategic. Just as you must *rally key players* around your strategic vision, enlist key allies to support your personal growth plan. Choose wisely. Supportive, empathetic colleagues can be invaluable as you work through change and overcome obstacles. You also want colleagues who will push and challenge you. Who in your circle is most likely to *open your window* or *hold up the mirror*, as Dr. Watson did for Sherlock Holmes? Who will tell you what you don't want to hear, as John Dewey did with Barnes? Who will push you to look out further or wider, experiment, and take more risks? Maybe your manager can help. In Jane's case, Lee wanted to help but lacked the strategic acumen to do so and thus was not able to analyze her weak points or guide her about how to strengthen them.

There are times when you need a more detached and objective third party to challenge your deepest assumptions and help you reframe issues in a more strategic light. This mentor could be a senior leader from another part of the business or even from outside, as long as he or she is willing and available to spend time with you. Many successful executives who become strategic leaders have a coach. So do nearly all top athletes and entertainers. If your company implores you to *be more strategic*, then by all means ask for a coach or mentor to guide you. Share the Strategic Leadership Assessment with your mentor or coach. Discuss the gaps you intend to address and the blind spots where you need help. With or without a coach, craft a clear development plan tailored to your gaps, with periodic reviews and tactical adjustments as needed.

Another way to support your plan is to seek internal or external training. Most executive education programs at leading universities have seminars that address strategic leadership. Alternatively, ask your firm to design a program for you and others to build strategic leadership. You are not alone. Strategic thinking remains the biggest competency gap in most companies. Remember, when executives were asked to select the leadership behaviors most critical to their organizations' future success, they chose *being strategic* 97 percent of the time."[1] Interestingly, in another recent study, women outperformed men on almost every leadership capability except strategic acumen.[2]

Read more about the strategic leaders profiled in this book. Draw insights and lessons from their successes and failures—especially the latter. Use our endnotes to find articles and books that delve more deeply into topics that interest you. Attend lectures or seminars on related topics, or just to expand your horizons in general. Above all, seek input from people beyond your industry and broaden your networks. Successful strategic leaders are students of business, economics, politics, technology, strategy, disruption, culture, and so on. They keep abreast of key trends and uncertainties that may impact their marketplace, as well the world beyond it. Develop a passion for learning, experimenting, exploring other cultures, and challenging assumptions among the varied aspects of strategic leadership.

POSTSCRIPT

Our book is especially aimed at leaders who want to make a big difference as well as those, such as Jane, who get thrust into a situation demanding more strategic leadership. Like many in these circumstances, Jane was determined to rise to the occasion and to make a strategic impact. Leaders with such aspirations can learn from Blakely, Branson, Musk, and the others we profiled to shape the future of their company or industry. Each of these leaders re-imagined their business or industry and created a transformational agenda. They aimed high, acted boldly, and upset the apple cart as needed. Because they bucked convention, they encountered resistance and faltered at times. But opposition never deters true strategic leaders; it *informs* and *strengthens* their leadership. Strategic leaders expect setbacks, willingly change course, learn from mistakes, and bounce back. Over the long run, all organizations and leaders compete on their ability to learn and adapt. Without strategic leaders, organizations fail to adapt and eventually become irrelevant. Although they may coast for a few years on past success, over time such companies become the walking dead.

Charles Darwin observed that "it is not the strongest of the species who survive, nor the most intelligent, but the ones most responsive to change."[3] This is why organizations need to develop strategic leadership capacity deep and wide throughout. We wrote this book to help demystify this crucial adaptive capability, and we deconstructed it into six disciplines. In each chapter, we've profiled remarkably gifted leaders who would be among our personal candidates for the Strategic Leader Hall of Fame. These are people who are transforming their company, industry, and, at times, the world. We know from firsthand experience that nearly all managers and professionals can become more strategic, *and that includes you.* What matters is not the stage you play on but your personal commitment to mastering these six disciplines in order to win the long game.

✦ ✦ ✦

Everyone can rise above their circumstances and achieve success if they are dedicated to and passionate about what they do.

—Nelson Mandela

APPENDIX

Research Foundation of this Book

A WIDE RANGE OF BEHAVIORS THAT ARE CRITICAL FOR leaders to be successful have been identified by scholars and practitioners. Our book examines the special challenges facing leaders who are confronted with deep uncertainty. The business media consider uncertainty to be a significant cause of low consumer confidence across the economy. Economists view it as an impediment to long-term investment or winning the long game.[1] But it's also true that entrepreneurs feed on uncertainty, and that without their ferocious appetites many of the most agile and future-focused companies would not aspire to greatness.

Whether you hate or love uncertainty, as a strategic leader you must deal with it. And here is the rub: in uncertain times, experience is not necessarily an asset. Surprise becomes a constant companion and the best course of action is often elusive or counterintuitive. Our research surfaced six broad disciplines essential for success in environments characterized by volatility, uncertainty, complexity, and ambiguity (VUCA). Mastering just four or even five of these six may not be enough. Just as a captain and crew need every available skill—and then some—when their ship sails into turbulent waters, so, too, normal routines no longer suffice as leaders encounter a world of VUCA. When all hell breaks loose, the leaders who master all six disciplines are the ones who will likely win the long game.

Researchers have examined each of our six components in isolation, although usually not in the special context of high uncertainty. Moreover, few studies have recognized the joint value of these components in times of ambiguity and volatility. The more uncertain the environment becomes, the more a leader needs these six disciplines *in combination* because they possess self-reinforcing qualities when deployed as an interdependent leadership system. Conversely, if some disciplines are wanting, a destructive spiral of doubt and confusion may set in during times of deep uncertainty. In cases where a leader does not master all six disciplines, it is wise to build complementary teams to address these weak spots collectively and cover key deficiencies. But like an orchestra conductor, the leader needs to know the finer points of each discipline and then harmonize them to suit the occasion. This critical role cannot be delegated since it is the essence of strategic leadership.

Our book draws on multiple sources, including our ongoing research at the Wharton School's Mack Institute for Innovation Management plus our consulting work and research at Decision Strategies International (DSI). The six-component framework developed here began as a conceptual adaptation of broad findings in the domains of leadership, strategy, and behavioral decision-making. We pre-tested the conceptual model via draft surveys of managers in companies and then collected data from over twenty thousand managers representing diverse geographies, companies, functions, and backgrounds. Using factor analysis as well as various tests of validity (see page 275), we refined the survey questions and identified remedies.

Our overall aim is to define and measure "strategic leadership" so that we can isolate specific gaps and design custom solutions to address the largest gaps of individual leaders and teams. Given the interdependencies among the six factors, major gaps and deficiencies deserve far more attention than minor ones in our model, beyond what a linear weighing approach would suggest. In most of the cases we encountered in practice, the top priority was to shore up a leader's weakest disciplines before addressing any others. This allowed for a *precision* rifle-shot approach to developing leadership as opposed to a scattered shot-gun approach characterized by many misses and an occasional hit. Unfortunately, the latter is still the most common organizational practice in learning and development today.

OUR USE OF TERMS

The term *strategy* originated in the military (referring to "the art of the general") but evolved into a broader notion about how leaders and organizations achieve a stated goal or vision. *Strategy* can be applied to chess games, with one player against another, as well as to team sports in which many players or teams compete, as in a boat race. The term can also be applied to contests with nature, such as devising a strategy for climbing a mountain or curing a disease. In business, the phrase *being strategic* can refer to decisions or problems arising at many levels—corporate, divisional, business unit, functional, project. The defining characteristic is not the type of problem being addressed or the organizational vantage point being adopted but, rather, that the problem at hand must be examined broadly, from multiple angles, with an open mind.

Strategic decisions typically reside above the routine tactical level and thus cannot be readily delegated one level lower down in the organization. Also, strategy concepts developed for one level (e.g., a business unit versus a corporate strategy) or one domain (e.g., politics versus business) will generalize in only limited ways across those domains. Consequently, the strategy concepts used in, say, business, warfare, and evolutionary biology employ different viewpoints and paradigms. Thus we define *strategy* in a broad sense, beyond the more focused perspectives of corporate strategy, game theory, or business models. To us, strategy is about the disciplined as well as creative search for solutions in problem situations where judgment, insight, goals, creativity, self-awareness, simplification, approximation, efficient search, and learning are essential.

The academic field of business strategy evolved multiple schools of thought. An early influential one was the rational-design school, whereby strategy in organizations is formulated analytically from the top down, as in a carefully planned military campaign.[2] This school's roots lie in micro-economics and operations research, with Michael Porter's five-forces model being a crowning example, supported by management science and decision analysis. Assuming rational players and stable market structures, Porter's model offers leaders three generic strategies (low cost, differentiation, and niche), one of which they must choose for their business unit. By analyzing the structure of their industry—in terms of entry barriers; the nature of rivalry; customer and supplier power; economies of scale, scope, or experience; and the role of technology or governments—leaders can deduce the best strategy for their firm. If they fail to clearly choose and execute one of the three generic strategies offered, the firm will be stuck in the middle without a sustainable competitive advantage since its competitors will specialize and defeat it on either cost, differentiation, or niche plays. The role of leadership in this view is limited; once the strategic game has been figured out, managers must just execute the plan and leaders become largely interchangeable. They are for hire in the open market as needed.

In contrast to the rational-design school is the emergent view of strategy, which focuses strongly on the specific context of the situation as well as on the largely incremental nature of decision-making. This influential perspective draws more on organization theory, sociology, and even politics, recognizing that organizations seldom rise to the level of rationality assumed in the rational-design model. The emergent view of strategy has been promulgated by researchers such as James Brian Quinn, Henry Mintzberg, and Jim March, for both descriptive and prescriptive purposes.[3] From their perspective, the top-down rational-design view is largely an organizational fiction since strategies seldom play out as intended. To them, the "plan" has to be viewed with considerable skepticism since no plan survives contact with reality. What matters is not the plan but, rather, the act of planning itself since that is where dialogue, learning, and adjustment to unexpected change take place. The focus is much more on what happens deep inside the organization, in terms of process, context, people, hidden agendas, incentives, culture, and decisions. This contextual view recognizes more fully the uniqueness of each organization and the decisive roles that leaders play in determining where companies end up.[4]

A third strategy paradigm, which flourished in the 1980s, further shifted the focus toward the inner working of the firm but with a strong strategic focus on the role of resources and deeply embedded capabilities.[5] Resources such as human and financial capital, technology, and leadership talent are viewed as potentially important sources of competitive advantage. The firm's capacity to deploy such resources, through information-rich organizational processes that develop over time, can bestow sustainable competitive advantages. These processes can be thought of as intermediate goods generated by the firm to provide not only enhanced productivity of its resources but also strategic flexibility and protection of its final products and services.[6] The strategic advantage of resources and capabilities lies in their unique characteristics, such as the time it takes to develop them, their complementary nature in the sense of functioning as a system, and their often tacit nature due to being rooted in the skills, knowledge bases, and personal relationships inside the firm. Based on these characteristics, capabilities can become core competencies that are proprietary to the firm (they can't easily "walk away") and hard to imitate by rivals. The more difficult the firm's resource and capabilities are to buy, sell, imitate, or substitute, the greater their strategic value to the firm. For example, investing in strategic leadership capacity, as our book proposes, can be a very powerful way to build sustainable advantage over time.

Dave Teece and his colleagues blended elements of this resource-based view of leadership with an evolutionary perspective of business to develop a dynamic-capabilities view of strategy.[7] The evolutionary component emphasizes the importance of adaptation in continually changing environments through the processes of mutation and natural selection. The basic argument of Teece et al. is that successful firms need a set of meta-capabilities—which operate at a higher level than their standard operational capabilities—to integrate, build, and reconfigure competencies in order to succeed in rapidly changing environments.[8] Whereas Porter emphasizes the static structural elements of the firm's environment (such as entry barriers, cost structures, and the nature of rivalry), Teece emphasizes its uncertain Darwinian context. Key elements in this latter view are the firm's ability to sense, shape, and create opportunities that will stimulate future success.[9] To do so, firms need to develop leaders who have the requisite skills and values to evolve dynamic capabilities that connect deeply with their organization's tacit knowledge base and internal organizational processes. For the individual leader, this means becoming more strategic, beyond the confines of narrow mindsets, fixed game plans, or rigid solutions. We have addressed this urgent call by enumerating six disciplines we deem crucial to the ability of firms and leaders to thrive in uncertain times. As such, our book is closest to the dynamic-capabilities view of business, followed by the emerging school of strategy, but we recognize that leaders must incorporate other schools as well in their thinking.

✦ ✦ ✦

The broadly used term *leadership* refers to the process by which a single person, or a group of people, influences the behavior or beliefs of others, in a spirit of followership. How and why this influence is exerted is central in the study of leadership. What complicates research is that followers may be in close proximity to the leader (as in families, tribes, or traditional organizations) or widely dispersed in time and space (as in art, science, or politics). For example, intellectual, inspirational, or artistic leaders can exert influence well past their death, with the Bible as a striking example. Diverse research fields, from anthropology and sociology to business and economics, touch on the important topic of leadership. However, to date, there is no unified view, nor even a dominant deep theory, as to what successful leadership fundamentally entails. When adding our special conditions of high stakes and turmoil, which are often encountered in business today, the enigmatic nature of leadership becomes even more obvious.

Research efforts to find general leadership traits have largely failed, in part because the roles of the person, the situation, and the broader organizational context interact in complex ways across time, place, circumstance, and culture. This difficulty has steered research away from unified general theories of leadership to ones that offer only contingent advice.[10] A prime example of a contingency model is Blake and Mouton's well-known managerial grid, which distinguishes between task- and people-oriented leadership situations.[11] Hersey, Johnson, and Blanchard, as well as Goleman, while working with the Hay Group, evolved this model to give practical advice to leaders about which styles would be most effective in what kind of circumstances.[12] Such contingency models, which combine the role of personal as well as situational factors, are by definition hard to generalize across time, culture, and space.

Accordingly, practical advice usually comes from clinical observations about what works well, or not, in a specific application domain, such as music, business, sports, politics, or science. Furthermore, within each of these domains many variations exist about when leadership works or fails. This lack of generality reflects the complexity of human interactions as well as the powerful roles played by place, time, circumstance, context, and culture. In a large-scale multicountry study, Robert House and his colleagues correlated leadership approaches with country-specific as well as company- or organization-specific dimensions of culture.[13] This research highlights not only the complexity of leadership in real-world settings but also its enigmatic nature. The latter has prompted some critics to view leadership as a convenient but rather opaque fallback category for what researchers can't explain in organizational success or failure. To most people, therefore, leadership remains a complex and somewhat mysterious mixture of art, science, and culture.

Although the leadership field is too large to review adequately in this Appendix, we do wish to mention some of the major streams to which our work connects.[14] Many of today's leadership models still reflect those of the previous century, when products were generally produced by top-down bureaucratic organizations. Although well suited to manufacturing and mass production, such models work less well in a knowledge-based economy where human capital, business networks, empowerment, and innovation play key roles.[15] Recent developments in leadership theories reflect this shift. They evolved from trait, situational, transformational, and contingency models to a new leadership paradigm focused on *adaptive leadership*.[16] Our book closely aligns with this new stream, blending a variety of perspectives with a practical focus.

Leadership experts such as Warren Bennis, Ronald Heifetz, Mike Useem, and Gary Yukl, among others, have given this approach both conceptual as well as practical definition. They emphasize the limits of technical expertise and recognize that technocrats can seldom solve today's most demanding management problems. Technical expertise resides in the head, as Heifetz notes, whereas adaptive challenges engage the stomach and the heart as well.[17] We need to understand leaders in the full context of their life course, including the psychodynamic perspectives on leadership.[18] Heifetz argues that many people confuse leadership with authority or expertise. But leadership in times of change often requires a deep challenge of authority in order to remain viable. This is why Mike Useem's work on "leading up" is so important and timely.[19] Effective leaders manage downward, upward, sideways, and through the middle. They exert influence wherever it is needed in their complex environment, without too much regard for hierarchy or formal roles. Our book emphasizes the roles of challenge, anticipation, and alignment for these very reasons.

We also recognize that courage is needed for those who lead organizations in times of change.[20] *Looking in the mirror* or *opening the window* requires that leaders take risks and try new things. Jay Conger notes that many other factors also influence leaders, such as genetic makeup, family background, education, life experiences, role models, incentives, and ability to learn.[21] Leaders are both born and made. Likewise, Warren Bennis emphasizes the role of crucibles in shaping a leader's character, values, and capabilities. Crucibles are life experiences that test you at a very deep level, confront you with who you really are. This can happen when you get fired, face a deep moral dilemma, encounter a crisis at work, experience personal hardship (illness, divorce, death of a child), or need to confront abject failure.[22] From such difficult experiences, leaders grow and may develop deep resolve, strong self-confidence, drive, and the courage to swim against the tide. Adaptive leadership is about managing a complex, open social system in times of change, using flexible relationships between leaders and followers, in ways that are far more fluid than the hierarchical model would ordinarily permit.[23] Mike Useem describes, for example, how the US military evolved its leadership model, which was previously based on a Cold War environment. A new approach was needed in order to better accommodate asymmetric and highly uncertain warfare with poorly understood adversaries.[24] Additional real-life examples of adaptive leadership, beyond the confines of business, are profiled by Heifetz, Grashaw, and Linsky.[25]

✦ ✦ ✦

The focus of our book is at the intersection of the two connected but largely distinct academic fields of strategy and leadership.[26] We believe that this convergence is particularly critical in a VUCA world where a long-term view is often required. Many leadership models focus on leading in the moment, and strategy models often divorce the interplay of leadership and organizational dynamics. Strategies fail, or just sit on the shelf, because leaders don't know how to deliver them. They lack the strategic leadership skills needed to navigate uncertainty and win the long game. The ability to fashion an adaptive strategy (in order to play the long game well) and to exhibit dynamic leadership (by orchestrating and mobilizing teams to execute the long game) is rare indeed. Those special leaders who can thrive at this intersection will have a distinct competitive advantage. Not only will their strategic acumen create a synergistic business effect whereby 1+1=3, but their dynamic leadership skills will unleash energy and talents whereby 1+1=5.

The essence of *strategic leadership* is to blend two complementary orientations that at their roots also entail antithetical reflexes, skills, and values. The adjective *strategic* here refers to the main characteristics of strategy—namely, its heuristic nature when searching for or devising solutions to achieve complex goals or objectives.[27] The noun *leadership* implies that organizations conduct this heuristic search in a human context, where leader-follower relationships matter greatly. The Venn diagram in the figure below itemizes some of the topics typically associated with either the field of strategy or that of leadership. Our contention is that the intersections among these fields are not sufficiently explored. The effective use of strategy concepts, principles, or tools usually requires teamwork to conceive and to implement them. And the teams in turn require leadership. In some instances, as when constructing a value chain or devising a segmentation map, the strategy tool can be developed by one person. But in most cases, as when developing a share strategic vision or orchestrating a network of business partners, a team approach is needed to do it well.

Conversely, we believe that leadership efforts bereft of strategic insight or acumen are bound to fail eventually since they undermine the long game. Yes, leaders may be able to rally their troops for a

Bridging the Fields of Strategy and Leadership

Strategy
- Business model
- Competitive advantage
- Asset optimization
- Business segmentation
- Contingency planning
- Value chain
- Ecosystem partnership
- Governance

Anticipate
Challenge
Interpret
Decide
Align
Learn

Leadership
- Vision & mission
- Organizational structure
- Organizational culture
- Ethics
- Talent management
- Communication
- Strategy execution
- Succession

while even as they pursue a deeply flawed goal or strategy. But this approach will soon run into major obstacles ranging from operational setbacks and lack of resources to poor team morale and the outright rejection of the leader or plan. A lack of strategic capability is especially damning for leaders who are facing uncertainty since frequent revisions of the plan will be needed as surprises heap on. This intersection is an underdeveloped area because the efficacy of strategy tools or methods is seldom studied within the context of high uncertainty and diverse leadership styles.

Our conceptual model of strategic leadership entails trait and situational elements as well as transformational and adaptive ones. We believe that effective leaders, rather than reacting to events, shape and even create their own future. In that sense, the term *adaptive leadership* has more of a reactive connotation than we would like, although much depends here on how you define what leaders are adapting to. The view that leaders adapt to a fixed, exogenous environment is too passive for us, although we acknowledge that real obstacles and immutable realities exist in the world, starting with the laws of physics. And we also know, of course, that humans can do little more than adapt to their experiences, imagination, hopes, fears, instincts, and reason. But as Russell Ackoff emphasizes, most managers and even leaders underestimate the influence they can have on their environment. Instead of planning *for* the future, he counsels, they should plan the future.[28] This is what winning the long game is about: leaders shaping the future.

Leaving aside free will and deep philosophical questions about how much we can control our destinies, strategic leadership entails mastering six core disciplines so as to shape or even change the future. The key is to deploy these disciplines flexibly in order to accommodate a wider variety of situations, some anticipated but many not. It is often the unanticipated situation that offers the greatest opportunity, but only if that is the leader's mindset to begin with. Surprises, especially deep crises, give leaders implicit permission to be creative and to reimagine their organizations. Conditions of instability and turmoil hide within them new possibilities and provide organizational legitimacy to seize the moment. Our book unpacks the main elements that leaders must master to do this, to be ready when the unexpected happens. We provide diagnostics for assessing where specific leaders are currently strong or weak along with insights, tools, and tips for remedying the greatest shortfalls. Unpacking strategic leadership into basic disciplines, while drawing on an array of general tools and methods, allows us to develop customized solutions for an individual leader facing specific career challenges. In fact, teams, divisions, and entire organizations can be assessed as well, since it is the combined mastery of our six disciplines across the organization that will ultimately dictate its success. But if key leaders are notably lacking in either their understanding or appreciation of these six disciplines, they will not do well in the long game.

STATISTICAL VALIDATIONS

Our Strategic Aptitude Assessment (SAA) survey was designed to measure our six disciplines, each of which calls for behaviors that connect the domains of strategy and leadership. These six disciplines are *Anticipate, Challenge, Interpret, Decide, Align,* and *Learn*. The SAA framework reflects our twenty-plus years of consulting experience working with a wide variety of clients across multiple industries around the globe. It also incorporates learnings from the organizational development, leadership, and strategic management literatures—both applied and academic. We use the associated survey to provide targeted feedback to leaders, teams, and organizations, since such feedback is often lacking—as we illustrate with the case of Jane throughout the book. Instead of taking a broad-brush approach to developing strategic leadership and thinking, we have designed a *targeted* plan of development based on the SAA instrument (as outlined in the Epilogue).

Our six-disciplines framework has what researchers refer to as face validity. It is based on prior research, teaching, and coaching models, as well as on inputs from many managers and leaders grappling with strategic thinking challenges. When we share it with experienced executives and talent professionals, we usually receive comments such as "This makes sense," "I get it," "This is easy to grasp," "You have made the complex into something simple." When we unveil it to clients or leaders who have taken the assessment, there is immediate recognition of the relevance and need to address these disciplines. And, given our backgrounds in academic research and our desire to use robust and validated instruments, we have subjected our assessment tool to statistical tests by a third-party statistician specializing in instrument construction and testing.[29]

The full-length version of our SAA survey has thirty-nine questions and has been used for self-assessment, peer-assessment, and 360-degree feedback ($N = 278$). In addition, we have used a shorter version of the self-assessment survey with just twelve question items. This version was published in March 2012 at www .Inc.com, with a web link (still available) that allows readers to complete the assessment at www.decisionstrat.com. This shorter survey resulted in a data set of 20,690 respondents. Using the above data sets, a study of the reliability and validity of the SAA was completed in the fall of 2012. The aim was to assess the reliability and validity of the SAA instrument as an appropriate tool for understanding, measuring, and developing strategic aptitude. For readers interested in the statistical results, here are the main conclusions of our tests in brief.

Internal consistency—a measure of reliability—was measured by Cronbach's Alpha, a statistic that represents the degree to which items on a scale consistently measure the same underlying construct. The Cronbach's Alpha levels for the SAA elements show that all of the six elements have high Alpha levels (in the range of .70 to .80). This means that each of the elements consistently and reliably measures the underlying construct that it is intended to represent. In short, the SAA can generally be considered a reliable measure of strategic aptitude (SA).

Criterion-related validity is a measure of how well one set of variables (e.g., the SA elements) predicts results about an important outcome (e.g., strategic leadership effectiveness). If scores on the SA elements are shown to be correlated with overall effectiveness as a strategic leader, then making improvements on the elements is likely to lead to greater effectiveness as a strategic leader.

Multiple regression analyses show that frequent use of the elements is strongly correlated with perceived overall effectiveness as a strategic leader. All of the six elements are statistically significant drivers of effective strategic leadership. This finding supports the criterion-related validity of the SAA as a predictor of overall strategic effectiveness. By building further competence in each of the SA elements—and by using the associated skills and habits more frequently and consistently—people are very likely to improve their effectiveness as strategic leaders.

Further support for the criterion-related validity of the SAA is provided by the strong and statistically significant correlation between ratings of overall effectiveness and ratings of strategic leadership effectiveness ($r = .75, p < .0001$). This suggests that by building capability on the SA elements, leaders as well as managers are likely to be rated as more effective in their jobs, overall.

These analytic results confirm the feedback and reactions we received from colleagues in academic as well as clinical settings, including talent and learning professionals, instrument users, and our own team of experienced consultants on strategy and leadership. The Strategic Aptitude Assessment is a focused, practical, and developmentally focused tool that can help leaders, teams, and organizations become more effective at strategic leadership and thus better positioned to win the long game. We hope that our instrument, the book, and the many tips provided throughout can serve this same purpose for you as well.

ACKNOWLEDGMENTS

T HIS BOOK IS AN OUTGROWTH OF OUR WORK AT DECISION Strategies International (DSI), the company where we serve as CEO and chairman respectively. Our Strategic Leadership framework reflects the thinking and inputs of the current DSI team as well as those of many who came before. It is our deep belief that leaders must become far more strategic when navigating the uncertain currents surrounding them. This means playing the long game, seeing the world from the outside in, challenging outdated assumptions, and learning faster, among other skills we describe.

Many DSI colleagues played very meaningful roles in shaping the point of view, framework, tools, and stories in this book. We wish to acknowledge several in particular here. Samantha Howland was a valued co-author of some of our original articles on strategic thinking in such outlets as *Inc.com*, *Chief Learning Officer*, and the *Harvard Business Review*. Sam has helped articulate, refine, and advocate for the DSI point of view over many years. Yulia Barnakova co-created many of the tools, techniques, title options, and creative touches found in the book. Mike Nowak worked tirelessly on story development, research, and endnotes. Roch Parayre developed and has applied the concepts in this book in boardrooms and classrooms for several decades. He has been an invaluable partner in the evolution of thought leadership within DSI as well as on behalf of DSI's clients and partners.

Matt Acconciamessa, with the help of summer interns Elissa Cook and Kristin Kirby, developed some of the early cases, and Franklin Shen as well as Toomas Truumees built out others. The rest of the team weighed in on story refinement, writing clarity, title suggestions, and inspirational support. Nicole Adams, Jim Austin, John Austin, Janet Castricum, Jacqueline Claudia, Henry Davies, Mike Hoherchak, Vivek Kumar, Eric Lerch, Rob Lippert, Charles MacDonald, Viraj Narayanan, Michelle Parks, Corey Phelps, Camelia Ram, Jarrad Roeder, Franck Schuurmans, Karin Stawarky, Nick Turner, and Arjen Van den Berg provided valuable inputs and energy to keep the book project moving forward.

We also appreciate contributions from Mary Ciocca for editing, managing schedules, and copying as well as distributing draft manuscripts. Howard Cohen and Liz Gubin stayed on top of the financial and contractual matters related to this multiyear project. We are grateful to the entire DSI team for supporting the book and weaving its content into the fabric of our offerings. We thank Terri Axtell for her statistical research of the data we collected from many companies via our Strategic Aptitude Assessment survey.

We have been fortunate to engage with many thoughtful practitioners over the past two decades. Their stories, lessons, and insights are woven throughout the chapters. Beyond our clients, we owe intellectual debts to many colleagues in academia and consulting who have advanced and challenged our thinking over multiple decades. Paul has benefited from frequent conversations and joint publications with George Day, J. Edward Russo, and Tom Donaldson about strategic decision-making and from Harbir Singh, Phil Tetlock, and Mike Useem for stimulating discussions about management and leadership. Steve is grateful to Merom Klein, Beverly Burton, Seth Lieberman, Rick Lepsinger, David Nadler, Peter Cairo, Rick Ketterer, and Deborah Brecher for many insights and debates about what separates the most strategic leaders from the rest.

We are also much indebted to friends, clients, and relatives outside of DSI, especially Brent Alderfer, Ben Golub, Ross Mitchell, Fred Krupp, and Laurie Krupp, who were kind enough to be interviewed and add great insights to this book. We thank J. P. Garnier, Gerard van Grinsven, Kent Masters, and Beth Sexton for their kind permission to share some of their stories.

Our book would not have its style, flair, and dynamic story telling without the invaluable contributions of Kirsten Sandberg, who helped us conceive and rework every chapter from beginning to end. Kirsten was a genuine intellectual partner in bridging the world of ideas and the real-world realities facing leaders. She conducted independent research and went more than the extra mile in other ways as well. We also thank Gretchen Anderson for her high-quality editing of Chapter 4 as well as for her broader editorial suggestions.

John Mahaney, our editor from PublicAffairs, has been the type of editorial partner that authors hope for but seldom get. John set the expectations high for this book and provided thoughtful guidance, comprehensive edits, and welcome encouragement throughout. He also challenged us to build out our main stories and sharpen the writing, ideas, and lessons of the book. We also thank Melissa Veronesi, who served as senior project editor, as well copyeditor Christine J. Arden, who was as punctilious as we had hoped. Her careful review caught errors, omissions, and stylistic miscues, with many helpful suggestions to improve writing.

Acknowledgments

Lastly, we owe much to our families. Deborah Krupp was the inspiration for and collaborator on the Barnes story in Chapter 7, reflecting her close teaching connections to the Violette de Mazia Foundation and the Barnes Foundation. David Krupp arranged the Community Energy interview and provided input and constructive challenge on everything from content to title. Olive Prince suggested the Oprah Winfrey story that became central to our opening chapter. Soren Krupp has been a calm and reasoned voice of practical guidance, thoughtful opinions, and personal support throughout.

Joyce Schoemaker was a great help in carefully reviewing our first full manuscript draft, with her incisive observations, good questions, and supportive comments. Kim Schoemaker provided helpful editorial feedback early on, and Paul Schoemaker Jr. provided detailed reviews of multiple drafts. He was also very helpful with background research on some of our more complex case studies.

As should be clear by now, it took a village to write this book. We thank all the villagers involved and hope we can buy them the drink of their choice in gratitude at the town square of our imaginary village. They more than deserve it.

NOTES

INTRODUCTION: THRIVING IN A WORLD OF VUCA: WHY STRATEGIC LEADERSHIP IS SO CRUCIAL NOW

1. "Wayne Gretzky," http://en.wikipedia.org/wiki/Wayne_Gretzky.

2. Robert Kabacoff, "Develop Strategic Thinkers Throughout Your Organization," HBR Blog Network, *Harvard Business Review*, February 7, 2014.

3. Peter F. Drucker, *The Essential Drucker: The Best of Sixty Years of Peter Drucker's Essential Writings on Management* (New York: Collins Business Essentials Series, HarperBusiness, 2008); see also Warren Bennis, *On Becoming a Leader* (Reading, MA: Addison-Wesley, 1989).

4. "Bernanke Open to New Steps to Keep Recovery Going," *CNBC.com*, July 21, 2010.

5. This is a quote from Bernanke's PhD thesis that Representative Jeb Hensarling (R, Texas) read to Bernanke during a 2010 session on Capitol Hill: http://blogs.wsj.com/economics/2010/07/22/bernanke-an-excellent-thesis-on-business-uncertainty/.

6. Goldman Sachs, *United States S&P 500 Beige Book*, which is a quarterly analysis of CEO statements.

7. "Tesla and SpaceX: Elon Musk's Industrial Empire," *60 Minutes*, March 31, 2014, http://www.cbsnews.com/videos/tesla-and-spacex-elon-musks-industrial-empire/.

8. Buckley's CEO quote is from "A Series of Interviews with 14 CEOs and Chairmen of Major Companies Sheds Light on the Foundations of Corporate Leadership," by Dennis Carey, Michael Patsalos-Fox, and Michael Useem, *McKinsey Quarterly* (2009): 1–9, http://www.mckinsey.com/insights/leading_in _the_21st_century/leadership_lessons_for_hard_times.

9. Giovanni Gavetti, Rebecca Henderson, and Simona Giorgi. "Kodak (A)," *Harvard Business School*, February 18, 2004.

10. Claudia H. Deutsch, "Chief Says Kodak Is Pointed in the Right Direction," *New York Times*, December 24, 1999.

11. Inder Sidhu, "For Your Consideration: The Twin Qualities That Made Oprah One of TV's Best," *Forbes*, May 23, 2011, http://www.forbes.com/sites /indersidhu/2011/05/23/for-your-consideration-the-twin-qualities-that-made -oprah-one-of-tvs-best/ (accessed April 17, 2014).

12. "Oprah Winfrey," *Academy of Achievement*, November 11, 2013, http:// www.achievement.org/autodoc/page/win0bio-1 (accessed April 18, 2014).

13. Eva Illouz, *Oprah Winfrey and the Glamour of Misery: An Essay on Popular Culture* (New York: Columbia University Press, 2003).

14. Brian Stelter, "Daytime TV's Empty Throne After 'Oprah,'" *New York Times*, June 10, 2012, http://www.nytimes.com/2012/06/11/business/media/end -of-oprahs-show-tightens-races-for-tv-ratings.html?_r=0 (accessed April 4, 2013).

15. J. Max Robins, "Oprah's OWN Makeover: From Failure to Success," *Forbes*, December 12, 2013, http://www.forbes.com/sites/maxrobins/2013/12/12 /oprahs-own-makeover-from-failure-to-success/ (accessed April 17, 2014).

16. Jenna Goudreau, "How to Lead Like Oprah," *Forbes*, October 22, 2010, http://www.forbes.com/sites/jennagoudreau/2010/10/22/how-to-lead-like-oprah -winfrey-own-rachael-ray-dr-oz-phil/ (accessed April 17, 2014).

17. "How She Did It: Oprah's Success Factors," *EvanCarmichael.com*, http:// www.evancarmichael.com/Famous-Entrepreneurs/514/How-She-Did-It-Oprahs -Success-Factors.html (accessed April 17, 2014).

18. Fritz Redlich, "Payments Between Nations in the Eighteenth and Early Nineteenth Centuries," *Quarterly Journal of Economics* 50, no. 4 (August 1936): 704.

19. Daniel Myers and Investopedia, "Buy When There's Blood in the Streets," *Forbes*, February 23, 2009, http://www.forbes.com/2009/02/23/contrarian-markets -boeing-personal-finance_investopedia.html (accessed March 21, 2013).

20. John Ilkiw, "Battle of the Bonds," *Canadian Investment Review* 20, no. 4 (Winter 2007): 7; see also Business Source Premier, EBSCOhost, March 21, 2013. Ilkiw cites Niall Ferguson's *The House of Rothschild: Money's Prophets 1798–1848* (New York: Penguin Group, 1998) and Herbert Kaplan's *Nathan Mayer Rothschild and the Creation of a Dynasty: The Critical Years 1806–1816* (Stanford, CA:

Stanford University Press, 2006) to reinforce the idea that N. M. had no advance warning. He was speculating.

21. Eduardo Braun, "Decision-Making: A Key Role for Leaders and Its Emotional Impact"; see also "Practicing Leadership," *CEO Magazine* (May 2012).

22. Richard Lepsinger, *Closing the Execution Gap: How Great Leaders and Their Companies Get Results* (San Francisco: Jossey-Bass, 2010).

23. Letter from Reed Hastings via e-mail (subject heading: "An Explanation and Some Reflections"), September 19, 2011. See also Brian Stelter, *New York Times* blog, October 10, 2011, and Reed Hastings, "DVDs Will Be Staying at Netflix.com," *The Official Netflix Blog: US & Canada*, Netflix, Inc., October 10, 2011, http://blog.netflix.com/2011/10/dvds-will-be-staying-at-netflixcom.html (accessed March 28, 2013).

24. Robert Frank, "Billionaire Sara Blakely Says Secret to Success Is Failure," *CNBC.com*, October 16, 2013, http://www.cnbc.com/id/47445683.

CHAPTER 1: ELEPHANTS AND BLACK SWANS: THE DISCIPLINE TO ANTICIPATE

1. Quoted in Peter Valdes-Dapena, "Tesla Gets Near-Perfect Score from Consumer Reports," *CNNMoney*, Cable News Network, May 9, 2013, http://money.cnn.com/2013/05/09/autos/tesla-model-s-consumer-reports/index.html.

2. Quoted in Jeff Plungis, "Tesla Model S Is Ranked Best Overall Car by Consumer Reports," *Bloomberg Businessweek*, February 25, 2014, http://www.businessweek.com/news/2014-02-25/tesla-model-s-is-ranked-best-overall-car-by-consumer-reports.

3. David Zenlea, "2013 Automobile of the Year: Tesla Model S," *Automobile* magazine, August 1, 2012, http://www.automobilemag.com/features/awards/1301_2013_automobile_of_the_year_tesla_model_s/viewall.html.

4. Antony Ingram, "Tesla Model S: Is It Really the Safest Car Ever?" *Christian Science Monitor*, August 26, 2013, http://www.csmonitor.com/Business/In-Gear/2013/0826/Tesla-Model-S-Is-it-really-the-safest-car-ever.

5. Peter Valdes-Dapena, "Tesla Sales Beating Mercedes, BMW and Audi," *CNNMoney*, Cable News Network, May 13, 2013, http://money.cnn.com/2013/05/13/autos/tesla-sales-bmw-mercedes-audi.

6. Brian Pereira, "Tesla CEO Elon Musk Confident About Return of Electric Cars," Tech Wow! blog, January 8, 2014, http://techwow.wordpress.com/2014/01/08/tesla-ceo-elon-musk-confident-about-return-of-electric-cars/.

7. Terry Dawes, "Why Critics Love to Hate Elon Musk," *Cantech Letter*, July 10, 2013, http://www.cantechletter.com/2013/06/why-critics-love-to-hate-elon-musk0610/ (accessed September 3, 2013).

8. David Kestenbaum, "Making a Mark with Rockets and Roadsters," *NPR*, August 9, 2007.

9. Ashlee Vance, "Tesla Pays Off Its $465 Million 'Loser' Loan," *Bloomberg Businessweek*, May 22, 2013, http://www.businessweek.com/articles/2013-05-22 /tesla-pays-off-its-465-million-loser-loan.

10. Stacy Curtin, "Why the Electric Car Is Doomed to Fail," Yahoo! Finance, March 2, 2012, http://finance.yahoo.com/blogs/daily-ticker/why-electric-car -doomed-fail-150050289.html.

11. Wynton Hall, "'Father of the Prius' Declares Electric Cars 'Not Viable,'" *Brietbart*, February 4, 2013, http://www.breitbart.com/Big-Government/2013/02 /04/Father-of-the-Prius-Declares-Electric-Cars-Not-Viable.

12. Quoted in Brian Pereira, "Tesla CEO Elon Musk Confident About Return of Electric Cars," *InformationWeek*, January 7, 2014.

13. Ryan Lawler, "Tesla CEO Elon Musk Says He Got into the Electric Car Business Because No One Else Would," *TechCrunch*, May 29, 2013, http:// techcrunch.com/2013/05/29/elon-musk-d11/.

14. "Elon Musk at D11: 'On Naysayers,'" http://videos.huffingtonpost.com /elon-musk-at-d11-on-naysayers-517797734.

15. Matt Hardigree, "Elon Musk Challenges Self to Build Affordable Car as Tesla Hits $100," Jalopnik, May 28, 2013, http://jalopnik.com/elon-musk -challenges-self-to-build-affordable-car-as-te-510078163.

16. Scott Pelley, "Tesla and SpaceX: Elon Musk's Industrial Empire." *60 Minutes. CBS News*, March 30, 2014.

17. Tom Cheredar, "Tesla Revs Its Engines with a Record 22,477 Cars Sold in 2013 and Big Expansion Plans on the Road Map," VentureBeat, February 19, 2014, http://venturebeat.com/2014/02/19/tesla-revs-its-engines-with-a-record -22477-cars-sold-in-2013-big-expansion-plans-on-the-road-map/.

18. Christina Rogers and Mike Ramsey, "Tesla to Stop Selling Electric Cars in New Jersey," *Wall Street Journal*, March 11, 2014.

19. Elon Musk, "All Our Patent Are Belong to You," June 12, 2014, http://www .teslamotors.com/blog/all-our-patent-are-belong-you.

20. Thomas Donaldson and Paul J. H. Schoemaker, "Self-Inflicted Industry Wounds: Early Warning Signals and Pelican Gambits," *California Management Review* 55, no. 2 (Winter 2013): 24–45.

21. Victor Mora, "Will Tesla Motors Surge Higher After Recent News?," Wall St. Cheat Sheet, March 4, 2014, http://wallstcheatsheet.com/business/will-tesla -motors-surge-higher-after-recent-news.html/?ref=YF.

22. Tesla Motors, Inc., Fourth Quarter and Full Year 2013 Shareholder Letter, February 2014.

23. Cheredar, "Tesla Revs Its Engines with a Record 22,477 Cars Sold in 2013 and Big Expansion Plans on the Road Map."

24. "Tesla Motors Co-founder Elon Musk's $5 Billion 'Gigafactory' May Start Bidding War Among US States," *The Economic Times*, February 2014, http://articles.economictimes.indiatimes.com/2014–02–28/news/47774389 _1_tesla-motors-elon-musk-model-s.

25. "Microsoft Anti-Trust Trial Archive: 1990–2000 Timeline," *Washington Post*, December 2000, http://www.washingtonpost.com/wp-srv/business /longterm/microsoft/timeline.htm (accessed September 24, 2013); Ken Auletta, "World War 3.0," *Random House Hardcover Books*, December 2000, http://www .randomhouse.com/features/auletta/links.html (accessed September 24, 2013).

26. Michele Matassa Flores, "Gates: Internet Battle Just Starting—Microsoft Presents Confident Strategy," *Seattle Times*, December 7, 1995, http://community .seattletimes.nwsource.com/archive/?date=19951207 (accessed September 24, 2013).

27. Quoted in "CEO Forum: Microsoft's Ballmer Having a 'Great Time,'" by David Lieberman, *USA Today*, April 29, 2007, http://usatoday30.usatoday.com /money/companies/management/2007–04–29-ballmer-ceo-forum-usat_N.htm.

28. Adam Hartung, "Oops! Five CEOs Who Should Have Already Been Fired (Cisco, GE, WalMart, Sears, Microsoft)," *Forbes*, May 12, 2012, http://www .forbes.com/sites/adamhartung/2012/05/12/oops-5-ceos-that-should-have-already -been-fired-cisco-ge-walmart-sears-microsoft/3/ (accessed August 21, 2013).

29. Quoted in Jay Yarow, "In a Six-Day Period, Microsoft's New CEO Satya Nadella Completely Changed the Company," *Business Insider*, April 3, 2014.

30. Peter Burrows and Dina Bass, "Microsoft Gets Style Shift With Nadella Replacing Ballmer," *Bloomberg.com*, February 5, 2014, http://www.bloomberg.com /news/2014-02-05/microsoft-gets-style-shift-with-nadella-replacing-ballmer.html.

31. Philip Beeching, "Why Did HMV Fail?" *The Guardian*, January 15, 2013, http://www.guardian.co.uk/commentisfree/2013/jan/15/why-did-hmv-fail (accessed March 29, 2013).

32. Sören Billing, "Lego to Build on Movie Success, Tackle Globalization Challenge," *Rappler.com*, March 12, 2014, http://www.rappler.com/life-and-style /52794-lego-build-movie-success-globalization-challenge.

33. Ron Metzger, "The Lego Story Part III—Lego Fights for Survival," *ToysPeriod*, n.d., http://www.toysperiod.com/blog/Lego/the-Lego-story-part-iii-Lego -fights-for-survival/ (accessed September 24, 2013).

34. David C. Robertson, with Bill Breen, *Brick by Brick: How Lego Rewrote the Rules of Innovation and Conquered the Global Toy Industry* (New York: Random House, 2013).

35. Ibid., p. 39.

36. Charles Fishman, "Why Can't Lego Click?" Fast Company, August 31, 2001, http://www.fastcompany.com/43497/why-cant-lego-click.

37. Robertson, *Brick by Brick.*

38. Quoted in Ben Fritz, "Warner Bros. CEO Guards the Old, Tests the New," *Wall Street Journal,* March 25, 2013.

39. Brooks Barnes, "Bullish on the Big Screen," *New York Times,* March 30, 2014.

40. George Day, *Innovation Prowess: Leadership Strategies for Accelerating Growth* (Philadelphia: Wharton Digital Press, 2013).

41. Jay Yarow, "The Best Steve Jobs Quotes from His Biography," *Business Insider,* October 26, 2011, http://www.businessinsider.com/best-steve-jobs-quotes -from-biography-2011-10?op=1.

42. Anna-Marie Lever, "Medical Drama: Playing Sick to Teach Doctors," *BBC News,* June 17, 2010, http://www.bbc.co.uk/news/10267228 (accessed February 18, 2014).

43. Xuewei Liu, "My Four Days of Experience at GE Training," *Harvard Business Review,* Chinese edition (Beijing: Harvard Business Publishing Group, February 2012), pp. 138–148, http://www.hbrchina.org.

44. Robertson, *Brick by Brick.*

45. Steve Krupp and Toomas Truumees, "Competitive Anticipation: How to Enhance Leadership by Sharpening Your Competitive Edge," *Leadership Excellence,* April 22, 2014.

46. Robertson, *Brick by Brick.*

47. This quotation and the related ones below are taken from Brent Alderfer (Community Energy), personal interview, March 11, 2014.

48. Kiyoshi Kurokawa, "Message from the Chairman," in The National Diet of Japan, *The Fukushima Nuclear Accident Independent Investigation Commission,* July 2012.

49. Thomas Donaldson and Paul J. H. Schoemaker, "Self-Inflicted Industry Wounds: Early Warning Signals and Pelican Gambits," *California Management Review* 55, no. 2 (Winter 2013): 24–45.

50. Testimony of Deven Sharma, President Standard & Poor's, Before the Committee on Oversight and Government Reform, United States House of Representatives (2008), http://oversight-archive.waxman.house.gov/documents /20081022125052.pdf.

51. Paul Krugman, "That Hissing Sound," *New York Times,* August 7, 2005.

52. Michael Lewis, *The Big Short: Inside the Doomsday Machine* (New York: W.W. Norton, 2010); see also Gregory Zuckerman, *The Greatest Trade Ever: The Behind-the-Scenes Story of How John Paulson Defied Wall Street and Made Financial History* (New York: Broadway Books, 2009).

53. Nate Silver, *The Signal and the Noise: Why So Many Predictions Fail* (New York: Penguin Press, 2012), p. 46.

54. Richard Foster and Sarah Kaplan, *Creative Destruction* (New York: Currency, 2001).

55. "True North Groups," *Bill George*, n.d., http://www.billgeorge.org/page/true-north-groups (accessed February 18, 2014).

56. Phil Terry (CEO), "About Collaborative Gain," *The Councils: Home for Product, General Management and Marketing Executives*, Collaborative Gain, Inc., January 2014, https://cgcouncils.com/about/ (accessed May 6, 2014).

57. Paul J. H. Schoemaker, George S. Day, and Scott A. Snyder, "Integrating Organizational Networks, Weak Signals, Strategic Radars and Scenario Planning," *Technological Forecasting and Social Change* 80 (2013): 815–824.

58. Paul J. H. Schoemaker, *Profiting from Uncertainty: Strategies for Succeeding No Matter What the Future Brings* (New York: Free Press, 2002).

59. For details on scenario planning, see Schoemaker, *Profiting from Uncertainty*.

CHAPTER 2: WHAT ARE YOU AFRAID OF?
THE DISCIPLINE TO CHALLENGE

1. Bradley Brooks, "Brazil's Roman Catholics Shrink as Secular Rise," Yahoo News, October 8, 2011, http://news.yahoo.com/brazils-roman-catholics-shrink-secular-rise-071216935.html.

2. "The Global Catholic Population," *Religion and Public Life Project*, Pew Research Center, February 13, 2013, http://www.pewforum.org/2013/02/13/the-global-catholic-population/ (accessed September 2, 2013).

3. "Pope Leads Way of the Cross: What Does the Cross Teach Us? Much More than Sacrifice," Rome Reports, July 27, 2013, http://www.romereports.com/pg153886-pope-leads-way-of-the-cross-what-does-the-cross-teach-us-much-more-than-sacrifice-en.

4. Francis X. Rocca, "Pope's Simple Actions Resonate," *Catholic Courier*, August 2013, p. A6.

5. Pope Francis, quoted by Cindy Wooden, "Pontiff Answers Media Questions," *Catholic Courier*, August 2013, p. A2.

6. Ibid.

7. Carol Glatz (CNS), "Vatican Bank Aims for Transparency," *Catholic Courier*, August 2013, p. A13; see also Avi Jorisch, "The Vatican Bank: The Most Secret Bank in the World," *Forbes*, June 26, 2012, http://www.forbes.com/sites/realspin/2012/06/26/the-vatican-bank-the-most-secret-bank-in-the-world/ (accessed January 5, 2014).

8. Jorisch, "The Vatican Bank."

9. Pope Francis, quoted by Carol Glatz (CNS), "Vatican Bank Aims for Transparency," *Catholic Courier,* August 2013, p. A13.

10. Pope Francis in *Lumen Fidei* [the pope's first encyclical], quoted by Francis X. Rocca (CNS), "Guiding Light of Faith Celebrated," *Catholic Courier,* August 2013, p. A7.

11. Eric Marrapodi, "Is This the First Papal Selfie?" CNN Belief Blog, August 30, 2013, http://religion.blogs.cnn.com/2013/08/30/could-it-be-the-first-papal-selfie/comment-page-2/ (accessed September 2, 2013).

12. Pope Francis, "Press Conference During the Return Flight from World Youth Day," *The Holy See,* Libreria Editrice Vaticana, July 28, 2013, http://www.vatican.va/holy_father/francesco/speeches/2013/july/documents/papa-francesco_20130728_gmg-conferenza-stampa_en.html (accessed September 2, 2013).

13. John Cassidy, "Pope Francis's Challenge to Global Capitalism," *The New Yorker* blog, December 3, 2013, http://www.newyorker.com/rational-irrationality/pope-franciss-challenge-to-global-capitalism.

14. Elisabetta Povoledo, Alan Cowell, and Rick Gladstone, "Pope Setting Up Commission on the Sexual Abuse of Children by Priests," *New York Times,* December 5, 2013, http://www.nytimes.com/2013/12/06/world/europe/pope-setting-up-commission-on-clerical-child-abuse.html?pagewanted=all&_r=0.

15. Abu M. Jalal and Alexandros P. Prezas, "Outsider CEO Succession and Firm Performance," *Journal of Economics and Business* 64, no. 6 (2012): 399–426.

16. "Comcast CEO: 'We Reinvent Ourselves Every Couple Years,'" interview by Kai Ryssdal, *Marketplace.org,* November 21, 2013, http://www.marketplace.org/topics/business/corner-office/comcast-ceo-we-reinvent-ourselves-every-couple-years (accessed March 17, 2014).

17. "PWC 16th Annual Global CEO Survey 2013," interview with Larry Fink, http://www.pwc.com/gx/en/ceo-survey/2013/pdf/us-ceo-survey-2013.pdf.

18. Ken Favaro, Per-Ola Karlsson, and Gary Neilson, "CEO Succession 2011: The New CEO's First Year," *Strategy+Business,* Issue 67 (Summer 2012), http://www.booz.com/media/uploads/BoozCo_CEO-Succession-Study-2011-3.pdf.

19. Stan Sorscher, "Group-Think Caused the Market to Fail," *The Huffington Post,* June 9, 2010.

20. Alison Fitzgerald, "Ex-Wall Street Chieftains Living Large in Post-Meltdown World," The Center for Public Integrity, September 10, 2013, http://www.publicintegrity.org/2013/09/10/13326/ex-wall-street-chieftains-living-large-post-meltdown-world.

21. Ben Golub (BlackRock CRO), personal interview, January 2014.

22. Ibid.

23. "The Rise of BlackRock," *The Economist,* December 7, 2013.

24. Ben Golub (BlackRock CRO), personal interview, January 2014.

25. The National Diet of Japan, *The Fukushima Nuclear Accident Independent Investigation Commission*, July 2012, p. 16.

26. Ibid.

27. Ibid.

28. Ibid.

29. Ibid., p. 20.

30. Ibid., p. 28.

31. Richard Harris, "What Went Wrong in Fukushima: The Human Factor," *NPR*, July 5, 2011, http://www.npr.org/2011/07/05/137611026/what-went-wrong-in-fukushima-the-human-factor.

32. Jared Bleak and Tony O'Driscoll, "The Changing Leadership Context: Inside the CEO's Mind," *Developing Leaders: Executive Education in Practice*, Issue 13 (2013).

33. Christina Farr, "Richard Branson and Elon Musk on Fear Failure and Reinventing the Future," VentureBeat, August 8, 2013, http://venturebeat.com/2013/08/08/richard-branson-and-elon-musk-on-fear-failure-and-reinventing-the-future/ (accessed September 2, 2013).

34. "Richard Branson: The P.T. Barnum of British Business," *Entrepreneur*, October 10, 2008, http://www.entrepreneur.com/article/197616.

35. "History: The Eighties, the Nineties, and the Naughties," *Virgin Atlantic*, n.d., http://www.virgin-atlantic.com/en/us/allaboutus/ourstory/history.jsp (accessed September 2, 2013).

36. Mallory Russell, "Richard Branson's Fails: 14 Virgin Companies That Went Bust," *Business Insider*, April 21, 2012, http://www.businessinsider.com/richard-branson-fails-virgin-companies-that-went-bust-2012-4?op=1 (accessed September 2, 2013).

37. Branson, *Screw Business as Usual*.

38. Russell, "Richard Branson's Fails."

39. Andrew J. Campell, *Friendly Opposition: The Red Team's Role in Strengthening Operation Design* (Houston, TX: BiblioScholar, 2012).

40. "Red Team," http://redteamjournal.com/about/; see also http://en.wikipedia.org/wiki/Red_team.

41. Amos Tversky and Daniel Kahneman, "The Framing of Decisions and the Psychology of Choice," *Science* 211, no. 4481 (1981): 453–458.

42. Daniel Kahneman, *Thinking, Fast and Slow* (New York: Farrar, Straus and Giroux, 2011).

43. Siddhartha R. Dalal, Edward B. Fowlkes, and Bruce Hoadley, "Risk Analysis of the Space Shuttle: Pre-*Challenger* Prediction of Failure," *Journal of the American Statistical Association* 84, no. 408 (December 1989): 945–957.

44. Upton Sinclair, *I, Candidate for Governor: And How I Got Licked* (Berkeley: University of California Press, 1994).

45. The full quote reads: "Conflict is the gadfly of thought. It stirs us to observation and memory. It instigates invention. It shocks us out of sheep-like passivity, and sets us at noting and contriving. . . . [C]onflict is a sine qua non of reflection and ingenuity." See http://www.goodreads.com/author/quotes/42738.John_Dewey.

46. Alfred Pritchard Sloan, *My Years with General Motors* (New York: Random House LLC, 1964). Quoted in Peter F. Drucker, *The Effective Executive*, Vol. 967 (London: Heinemann, 1964), p. 148.

47. Charlan J. Nemeth, Bernard Personnaz, Marie Personnaz, and Jack A. Goncalo, "The Liberating Role of Conflict in Group Creativity: A Study in Two Countries," *European Journal of Social Psychology* 34 (2004): 365–374, published online in Wiley InterScience (www.interscience.wiley.com), DOI: 10.1002/ejsp.210.

48. Jonah Lehrer, *Imagine: How Creativity Works* (Boston: Houghton Mifflin Harcourt, 2012).

49. Dan Senor and Saul Singer, *Start-Up Nation: The Story of Israel's Economic Miracle* (New York: Twelve, 2009).

50. Leon Lazaroff, "China to Capitalize on NASDAQ Jump with Tech IPOs, BNY Says," *Bloomberg Businessweek*, May 7, 2012.

51. Sheryl Sandberg, *Lean In: Women, Work, and the Will to Lead* (New York: Knopf, 2013).

52. Belinda Luscombe, "Confidence Woman: Facebook's Sheryl Sandberg Is on a Mission to Change the Balance of Power. Why She Just Might Pull It Off," *Time*, March 7, 2013.

53. Sandberg, *Lean In*, p. 23.

54. Amos Tversky and Daniel Kahneman's "Judgment Under Uncertainty: Heuristics and Biases" (*Science* 185 [1974]: 124–130) is a classic in behavioral decision theory; for a broader treatment, see Rüdiger F. Pohl, *Cognitive Illusions: A Handbook on Fallacies and Biases in Thinking, Judgment and Memory* (Hove, UK: Psychology Press, 2004).

55. Peter A. Diamond and Hannu Vartiainen, *Behavioral Economics and Its Applications* (Princeton, NJ: Princeton University Press, 2007); for a textbook version, see David R. Just, *Introduction to Behavioral Economics* (Oxford: Wiley-Blackwell, 2013).

CHAPTER 3: THE DOG THAT DID NOT BARK: THE DISCIPLINE TO INTERPRET

1. Nicholas Meyer, *The Seven Percent Solution: Being a Reprint from the Reminiscences of John H. Watson, M.D.* (New York: Ballantine Books, 1975); a movie adaptation was released in 1976.

2. Paraphrased and abridged from the dialogue in the movie; see ibid.

3. Ibid.

4. "Malcolm Gladwell Looks at Technology Innovations," interview by Robert Siegle, *NPR*, May 16, 2011.

5. "Perception," http://www.philosophy-dictionary.org/perception.

6. Ram Charan, "DuPont's Swift Response to the Financial Crisis," *Bloomberg Businessweek*, January7, 2009, http://www.businessweek.com/stories/2009-01-07/duponts-swift-response-to-the-financial-crisis#rshare=email_article (accessed December 11, 2013).

7. "Abilene Paradox," http://en.wikipedia.org/wiki/Abilene_paradox.

8. Jerry B. Harvey, "The Abilene Paradox: The Management of Agreement," *Organizational Dynamics* (Summer 1974): 63–80.

9. "Tasty Baking Company History," http://www.fundinguniverse.com/company-histories/tasty-baking-company-history/.

10. Robert C. Atkins, *Dr. Atkins' New Diet Revolution* (New York: M. Evans, 2002); Arthur Agatston, *The South Beach Diet* (New York: Random House, 2003).

11. This Tastykake case was adapted from George S. Day and Paul J. H. Schoemaker's *Peripheral Vision* ([Boston: Harvard Business School Press, 2006], pp. 9–13), which provides more detail.

12. George Santayana, *Scepticism and Animal Faith: An Introduction to Philosophy* (London: Constable, 1923).

13. Christopher Chabris and Daniel Simons, *The Invisible Gorilla: And Other Ways Our Intuitions Deceive Us* (New York: Random House, 2011).

14. "Silver Blaze," http://en.wikipedia.org/wiki/Silver_Blaze.

15. Hunter Davies, *The Beatles: The Authorized Biography* (New York: McGraw-Hill, 1968), p. 131.

16. "Grolier," http://en.wikipedia.org/wiki/Grolier.

17. For further details, see "Encyclopedia Britannica," Harvard Business School Case N9-396-051, December 1995; for an update, see Richard A. Melcher, "Dusting Off the Britannica," *BusinessWeek*, October 20, 1997, and Adam Davidson, "Bound For Glory? The Venerable Encyclopaedia Britannica Struggles to Survive in an Electronic Age," *Chicago Tribune*, March 1, 1998.

18. Gary Klein, *Sources of Power* (Cambridge, MA: MIT Press, 1998); see also Robin M. Hogarth, *Educating Intuition* (Chicago: University of Chicago Press, 2001).

19. For fascinating examples of thin slicing and thinking without thinking, see Malcolm Gladwell, *Blink: The Power of Thinking Without Thinking* (New York: Little, Brown, 2005), and Robin M. Hogarth, *Educating Intuition* (Chicago: University of Chicago Press, 2001).

20. Quoted in Eduardo Braun, "Decision-Making: A Key Role for Leaders and Its Emotional Impact"; see also "Practicing Leadership," *CEO Magazine*, May 2012.

21. This example comes from Charles Duhigg, "How Companies Learn Your Secrets," *New York Times*, February 18, 2012, http://www.nytimes.com/2012/02/19 /magazine/shopping-habits.html?pagewanted=1&_r=0&adxnnl=1&adxnnlx =1387261006-o1ELIP9IKrnrzGzW1lnMDA (accessed December 15, 2013).

22. Ibid.

23. Leonardo da Vinci's observation is cited in Michael Michalko, *Cracking Creativity* (Berkeley: Ten Speed Press, 2001).

24. "Escaping Flatland," http://www.edwardtufte.com/tufte/advocate_1099; see also chapter 2 in Edward R. Tufte, *Visual and Statistical Thinking: Displays of Evidence for Making Decisions* (Cheshire, CT: Graphics Press, 1997).

25. "Outbreak of Cholera in 1854," http://www.homeoint.org/morrell /londonhh/outbreak.htm.

26. James Surowiecki, *The Wisdom of Crowds* (New York: Anchor Books, 2005).

27. This example is more fully discussed in Paul J. H. Schoemaker and Michael V. Mavaddat, "Scenario Planning for Disruptive Technologies," in George S. Day and Paul J. H. Schoemaker (eds.), *Wharton on Managing Emerging Technologies* (New York: Wiley, 2000).

28. Quoted in Ken Favaro, Per-Ola Karlsson, and Gary L. Neilson, "Captains in Disruption," *Strategy+Business*, Issue 71 (Winter 2013), http://www.strategy -business.com/article/00182?gko=2eb37.

29. Ibid.

CHAPTER 4: SAILING INTO THE STORM:
THE DISCIPLINE TO DECIDE

1. "Leading the Rescue of the Miners in Chile," case study by Michael Useem (The Wharton School, University of Pennsylvania) and Rodrigo Jordán and Matko Koljatic (both from the School of Business Administration at the Pontifical Catholic University of Chile), May 10, 2011.

2. Quoted in Michael Useem, Rodrigo Jordán, and Matko Koljatic, "How to Lead During a Crisis: Lessons from the Rescue of the Chilean Miners," *MIT Sloan Management Review*, August 18, 2011.

3. Ibid.

4. Robert Mundle, *Fatal Storm: The Inside Story of the Tragic Sydney-Hobart Race* (Camden, ME: International Marine/McGraw-Hill, 1999).

5. Oliver Wyman and The Syncretics Group, *Racing Through the Storm: Building Exceptional Teams for Extraordinary Times, A Special Report* (2009), http:// syncreticsgroup.com/wp-content/uploads/RacingThroughtheStorm_WP _Syncretics.pdf.

6. See Hillel Einhorn and Robin M. Hogarth, "Decision Making Under Ambiguity," *Journal of Business* 59, no. 4 (1986): S225–S255, or the original study by Daniel Ellsberg that became a classic in the field: Daniel Ellsberg, "Risk, Ambiguity, and the Savage Axioms," *Quarterly Journal of Economics* 75, no. 4 (1961): 643–669.

7. W. Chan Kim and Renee Mauborgne, *Blue Ocean Strategy: How to Create Uncontested Market Space and Make the Competition Irrelevant* (Boston: Harvard Business School Press, 2005).

8. "Hastings," http://en.wikipedia.org/wiki/Reed_Hastings.

9. Greg Sandoval. "Netflix's Lost Year: The Inside Story of the Price-Hike Train Wreck," CNET, July 11, 2012.

10. Letter from Reed Hastings via e-mail, September 19, 2011 (subject heading: "An Explanation and Some Reflections"), quoted in Brian Stelter, *New York Times* blog, October 10, 2011.

11. Andrew Goldman, "Reed Hastings Knows He Messed Up," *New York Times*, October 20, 2011.

12. Quoted in Brian Stelter, "Netflix, in Reversal, Will Keep Its Services Together," *New York Times*, October 10, 2011.

13. Kathleen M. Eisenhardt, "Making Fast Strategic Decisions In High-Velocity Environments," *Academy of Management Journal* 32, no. 3 (1989): 543–576.

14. Personal conversation.

15. A. Tversky and D. Kahneman, "The Framing of Decisions and the Psychology of Choice," *Science* 211, no. 4481 (1981): 453–458.

16. Confidential survey and interviews conducted by our company Decision Strategies International with this anonymous client.

17. Personal conversation.

18. Jennifer Reingold, "How Free Shipping Saved Zappos," chapter 2 in Verne Harnish et al. (eds.), *The Greatest Business Decisions of All Time: How Apple, Ford, IBM, Zappos, and Others Made Radical Choices That Changed the Course of Business* (New York: Fortune, 2012), pp. 39–46.

19. Quoted in blog by Jeanne Gray in *American Entrepreneurship Today*, http://www.americanentrepreneurship.com/news/my-blog/blogger/listings/jeannegray.html.

20. Quoted in Mary Vinnedge, "Richard Branson: Virgin Entrepreneur," *Success*, May 31, 2009.

21. "Reichmann, Developer Who Transformed Skylines, Dies," *The Chronicle Herald*, October 25, 2013, http://thechronicleherald.ca/world/1163064-reichmann-developer-who-transformed-skylines-dies.

22. Ibid.

23. Ibid.

24. "EBX Group," http://en.wikipedia.org/wiki/EBX_Group.

25. Joe Leahy and Samantha Pearson, "Eike Batista: Reversal of Fortune," *Financial Times*, August 7, 2013.

26. John Lyons and Luciana Magalhaes, "Brazil's Batista Says He'll Rise Again," *Wall Street Journal*, September 15, 2013.

27. Adrian Bridge, "A Conversation with Angela Merkel: Remembering Her Rise to Power," *The Telegraph*, September 20, 2013, http://www.telegraph.co.uk /news/worldnews/europe/germany/10322798/A-conversation-with-Angela -Merkel-remembering-her-rise-to-power.html.

28. "A Safe Pair of Hands," *The Economist*, September 14, 2013.

29. Ibid.

30. Ibid.

31. Harnish et al., *The Greatest Business Decisions of All Time*.

32. Geoff Colvin, "The Greatest Business Decisions of All Time," *Fortune Money*, October 1, 2012.

33. Vijay Murty, "Tata Steel on Drive to Cut Headcount by 7,600," *Hindustan Times*, December 4, 2008.

CHAPTER 5: THIS MATRIX IS KILLING ME: THE DISCIPLINE TO ALIGN

1. "Whole Foods Market History," http://www.wholefoodsmarket.com /company-info/whole-foods-market-history; "Whole Foods Market, Inc. (WFM)," http://uk.finance.yahoo.com/q?s=WFM; Gary Hamel, *The Future of Management* (Boston: Harvard Business School Press, 2007).

2. Whole Foods Market, Inc., *Annual Report for the Fiscal Year Ended September 25, 2011* (Washington, DC: US Securities and Exchange Commission, 2011), p. 2, http://www.sec.gov/Archives/edgar/data/865436/000110465911065946/a11 -28314_110k.htm.

3. S&P's Corporate Descriptions, Whole Foods Market, Inc., Revision Date: December 31, 2013.

4. Geoff Colvin, "Walter Robb: Whole Foods' Other CEO on Organic Growth," *CNNMoney*, May 6, 2013.

5. Kyle Stock, "Whole Foods Profits by Cutting 'Whole Paycheck' Reputation," *Bloomberg Businessweek*, May 8, 2013.

6. This quote is the journalist's paraphrase of Mr. Wolf's statement. See Brian Gaar, "Spotlight Shines on Whole Foods; Grocer Learning Many Lessons as It Becomes a Well-Known Brand," *Dayton Daily News* (Ohio), September 29, 2013, p. E1.

7. Tom Vilsack, "Developments in Federal Agricultural Law and Policy," *Drake Journal of Agricultural Law* (Spring 2013): 1–12, http://students.law.drake .edu/agLawJournal/docs/agVol18No1-Vilsack.pdf.

8. Andrew Hill, "John Mackey, Whole Foods Market," *Financial Times*, June

30, 2013, http://www.ft.com/intl/cms/s/2/ab2996e0-da9f-11e2-a237-00144feab7de .html#axzz35PcU5uj5.

9. Brian Gaar, "Whole Foods Opens First-Ever Store in Detroit," *Statesman .com*, June 5, 2013.

10. Neil Munshi, "Whole Foods Targets Low-Income Market in Chicago's Mean Streets," *Financial Times*, September 13, 2013.

11. David Shaywitz, "Five Take-Aways from Whole Foods CEO John Mackey's Surprising New Book," *Forbes*, February 16, 2013.

12. "SVN Courageous Conversations: SVN Interviews Errol Schweizer, Whole Foods Market," *Social Venture Network*, March 30, 2013, http://www.triple pundit.com/podium/svn-courageous-conversations-svn-interviews-errol-schweizer -foods-market/.

13. Colvin, "Walter Robb."

14. Charles Fishman, "Whole Foods Is All Teams," *Fast Company*, April 30, 1996; see also John Mackey and Rajendra Sisodia, *Conscious Capitalism: Liberating the Heroic Spirit of Business* (Boston: Harvard Business Review Press, 2013).

15. Brian Gaar, "At Whole Foods, Team Management Goes All the Way to the Top," *Statesman.com*, September 25, 2010.

16. *Whole Foods Market 2012 Annual Report*, 2012.

17. Mackey and Sisodia, *Conscious Capitalism*.

18. Ibid.

19. Ram Charan and Geoffrey Colvin, "Why CEOs Fail: It's Rarely for Lack of Smarts or Vision. Most Unsuccessful CEOs Stumble Because of One Simple, Fatal Shortcoming," *Fortune*, June 21, 1999.

20. Rich Horwath, *The Strategic Thinking Manifesto*, http://www.strategyskills .com/wp-content/uploads/2012/09/The-Strategic-Thinking-Manifesto.pdf.

21. Ibid.

22. Michael Beer and Russell Eisenstat, "The Silent Killers of Strategy Implementation and Learning," *Sloan Management Review*, Issue 41 (Summer 2000).

23. Richard Lepsinger, *Closing the Execution Gap: How Great Leaders and Their Companies Get Results* (San Francisco: Jossey-Bass, 2010).

24. "The Last Kodak Moment?" *The Economist*, January 14, 2012, http://www .economist.com/node/21542796.

25. Gavetti, Henderson, and Giorgi. "Kodak (A)."

26. Giovanni Gavetti, "Kodak: Interview with Dr. George Fisher," *Harvard Business Review*, October 1, 2005, http://hbr.org/product/kodak-interview-with -dr-george-fisher-video/an/706802-VID-ENG.

27. Geoffrey Smith, William C. Symonds, Peter Burrows, Ellen Neuborne, and Paul C. Judge, "Can George Fisher Fix Kodak?," *Bloomberg Businessweek*,

October 9, 1997, http://www.businessweek.com/1997/42/b3549001.htm (accessed March 25, 2014).

28. Gavetti, "Kodak: Interview with Dr. George Fisher."

29. Henry Lucas and Jie Mein Goh, "Disruptive Technology Lucas," *Journal of Strategic Information Systems*, February 25, 2009, http://www.scribd.com/doc/21686414/Disruptive-Technology-Lucas (accessed March 2014).

30. David Nadler and Mark B. Nadler, *Champions of Change: How CEOs and Their Companies Are Mastering the Skills of Radical Change* (San Francisco: Jossey-Bass, 1998).

31. Quoted in Claudia H. Deutsch, "Chief Says Kodak Is Pointed in the Right Direction," *New York Times*, December 24, 1999.

32. Andrew Hill, "Snapshot of a Humbled Giant," *Financial Times*, April 2, 2012.

33. Jared Bleak and Tony O'Driscoll, "The Changing Leadership Context: Inside the CEO's Mind," *Developing Leaders* (2013), Issue 13.

34. Ibid.

35. Chip Heath and Dan Heath, *Switch: How to Change Things When Change Is Hard* (New York: Broadway, 2010).

36. "The Boldness to Dream: An Interview with Olivia Lum, Group President and Chief Executive Officer, Hyflux Ltd.," *Leaders*, January–March 2012 edition, http://www.leadersmag.com/issues/2012.1_Jan/ROB/LEADERS-Olivia-Lum-Hyflux-Ltd.html; see also Jonathan Gifford, *100 Great Business Leaders: Of the World's Most Admired Companies*, Marshall Cavendish International Asia Pte Ltd. (2013), pp 135–136.

37. "The Boldness to Dream: An Interview with Olivia Lum," *Leaders* 35.1 (2012), pp. 18–19.

38. "Thomas Schelling," http://en.wikipedia.org/wiki/Thomas_Schelling.

39. "FedEx: Driving Toward Cleaner Trucks," Environmental Defense Fund, n.d., http://business.edf.org/casestudies/edf-and-fedex-driving-toward-cleaner-trucks.

40. Fred Krupp, telephone interview, January 2014.

41. Ibid.

42. "Fred Krupp," http://www.edf.org/people/fred-krupp.

43. "Q&A: Fred Krupp," interview by Eric Nee, *Stanford Social Innovation Review*, Fall 2009.

44. Fred Krupp, "The Making of a Market-Minded Environmentalist," *Strategy+Business*, Issue 51, June 10, 2008.

45. Fred Krupp, telephone interview, January 2014.

46. Joe Nocera, "Fracking's Achilles' Heel," *New York Times*, November 18, 2013.

47. Fred Krupp, telephone interview, January 2014; for further specifics about the Colorado agreement, see http://www.colorado.gov/cs/Satellite/GovHickenlooper/CBON/1251651127442; see also "Environmental Defense Fund," http://www.edf.org.

48. *Denver Post* editorial board, "Clean Air and Drilling Can Exist Together in Colorado," *Denver Post,* February 21, 2104.

49. *Washington Post* editorial board, "Methane, Friend and Foe for Climate Change," *Washington Post,* February 16, 2014.

50. Fred Krupp, telephone interview, January 2014.

51. Keith Poole, "H.R. 7152 PASSAGE—House Vote #128—Feb. 10, 1964," GovTrack.us. Civic Impulse, LLC, February 10, 1964, https://www.govtrack.us /congress/votes/88-1964/h128 (accessed June 23, 2014).

52. Amy C. Edmondson, "The Mistakes Behind Healthcare.gov Are Probably Lurking in Your Company, Too," *HBR Blog Network,* December 5, 2013.

53. Robert Pear, Sharon Lafraniere, and Ian Austen, "From the Start, Signs of Trouble at Health Portal," *New York Times,* October 12, 2013.

54. Howard V. Perlmutter, "Developing a Global Civilization Mindset," *Financial Times-Mastering Management* (2002), Reader 6; see also Howard V. Perlmutter, "On Deep Dialog" (mimeo), Emerging Global Civilization Project, The Wharton School, 1990.

55. Anita Elberse and Tom Dye, "Sir Alex Ferguson: Managing Manchester United," Harvard Business School Publishing, September 20, 2012, Case N9-513-051.

56. Ibid.; see also Colleen Walsh, "Sir Alex Leads the Way," *Harvard Gazette,* December 17, 2012, http://news.harvard.edu/gazette/story/2012/12/sir-alex -leads-the-way/.

57. Geert Hofstede, *Culture's Consequences: International Differences in Work-Related Values* (Newbury Park, CA: Sage Publications, 1980).

58. Robert J. House, Paul J. Hanges, Mansour Javidan, Peter W. Dorfman, and Vipin Gupta (eds.), *Culture, Leadership, and Organizations: The GLOBE Study of 62 Societies* (Beverly Hills, CA: Sage Publications, 2004).

59. "Data Mining," *IT Glossary,* Gartner, Inc., n.d., http://www.gartner.com /it-glossary/data-mining (accessed November 26, 2013).

60. "From Guard Shack to Global Giant," *The Economist,* January 12, 2013, http://www.economist.com/news/business/21569398-how-did-lenovo-become -worlds-biggest-computer-company-guard-shack-global-giant.

61. "Chinese Mirrors," CEO Forum Group, July 2011, http://www.ceoforum .com.au/article-print.cfm?cid=11565&t=/Alan-Munro—Lenovo-Australia— New-Zealand/Chinese-mirrors/.

62. "From Guard Shack to Global Giant."

63. Ibid.

CHAPTER 6: MY GIFT WAS NOT KNOWING: THE DISCIPLINE TO LEARN

1. "Fareed Zakaria GPS: Panel Looks Ahead to 2014; Interview with Bono;

Interview with Elon Musk," *CNN*, January 5, 2014, http://transcripts.cnn.com /TRANSCRIPTS/1401/05/fzgps.01.html.

2. "Vinod Khosla Denounces '60 Minutes' 'Cleantech Crash' Segment," *India West*, January 29, 2014, http://www.indiawest.com/news/business/article_daff 8922-34a2-5aae-8434-df9555a98ad3.html.

3. Ibid.

4. "Vinod Khosla," http://en.wikipedia.org/wiki/Vinod_Khosla.

5. "Thomas J. Watson," http://en.wikipedia.org/wiki/Thomas_J._Watson.

6. Robert Frank, "Billionaire Sara Blakely Says Secret to Success Is Failure," *CNBC.com*, October 16, 2013.

7. Clare O'Connor, "Undercover Billionaire: Sara Blakely Joins the Rich List Thanks to Spanx," *Forbes*, March 7, 2012.

8. Ibid.

9. Meredith Lepore, "How Sara Blakely 'Failed' Her Way to Billions," *Levo League*, April 9, 2013.

10. Robert Frank, "Spanx Billionaire's Secret to Success: Failure," *CNBC.com*, October 16, 2013.

11. Lepore, "How Sara Blakely 'Failed' Her Way to Billions."

12. Ibid.

13. Mary Vinnedge, "Richard Branson: Virgin Entrepreneur," *Success*, June 8, 2009, http://www.success.com/article/richard-branson-virgin-entrepreneur #sthash.pDGd9LzH.dpuf.

14. Peter M. Senge, *The Fifth Discipline: The Art and Practice of the Learning Organization* (New York: Doubleday/Currency, 1990).

15. "BlackBerry," http://en.wikipedia.org/wiki/RIM_BlackBerry.

16. Vin D'Amico, "Lessons Learned from BlackBerry's Decline and Fall," *BrainsLink.com*, October 1, 2013, http://brainslink.com/2013/10/lessons-learned -from-blackberrys-decline-and-fall/ (accessed January 28, 2014).

17. Charles Arthur, "BlackBerry Fires CEO Thorsten Heins as $4.7bn Fairfax Rescue Bid Collapses," *The Guardian*, November 4, 2013, http://www .theguardian.com/technology/2013/nov/04/blackberry-fires-ceo-thorsten -heins-fairfax-bid-collapses (accessed February 5, 2014).

18. Clayton Christensen, *The Innovator's Dilemma: When New Technologies Cause Great Firms to Fail* (Boston: Harvard Business Review Press, 2013).

19. Scott D. Anthony, "The Real Lessons from the Fates of BlackBerry and Nokia," *Bloomberg Businessweek*, October 8, 2013.

20. Tom Taulli, "Lessons from the Fall of BlackBerry," *Forbes*, September 23, 2013.

21. Chaitanya Kalbag and Josey Puliyenthuruthel, "The Personality of Xerox Is Not Gender-Based, But It Is One That Enables Women," *Ursula Burns on Xerox's Transformation to a Products and Services Company*, September 29, 2013.

22. Adam Bryant, *The Corner Office: Indispensable and Unexpected Lessons from CEOs on How to Lead and Succeed* (New York: Times Books, 2011), p. 63.

23. Ibid.

24. Arie de Geus, *The Living Company* (Cambridge, MA: Harvard Business Press, 2002).

25. Ibid.

26. Oliver Folkard, "Virgin Media Teams Up with THECUBE for Innovation Lab," uSwitch, November 10, 2011, http://www.uswitch.com/broadband/news/2011/11/virgin_media_teams_up_with_thecube_for_innovation_lab/.

27. Tom Jowitt, "Virgin Media Opens Superfast 'Innovation Lab,'" *Tech Week Europe*, November 10, 2011.

28. Diane Tang, Ashish Agarwal, Deirdre O'Brien, and Mike Meyer, "Overlapping Experiment Infrastructure: More, Better, Faster Experimentation," *Proceedings of the 16th Conference on Knowledge Discovery and Data Mining* (2010), Association for Computing Machinery, Washington, DC, http://static.googleusercontent.com/media/research.google.com/en/us/archive/papers/Overlapping_Experiment_Infrastructure_More_Be.pdf.

29. Ibid.

30. Ibid.

31. "Secret Google Lab 'Rewards Failure,'" *News Technology* (BBC News), January 24, 2014, http://www.bbc.co.uk/news/technology-25883016.

32. Steven Levy, *In the Plex: How Google Thinks, Works, and Shapes Our Lives* (New York: Simon & Schuster, 2011).

33. Sarah Kessler, "Here's a Google Perk Any Company Can Imitate: Employee-to-Employee Learning," *Fast Company*, March 26, 2013.

34. Quoted in Thomas L. Friedman, "How to Get a Job at Google," *New York Times*, February 22, 2014.

35. "History of Cancer Treatment Centers of America," http://www.cancercenter.com/about-us/history/.

36. Sabrina Rodak, "Should Hospitals Be Like Hotels? Q&A with Gerard van Grinsven, CEO of Henry Ford West Bloomfield Hospital," *Becker's Hospital Review* 29 (October 2012).

37. Gerard van Grinsven, "Putting Patients Back in the Health Care Conversation," *The Huffington Post*, December 3, 2013.

38. Sam Byford, "King of Samsung: A Chairman's Reign of Cunning and Corruption," *The Verge*, November 30, 2012.

39. Jay Yarow, "This Bizarre Story About a Three-Day Speech in a German Hotel Explains Samsung's Culture," *Business Insider*, March 28, 2013.

40. Nicholas Varchaver, "Why Samsung Pays Its Stars to Goof Off," chapter 3 in Verne Harnish et al., *The Greatest Business Decisions of All Time: How Apple,*

Ford, IBM, Zappos, and Others Made Radical Choices That Changed the Course of Business (New York, Fortune, 2012), pp. 47–56.

41. Quoted in Sam Grobart, "Samsung's Year Abroad," *Bloomberg Businessweek*, April 4, 2013.

42. Ibid.

43. Ibid.

44. Varchaver, "Why Samsung Pays Its Stars to Goof Off."

45. "Tesla Is Important as an Example to Us," *Reuters* Video, July 29, 2013, http://www.reuters.com/video/2013/07/29/tesla-is-important-as-an-example-to -us-b?videoId=244465998.

46. "BMW Eyes Internet Sales for All Models—Magazine," *Reuters*, July 21, 2013.

47. "After-Action Review," http://en.wikipedia.org/wiki/After_action_review.

48. Dan Senor and Saul Singer, *Start-Up Nation: The Story of Israel's Economic Miracle* (New York: Twelve, 2009).

49. Ibid.

50. Gary Klein, "Performing a Project Premortem," *Harvard Business Review* 85, no. 9 (2007): 18–19.

51. Quoted in Robert S. Root-Bernstein, "How Scientists Really Think," *Perspectives in Biology and Medicine* 32, no. 4 (Summer 1989): 472–488.

52. William Howard Hughes, *Alexander Fleming and Penicillin* (London: Priory, 1974).

53. Ibid.; see also Root-Bernstein, "How Scientists Really Think."

54. American Chemical Society International Historic Chemical Landmarks, "Discovery and Development of Penicillin," http://www.acs.org/content/acs/en /education/whatischemistry/landmarks/flemingpenicillin.html.

55. Paul J. H. Schoemaker, *Brilliant Mistakes: Finding Success on the Far Side of Failure* (Philadelphia: Wharton Digital Press, 2011).

56. You can read about the three winners of the Wharton competition in the *Wall Street Journal:* http://blogs.wsj.com/venturecapital/2012/02/15/wharton -tries-to-define-brilliant-mistakes/.

57. Paul J. H. Schoemaker and Robert E. Gunther, "The Wisdom of Deliberate Mistakes," *Harvard Business Review*, June 2006, pp. 109–114.

58. "C. F. Hathaway Company," http://en.wikipedia.org/wiki/C._F._Hathaway _Company.

59. Maria Dahvana Headley, *The Year of Yes* (New York: Hyperion, 2007).

60. Martin E. P. Seligman, *Authentic Happiness: Using the New Positive Psychology to Realize Your Potential for Lasting Fulfillment* (New York: Free Press, 2002).

61. "Failure Week," http://www.wimbledonhigh.gdst.net/blog/failure-week.html.

62. Senor and Singer, *Start-Up Nation*, p. 31.

63. Kathy Caprino, "Startup Investor Whitney Johnson Helps You Answer

the Question 'Are You a True Entrepreneur?,'" *Forbes*, June 5, 2012.

64. These insights were presented by Jesse Treu at a management conference at the Wharton School on portfolio strategies, held in Philadelphia on November 12, 2010, and organized by the Mack Center for Technological Innovation.

65. Adam Bryant, "Brad Smith of Intuit: Follow the Fastest Beat of Your Heart," *New York Times*, April 12, 2014.

66. Story reported by David Tanner in *Total Creativity in Business and Industry* (1997) and recounted by Charles W. Prather in "Use Mistakes to Foster Innovation," *Research Technology Management* 51, no. 2 (2008).

67. David A. Garvin, Amy C. Edmondson, and Francesca Gina, "Is Yours a Learning Organization?" *Harvard Business Review*, March 2008, http://hbr.org/2008/03/is-yours-a-learning-organization/ar/1.

CHAPTER 7: TWO VISIONARY LEADERS: MANDELA AND BARNES—COMBINING IT ALL

1. "Apartheid in South Africa," http://en.wikipedia.org/wiki/Apartheid_in_South_Africa.

2. "On This Day: March 21," *BBC News*, http://news.bbc.co.uk/onthisday/hi/dates/stories/march/21/newsid_2653000/2653405.stm.

3. "Security Council Resolutions" (1960), http://www.un.org/en/sc/documents/resolutions/1960.shtml.

4. For further details, see http://knowledge.wharton.upenn.edu/article/lasting-legacy-nelson-mandelas-evolution-as-a-strategic-leader/.

5. Clem Sunter, *The World and South Africa in the 1990s* (Cape Town: Human & Rousseau, 1987).

6. S. R. Ritner, "The Dutch Reformed Church and Apartheid," *Journal of Contemporary History* 2, no. 4 (1967): 17–37.

7. "The Internally Displaced in South Africa," http://www.law.kuleuven.be/jura/art/32n4/henrard.htm.

8. Stephen Ellis, *External Mission: The ANC in Exile, 1960–1990* (New York: Oxford UP, 2013).

9. "F. W. de Klerk's speech at the opening of Parliament 2 February 1990," http://www.nelsonmandela.org/omalley/index.php/site/q/03lv02039/04lv02103/05lv02104/06lv02105.htm; "The Rise and Fall of the Berlin Wall," http://www.history.co.uk/shows/the-rise-and-fall-of-the-berlin-wall.

10. "The Nobel Peace Price 1993," http://www.nobelprize.org/nobel_prizes/peace/laureates/1993/.

11. "Ian Smith," http://www.britannica.com/EBchecked/topic/549759/Ian-Smith.

12. David Smith, "Mugabe Celebrates 90th Birthday as Zimbabwe's International Pariah," *The Guardian*, February 19, 2014, http://www.theguardian.com

/world/2014/feb/21/mugabe-celebrates-90th-birthday-zimbabwe-international
-pariah.

13. Stella Mapenzauswa, "No Tears But Grudging Respect for Mandela in White Afrikaner Enclave," *Reuters*, December 7, 2013, http://in.reuters.com /article/2013/12/07/mandela-afrikaners-idINDEE9B607Y20131207.

14. For alternative scenarios regarding South Africa, see Adam Kahane, "Transformative Scenario Planning: Changing the Future by Exploring Alternatives," *Strategy and Leadership* 40, no. 5 (2012).

15. "Speech by Nelson Mandela at the Inaugural Laureus Lifetime Achievement Award, Monaco 2000," http://db.nelsonmandela.org/speeches/pub_view .asp?pg=item&ItemID=NMS1148.

16. "Murder Most Horrible," Searchlight South Africa no. 10 (April 1993), http://www.sahistory.org.za/archive/murder-most-horrible.

17. "Thembisile 'Chris' Hani," http://www.sahistory.org.za/people/thembisile -chris-hani.

18. Paul J. H. Schoemaker, "Nelson Mandela as a Strategic Leader" *The European Business Review*, January–February 2014, pp. 48–52.

19. "Speech by Nelson Mandela at the Inaugural Laureus Lifetime Achievement Award, Monaco 2000."

20. John Jeansonne, "South Africa," *Los Angeles Times*, July 26, 1992, http:// articles.latimes.com/1992-07-26/sports/sp-5307_1_south-africa.

21. Thomas L. Friedman, "Why Mandela Was Unique," *New York Times*, December 10, 2013.

22. Gerald Imray, "1995 Rugby World Cup Final Put Nelson Mandela's Belief in the Power of Sports on Display," *The Huffington Post*, December 5, 2013, http://www.huffingtonpost.com/2013/12/05/rugby-world-cup-nelson-mandela -sports_n_4394712.html.

23. "Africa on the Top of the World's Worst Despots List," Afronline, June 23, 2010, http://www.afronline.org/?p=6003 https://exploringafrica.matrix.msu.edu/ images/decolinization.jpg.

24. "Statement of Nelson Mandela at his Inauguration as President," http:// www.anc.org.za/show.php?id=3132.

25. Personal communication with Brian Isaacson, based in Johannesburg, South Africa. Thanks as well go to Professor Nick Binedell, dean of Gordon Institute of Business Science (GIBS), for sharing his insights in person.

26. Nelson Mandela, *Long Walk to Freedom: The Autobiography of Nelson Mandela* (New York: Hachette Digital, Inc., 2008).

27. For many years under white rule, there were no laws against cartel formation in South Africa, including the Anglo Americans' gold, diamond, wheat, and other price-fixing schemes; a cozy relationship existed between government

and business. See David Lewis, *Thieves at the Dinner Table—Enforcing the Competition Act* (Pretoria, South Africa: Jacana Media Ltd., 2012).

28. Quoted in Friedman, "Why Mandela Was Unique."

29. Ibid.

30. Andrew R. Sorkin, "How Mandela Shifted Views on Freedom of Markets," *DealBook: "How Mandela Shifted Views on Freedom of Markets" Comments*, December 9, 2013.

31. The role of historical context is examined critically by Hermann Giliomee, *The Last Afrikaner Leaders: A Supreme Test of Power* (Charlottesville: University of Virginia Press, 2013).

32. Richard J. Wattenmaker, *American Paintings and Works on Paper in the Barnes Foundation* (Merion, PA: Barnes Foundation, 2010).

33. Mary Ann Meyers, *Art, Education, and African-American Culture: Albert Barnes and the Science of Philanthropy* (New Brunswick, NJ: Transaction, 2004), p. xi.

34. Wattenmaker, *American Paintings and Works on Paper in the Barnes Foundation.*

35. Ibid.

36. Ibid.

37. Ibid.

38. Ibid.

39. Ibid.

40. Meyers, *Art, Education, and African-American Culture.*

41. Wattenmaker, *American Paintings and Works on Paper in the Barnes Foundation*, p. 2.

42. Ross Mitchell, executive director of the Violette de Mazia Foundation and former gallery director at the Barnes Foundation, personal interview, February 2014.

43. Ibid.

44. *The Art of the Steal*, directed by Don Argott, Independent Film Channel, 2009.

45. Wattenmaker, *American Paintings and Works on Paper in the Barnes Foundation.*

46. Meyers, *Art, Education, and African-American Culture*, p. 23.

47. Wattenmaker, *American Paintings and Works on Paper in the Barnes Foundation*, p. 16.

48. Howard Greenfeld, *The Devil and Dr. Barnes: Portrait of an American Art Collector* (New York: Viking, 1987), p. 126.

49. Ibid., p. 34.

50. Ross Mitchell, executive director of the Violette de Mazia Foundation and former gallery director at the Barnes Foundation, personal interview, February 2014.

51. Albert C. Barnes, *The Art in Painting: One Hundred and Six Illustrations* (New York: Harcourt, Brace, 1925–1926), p. 55.

52. Greenfeld, *The Devil and Dr. Barnes*, p. 27.

53. Ibid.

54. Interview with Violette de Mazia in *House & Garden* magazine, Vol. 8 (September 24, 1942); see also "Out of Solitary," http://articles.latimes.com/1992 -10-07/entertainment/ca-636_1_barnes-foundation/2.

55. Carl W. McCardle, "The Terrible-Tempered Dr. Barnes," *Saturday Evening Post*, April 4, 1942 (Vol. 214, Issue 40), p. 18.

56. Ibid., p. 22.

57. Ross Mitchell, executive director of the Violette de Mazia Foundation and former gallery director at the Barnes Foundation, personal interview, February 2014.

58. John Dewey, *Art as Experience* (New York: Berkley Publishing Group, 1935), p. viii.

59. Wattenmaker, *American Paintings and Works on Paper in the Barnes Foundation*, p. 27.

60. Ibid., p. 27.

61. Greenfeld, *The Devil and Dr. Barnes*.

62. Edward Sozanski, "What Albert C. Barnes Definitely Did Not Want," *Philly.com*, May 28, 2012.

63. Albert C. Barnes, "The Art in Painting" Manuscripts, The Barnes Foundation Archives, Merion, Pennsylvania. This collection resides at the foundation and consists of background materials, travel notes, manuscript and typescript drafts, galley proofs, page proofs, final printed text blocks, and promotional materials written by Barnes himself.

64. Ross Mitchell, executive director of the Violette de Mazia Foundation and former gallery director at the Barnes Foundation, personal interview, February 2014.

65. Cited in Meyers, *Art, Education, and African-American Culture*, p. 23.

66. Wattenmaker, *American Paintings and Works on Paper in the Barnes Foundation*, p. 23.

67. Ibid., p. 27.

68. McCardle, "The Terrible-Tempered Dr. Barnes."

69. Henry Hart, *Dr. Barnes of Merion: An Appreciation* (New York: Farrar, Straus, 1963), pp. 23–24.

70. Jessica Durando, "15 of Nelson Mandela's Best Quotes," *USA Today Network*, December 6, 2013, http://www.usatoday.com/story/news/nation-now/2013 /12/05/nelson-mandela-quotes/3775255/.

EPILOGUE: BE MORE STRATEGIC: YOUR PERSONAL PLAN

1. Robert Kabacoff, "Develop Strategic Thinkers Throughout Your Organization," HBR Blog Network, *Harvard Business Review*, February 7, 2014.

2. Bob Sherwin, "Why Women Are More Effective Leaders Than Men," *Business Insider*, January 24, 2014.

3. Charles Darwin, *The Voyage of the Beagle* (New York: Harper, 1959).

APPENDIX: RESEARCH FOUNDATION OF THIS BOOK

1. Goldman Sachs, *United States S&P 500 Beige Book*.

2. Charles W. Hofer and Dan Schendel, *Strategy Formulation: Analytical Concepts* (St. Paul, MN: West Publishing Company, 1978); Michael E. Porter, *Competitive Strategy: Techniques for Analyzing Industries and Competitors* (New York: Simon and Schuster, 2008); Arnoldo C. Hax and Nicolas S. Majluf, "The Concept of Strategy and the Strategy Formation Process," *Interfaces* 18, no. 3 (1988): 99–109.

3. D. Braybrooke and Charles E. Lindblom, *A Strategy of Decision* (New York: Free Press, 1963); Michael D. Cohen, James G. March, and Johan P. Olsen, "A Garbage Can Model of Organizational Choice," *Administrative Science Quarterly* 17 (1972): 1–25; James Brian Quinn, *Strategies for Change: Logical Incrementalism* (Homewood, IL: Richard D Irwin, 1980); James G. March, *Decisions and Organizations* (Oxford: Basil Blackwell, 1988); Henry Mintzberg, *Crafting Strategy* (Boston: Harvard Business School Press, 1987).

4. For references and more detailed discussions of competing views on strategic decision-making, see Paul J. H. Schoemaker, "Strategic Decisions in Organizations: Rational and Behavioral Views," *Journal of Management Studies* 30, no. 1 (1993): 107–129.

5. Here are four key academic references: Birger Wernerfelt, "A Resource-Based View of the Firm," *Strategic Management Journal* 5 (1984): 171–180; Ingemar Dierickx and Karel Cool, "Asset Stock Accumulation and Sustainability of Competitive Advantage," *Management Science* 35 (1989): 1504–1511; Jay B. Barney, "Firm Resources and Sustained Competitive Advantage," *Journal of Management* 17 (1991): 99–120; and Raffi Amit and Paul J. H. Schoemaker, "Strategic Assets and Organizational Rent," *Strategic Management Journal* 14 (1993): 33–46.

6. These are the three managerial references we recommend: Robert B. Grant, "A Resource-Based Theory of Competitive Advantage: Implications for Strategy Formulation," *California Management Review* 33 (1991): 114–135; Paul J. H. Schoemaker, "How to Link Strategic Vision to Core Capabilities," *Sloan Management Review* 34 (1992): 67–81; Gary Hamel and C. K. Prahalad, *Competing for the Future: Breakthrough Strategies for Seizing Control of Your Industry and Creating the Markets of Tomorrow* (Boston: Harvard Business School Press, 1994).

7. Constance F. Helfat et al., *Dynamic Capabilities: Understanding Strategic Change in Organizations* (Malden, MA: Blackwell, 2007).

8. Teece refers to this distinction as *dynamic* capabilities versus *ordinary* capabilities; see David J. Teece, *Dynamic Capabilities and Strategic Management* (Oxford: Oxford University Press, 2009), p. x.

9. David J. Teece and Amy Shuen, "Dynamic Capabilities and Strategic Management," *Strategic Management Journal* 18 (1997): 509–533.

10. Michael Useem, *The Leadership Moment: Nine Stories of Triumph and Disaster and Their Lessons for Us All*, Vol. 10 (New York: Random House LLC, 1998).

11. Robert Rogers Blake and Jane Srygley Mouton, *The Managerial Grid III: A New Look at the Classic That Has Boosted Productivity and Profits for Thousands of Corporations Worldwide* (Houston, TX: Gulf Publishing Company, Book Division, 1985).

12. Paul Hersey, Kenneth Blanchard, and Dewey E. Johnson, *Management of Organization Behavior* (England Cliffs, NJ: Prentice-Hall, 1979); Kenneth H. Blanchard et al., *Leadership and the One-Minute Manager: Increasing Effectiveness Through Situational Leadership* (New York: Morrow, 1985); Daniel Goleman, Richard Boyatzis, and Annie McKee, "Primal Leadership: The Hidden Driver of Great Performance," *Harvard Business Review* 79, no. 11 (2001): 42–53.

13. Robert J. House, Paul J. Hanges, Mansour Javidan, Peter W. Dorfman, and Vipin Gupta (eds.), *Culture, Leadership, and Organizations: The GLOBE Study of 62 Societies* (Beverly Hills, CA: Sage Publications, 2004).

14. A good textbook is Peter G. Northouse, *Leadership: Theory and Practice* (Thousand Oaks, CA: Sage Publications, 2013). Practical advice can be found in James M. Kouzes and Barry Posner, *The Leadership Challenge: How to Make Extraordinary Things Happen in Organizations* (San Francisco: Jossey-Bass, 2012), or Richard Lepsinger, *Closing the Execution Gap: How Great Leaders and Their Companies Get Results* (San Francisco: Jossey-Bass, 2010).

15. Mary Uhl-Bien, Russ Marion, and Bill McKelvey, "Complexity Leadership Theory: Shifting Leadership from the Industrial Age to the Knowledge Era," *The Leadership Quarterly* 18, no. 4 (2007): 298–318.

16. Nick Obolensky, *Complex Adaptive Leadership: Embracing Paradox and Uncertainty* (Surrey, England: Gower Publishing, 2010).

17. Ronald A. Heifetz and Marty Linsky, "When Leadership Spells Danger," *Educational Leadership* 61, no. 7 (2004): 33–37; see also Ronald Heifetz, Alexander Grashow, and Marty Linsky, "Leadership in a (Permanent) Crisis," *Harvard Business Review* 87, nos. 7/8 (2009): 62–69.

18. Manfred F.R. Kets de Vries, *Organizations on the Couch: Clinical Perspectives on Organizational Behavior and Change* (San Francisco: Jossey-Bass, 1991); Manfred F.R. Kets de Vries and Danny Miller, *The Neurotic Organization: Di-*

agnosing and Changing Counterproductive Styles of Management (San Francisco: Jossey-Bass, 1984); Manfred F.R. Kets de Vries (ed.), *Organizational Paradoxes: Clinical Approaches to Management,* Vol. 4. (New York: Routledge, 2013); Kiran Trehan, "Psychodynamic and Critical Perspectives on Leadership Development," *Advances in Developing Human Resources* 9, no. 1 (2007): 72–82.

19. Michael Useem, *Leading Up: Managing Your Boss So You Both Win* (New York: Random House LLC, 2001); see also Michael Useem, *The Leader's Checklist, Expanded Edition: 15 Mission-Critical Principles* (Philadelphia: Wharton Digital Press, 2011).

20. Merom Klein and Rod Napier, *The Courage to Act: 5 Factors of Courage to Transform Business* (Palo Alto, CA: Davies-Black Publishing, 2003).

21. Jay Conger, "Developing Leadership Capability: What's Inside the Black Box," *Academy of Management Perspectives* 18, no. 3 (August 2004): 136–139.

22. Warren Bennis, *On Becoming a Leader* (New York: Basic Books, 2009; see also Warren Bennis, "The Challenges of Leadership in the Modern World: Introduction to the Special Issue," *American Psychologist* 62, no. 1 (2007): 2.

23. D. Scott DeRue, "Adaptive Leadership Theory: Leading and Following as a Complex Adaptive Process," *Research in Organizational Behavior* 31 (2011): 125–150; see also Gary Yukl and Richard Lepsinger, *Flexible Leadership: Creating Value by Balancing Multiple Challenges and Choices* (San Francisco: John Wiley & Sons, 2004).

24. Michael Useem, "Four Lessons in Adaptive Leadership," *Harvard Business Review* 88, no. 11 (2010): 86–90.

25. Ronald Abadian Heifetz, Alexander Grashow, and Martin Linsky, *The Practice of Adaptive Leadership: Tools and Tactics for Changing Your Organization and the World* (Boston: Harvard Business Press, 2009).

26. For a thorough academic overview of the strategic leadership literature, see Sidney Finkelstein, Donald C. Hambrick, and Albert A. Cannella, *Strategic Leadership: Theory and Research on Executives, Top Management Teams, and Boards* (New York: Oxford University Press, 2009).

27. Richard P. Rumelt, *Good Strategy—Bad Strategy* (New York: Crown Business/Random House, 2011).

28. Russell L. Ackoff, *Re-creating the Corporation: A Design of Organizations for the 21st Century* (New York: Oxford University Press, 1999).

29. We thank Terri Axtell, PhD, for her help with some of the statistical analyses reported here. Terri is the president of Axtell Consulting, and she specializes in survey design, statistical validation, and research administration.

CREDITS

INDEX

Index

Index

STEVEN KRUPP is the CEO of Decision Strategies International, Inc. (DSI), an entrepreneurial firm devoted to helping leaders become strategic and decisive. DSI provides executive development, strategy consulting, and management training programs to the world's largest

organizations in six continents. DSI solutions and intellectual property not only equip executives to implement dynamic strategies suited for an uncertain world but also design adaptive organizations that flex to rapidly changing demands.

Steve is a thought leader on the strategic thinking, change, decision-making, collaboration, customer centricity, innovation, and risk-taking required to shape the future. He and his colleagues have created programs to build these capabilities for thousands of leaders at global organizations such as AIG, Australia National Bank, Bank of America, BlackRock, British Petroleum, CEMEX, Comcast, General Electric, GlaxoSmithKline, Lenovo, L'Oreal, Lockheed Martin, Merck, Microsoft, PepsiCo, Royal Bank of Scotland, Thomson Reuters, Total, and Transocean.

Before joining DSI, Steve was a senior partner at Oliver Wyman, where he headed the Executive Talent Management practice advising boards and CEOs on succession and enterprise change. Prior to that, Steve was senior managing vice president at Right Management Consultants, where he led the human capital consulting business for the Americas. Steve joined Right when it acquired his firm Key Management Strategies, where he was CEO and learned firsthand to practice leadership and entrepreneurship amidst uncertainty.

Steve holds a PhD from Temple University in Organizational Development. He is published in *Harvard Business Review, Harvard Management Update, CLO Magazine, Talent Management Magazine, Leadership Excellence, Inc.com*, the *Wall Street Journal*, and the *Philadelphia Business Journal*. Recent article titles include "Strategic Leadership: The Essential Skills"; "Competitive Anticipation: How to Enhance Leadership by Sharpening Your Competitive Edge"; "Wanted: Adaptive Leaders with the Right Stuff"; "How to Rally Your Team Around a Strategy"; and "5 Ways to Know What Your Customers Want Before They Do."

PAUL J. H. SCHOEMAKER is an author, educator, researcher, and entrepreneur in strategic management, decision-making, and leadership. He is the founder and executive chairman of Decision Strategies International, Inc. (DSI), a consulting and training firm  specializing in strategic management and leadership. The company's clients include several of the largest corporations worldwide, as well as over a hundred of the Fortune 500. Paul also serves as research director of the Mack Institute for Innovation Management at the Wharton School, where he teaches strategy and decision-making. Paul is internationally known for his many articles (he ranks in the top 1 percent of scholarly citations globally) and more than ten books on decision-making and strategy, including *Decision Traps; Winning Decisions; Wharton on Managing Emerging Technologies; Profiting from Uncertainty; Peripheral Vision; Chips, Clones and Living Beyond 100;* and, more recently, *Brilliant Mistakes.*

For twelve years, Paul was a professor at the University of Chicago's graduate school of business, where he did leading academic work in the Center for Decision Research on behavioral economics, decision theory, and strategy. During that period, he spent a two-year sabbatical with Royal Dutch Shell's corporate planning group in London, where he helped pioneer scenario planning. Paul pens a fortnightly column for *Inc.com* covering topics in strategy and decision-making. His most-viewed column had over 1.6 million visitors. Paul is also the chairman of Public Salt Co., a wholesale distribution company based in Ohio that serves several Midwestern states, as well as the chairman of Vaessen-Schoemaker BV, a food additives company based in the Netherlands with clients throughout Europe. Paul's hobbies include tennis, golf, and piano. He lives with his wife on the east coast of the United States, while retaining roots in the Netherlands, where he was born and raised through adolescence.

PublicAffairs is a publishing house founded in 1997. It is a tribute to the standards, values, and flair of three persons who have served as mentors to countless reporters, writers, editors, and book people of all kinds, including me.

I. F. STONE, proprietor of *I. F. Stone's Weekly*, combined a commitment to the First Amendment with entrepreneurial zeal and reporting skill and became one of the great independent journalists in American history. At the age of eighty, Izzy published *The Trial of Socrates*, which was a national bestseller. He wrote the book after he taught himself ancient Greek.

BENJAMIN C. BRADLEE was for nearly thirty years the charismatic editorial leader of *The Washington Post*. It was Ben who gave the *Post* the range and courage to pursue such historic issues as Watergate. He supported his reporters with a tenacity that made them fearless and it is no accident that so many became authors of influential, best-selling books.

ROBERT L. BERNSTEIN, the chief executive of Random House for more than a quarter century, guided one of the nation's premier publishing houses. Bob was personally responsible for many books of political dissent and argument that challenged tyranny around the globe. He is also the founder and longtime chair of Human Rights Watch, one of the most respected human rights organizations in the world.

.   .   .

For fifty years, the banner of Public Affairs Press was carried by its owner Morris B. Schnapper, who published Gandhi, Nasser, Toynbee, Truman, and about 1,500 other authors. In 1983, Schnapper was described by *The Washington Post* as "a redoubtable gadfly." His legacy will endure in the books to come.

Peter Osnos, *Founder and Editor-at-Large*